Digital Media in Education

"This book has a great deal to offer at several levels. Michelle Cannon provides a much-needed, richly-detailed account of media arts practices with younger children, updating debates and theories of media literacy and moving image work in the context of contemporary digital practices and technologies. She also has much to contribute to current research and practice about the nature of literacy more generally, tackling some notoriously difficult debates about creativity and learning in ways that will be valuable to practitioners and researchers alike. Finally, her book is an exemplary instance of interdisciplinary thought and method, integrating philosophical and anthropological enquiry with authoritative theorised practice. We can all—students, teachers, researchers—learn from her approach."

—Andrew Burn, *Professor of English, Media and Drama,*
University College London, UK

"Michelle Cannon's book is an important and well-written contribution to the field of media literacy and media education. Her examination of media production in schools raises critical questions that challenge our understanding of creativity and digital technology as they relate to literacy. The book serves multiple purposes, offering an introduction to media literacy, a critical perspective on student agency and support for teachers working with film and media production."

—Oystein Gilje, *Associate Professor, Department of Teacher*
Education and School Research, University of Oslo, Norway

"In this inspirational and timely book, Cannon adds her expert voice to calls for rethinking literacy education to account for digital media practices. Firmly grounded in extensive research and professional experience, Cannon combines thought-provoking and incisive commentary with rich, compelling examples of her own work with learners. Her book provokes the reader to see anew the complexities of young people's creative and critical media production and as such is rich with possibilities. It is a must-read for those already researching and practising in this field as well as those new to this area, and for all teachers who are committed, like Cannon, to "reimagining school's relationship to film"."

—Cathy Burnett, *Professor of Literacy and Education,*
Sheffield Hallam University, UK

"Michelle Cannon's book is a much-needed, interdisciplinary and thoughtful piece of work. Full of detailed research, drawing on a wide range of theories from anthropology through to multimodality and the new literacy studies, it paints a detailed picture of digital media production by children and young people. It is passionately argued, highly original in its thinking and proposals of models of new ways with pedagogy in the 21st century. It deserves the widest possible readership in academic circles, but also in schools, speaking to practitioners in accessible language and with examples to which they will relate. Most importantly of all, it enlarges all our thinking about the possibilities of the digital in primary education."

—John Potter, *Reader in Media in Education, University College London, UK*

Michelle Cannon

Digital Media in Education

Teaching, Learning and Literacy
Practices with Young Learners

Michelle Cannon
UCL Knowledge Lab, Institute of Education
University College London
London, UK

ISBN 978-3-319-78303-1   ISBN 978-3-319-78304-8   (eBook)
https://doi.org/10.1007/978-3-319-78304-8

Library of Congress Control Number: 2018942683

Cover illustration: © Mira / Alamy Stock Photo

Printed on acid-free paper

This Palgrave Macmillan imprint is published by the registered company Springer International Publishing AG part of Springer Nature.
The registered company address is: Gewerbestrasse 11, 6330 Cham, Switzerland

In memory of Neil Cannon (1959–1996) and his enthusiasm for life

Acknowledgements

I would like to thank the many individuals and organisations that have supported me throughout the production of this work. It was made possible in the first instance with a bursary from the Centre for Excellence in Media Practice (CEMP) at Bournemouth University, UK. Particular thanks go to my doctoral supervisors Mark Readman and Kip Jones whose consistently attentive, critical and creative guidance steered me through the thickets, especially in amongst those dark shadowy places with no discernible coordinates.

I would also like to express my gratitude to mentors and colleagues from other institutions whose constant encouragement has been, and continues to be invaluable, namely: John Potter and Andrew Burn at the UCL Knowledge Lab, Institute of Education, University of London, whose MA programme gathered together much of my prior personal and professional experience, rendering it useful in ways I had not thought possible. Their intellectual and moral support has been immense, and much of what follows builds on their inspiring work. Similarly, thanks to Mark Reid, Head of UK Teaching and Learning Programmes at the British Film Institute, whose generosity of spirit and strong advocacy of film education initiatives have facilitated and enriched my work.

Thanks are due to all the many participants in my research, to the teachers, educators, learning mentors, practitioners, film-makers, researchers, tutors, commentators, students, children and young people, without whose productive activity and willingness to reflect, there would be no study, and little in the way of rich qualitative cud to chew on. I am also particularly grateful to those East London primary Head Teachers, Sean Flood and Carolyn Lindsay, whose foresight and enabling ways made room for film and digital media experimentation in the early days of my creative practice.

I thank my family and friends, and finally my daughter, Maddie, who was supportive of a physically present but often 'absent' mother, with little motivation to maintain a fully stocked fridge. It has been an all-consuming journey and it is now time to pick up a few dropped balls and run with many more.

Contents

List of Figures

1

Media-Making: Researching, Teaching & Learning

The pages that follow explore teaching, learning and making with digital media, as they relate to practical film and moving image work in schools. It comes at a time of widespread use of digital media in western social worlds, and a perceived gulf separating many school practices from those in everyday living. The book argues for more personally relevant dynamic school experiences that embed film and media production in the curriculum as standard, rather than as optional or extracurricular. Of central importance is the investigation of an enlarged conception of literacy: one that includes not only the manipulation of moving image, sound and time, but also one that considers the socio-historical conditions of media production and issues related to practical 'ways of knowing'. In this account, creative expression and critical understanding are seen as interdependent dimensions of literacy: as entwined and inseparable as the surface of a Möbius strip. By articulating the particular characteristics of learning with digital media, I identify the ways in which pedagogy can be developed in order to accommodate more social and collaborative classroom practice. I also interrogate the tensions related to policymakers' educational interventions that are seen to obstruct the development of dispersed digital media-making, such as film-making in schools. This work seeks to

© The Author(s) 2018
M. Cannon, *Digital Media in Education*,
https://doi.org/10.1007/978-3-319-78304-8_1

position media production as a core entitlement adding to and enriching, rather than supplanting, established literacy practices, and one that supports primary learners as 'writers' of audiovisual media as well as 'readers'.

Drawing on theories related to Cultural Studies, anthropology, film and media education, new literacy studies, multimodality and moving image composition, I explore young learners' 'performance' with digital media in specific educational settings. Given the complex ways in which modern social actors use media representations to negotiate their identity and relationships within networks, I suggest that providing young learners, defined in this study as those aged between nine and twelve, with opportunities for creative digital media expression delivers a relevant, engaging and critically-oriented school experience. Whilst making no claims for creative media as a remedial, emancipatory silver bullet—given the many other economic factors affecting social advantage—it is proposed that practical media work does at the very least nurture the skills and disposition for inclusive, praxis-oriented cultural participation. It is hoped that learners and educators across sectors will find the energy and resources to embrace this socially-framed vision of literacy, which promises to be of benefit not only to individual everyday lives, but also to the cultural prosperity of local communities.

This vision of contemporary literacy encompasses the study of film language and the production of moving image as an important cultural dimension of education. This approach hinges on collaborative meaning-making practices that combine pupils' interests and popular cultural motifs with:

- iterative social and cognitive engagements with media forms
- concrete inscription and crafting of media assets with digital tools of production
- the proactive development of imaginative and conceptual leaps
- sensibility and criticality towards the social and environmental network of relations embedded in everyday living

These suggestions are rooted in years of largely non-formal teaching experience in urban primary school environments and provide a framework for this review of contemporary literacy practices.

Personal Motivations

My engagement in this field sprang from a former life as a 'new media' professional with an interest in education. From 2000 I had been working part-time in East London primary schools in a role that transformed over the years from in-house web designer/developer to 'creative media practitioner'. As the use and development of digital media and distribution platforms evolved, I began to take an interest in the particular learning affordances of projects with children that involved 'multimedia'. One particular school was unusual at the time in that its Head Teacher had invested in an iMac suite, upgrading hardware and software as it became available. He saw the value of a weekly slot for a freelancer such as myself to build the school website and involve the children in its maintenance: an embryonic model of a media-practitioner-educator began to emerge.

Media production work in schools largely takes place outside the formal curriculum in the non-formal spaces of extracurricular arts activities or after school projects, however, my experience began with coordinating such projects that were integrated into formal cross-curricular subject areas. After Mac software training via CPD (Continuing Professional Development), I began making simple edited video clips in iMovie with small groups of Key Stage 2 children (7- to 11-year olds). I remember noticing the children's enthusiasm for learning: intellectual and social engagement; a willingness to experiment with new digital modes; and strong motivation linked to public displays of their work. My impression was that some were experiencing a hitherto elusive fascination with and control over a creative process, in a medium that was at once strange and familiar. My sessions differed from most regular classes in a number of ways: there was a sense of shared purpose and ownership, the social arrangements were less hierarchical, their work was publicly valued and peer reviewed, and many were committed to iterative and improvisational revisions to simply make their work 'right' or 'better' in some way.

The personal disclosure with which I begin this section serves as a blueprint for much of what follows. These early experiences of making texts or 'writing' with digital media—experiences which were, importantly, as much a learning process for me as for the children—raise questions not only concerning school cultures and the premise on which mainstream practices are based, but also how meaning-making with digital media warrants an evolved concept of literacy and alternative classroom practices. This entreaty for more relevant approaches to learning—beyond the purchase and installation of new tools and technology (Buckingham 2007)—is nothing new and has been made repeatedly by media educators and new literacy advocates for decades (Bazalgette 1989, 2000; Bazalgette and Bearne 2010; Buckingham 1986, 1990, 2003; Buckingham and Sefton-Green 1994; Burnett 2016; Burnett and Merchant 2015; Lankshear and Knobel 2003, 2011; Marsh and Bearne 2008; Sinker 2000).

Media Education Conundra

The ways in which we make meaning and interact socially are changed by the participatory affordances of digital media (Ito 2009; Ito et al. 2013; Jenkins et al. 2006, 2016; Kafai and Peppler 2011; Reid 2014). These thus present a challenge to many educational institutions, whose priorities and practices are, for many, outdated (Burn 2009; Potter 2012), fraught as they are with bureaucratic political interventions (Pring 2004; Ball 2013) and hierarchies (Merrin 2009, 2014). The view is that while other sectors variously adapt, the school sector—increasingly shaped and monitored by central government—is not only slow to respond to changes in the social and media landscape, but is hampered by retrogressive reform measures that cleave towards 'the basics' and marginalise media (Buckingham 2014).

The traditional versus the progressive in educational discourse is nothing new, but with the uptake of new media technologies the debate emerges with a renewed vigour and spread of agendas. At the same time as consecutive Secretaries of State for Education and their acolytes push through 'back to basics' reforms (Gove 2013), a number of other competing lobbies complicate the media education debate. A range of discursive frames crisscross the field furrowing their own trajectories, for example, there are the proponents of: technological determinism and vocationalism (Hagel and Seely Brown 2005; Shirky 2009); the protectionist frame (Livingstone 2009; Livingstone and Bulger 2014); and those who either question (Banaji et al. 2006; Readman 2010) or support the 'rhetorics' of creativity (Gauntlett 2007, 2011; NACCE 1999; Robinson 2006, 2011, 2013). The fallout sees film and digital media production in schools developing unevenly in 'pockets of excellence' around the country (Mumford et al. 2013), located in extracurricular programmes or on the margins of statutory curricula, often as a function of enthusiastic hobbyists or geographic happenchance.

In order to examine this terrain in more detail, I look at the ways in which some cultural agencies and public bodies in the UK have advocated, and indeed implemented programmes of moving image literacy within and beyond formal school curricula, as a means of ensuring learners' critical, creative and cultural participation in social processes (FLAG—Film Literacy Advisory Group—2013, 2015; NI DOE 2010;[1] 2014; Reid 2009, 2013). If this expanded view of literacy is to become as universal an entitlement as print literacy (Bazalgette 1989, 2000, 2011; Dezuanni 2011) it will be necessary to investigate alternative pedagogies (Thomson et al. 2012) and the function of media production in schools through a range of perspectives that touch on the personal, the social, the academic, the vocational and the economic (Sefton-Green 2013a).

To throw more light on the conflicting dimensions outlined above this research sought deeper understandings of the following questions:

How does creative media work constitute a wider literacy in formal and non-formal school spaces?
What can established pedagogy learn from moving image production processes?
How do social discursive factors determine practical media work in schools?

At the same time as examining my own and others' creative media practice for relevance and any potential benefits to the individual and

---

[1] There is much to be learned from the devolved nations: the revised Northern Ireland curriculum (NI DOE 2010) implemented since 2007, mandates 'media rich' and 'active, hands on' learning experiences. Equally, within Welsh (Donaldson 2015) and Scottish (Curriculum Review Group 2004) curricula, the expressive arts, including digital media and moving image, claim to be of central importance.

community, this study looked for a balanced understanding of what happens in the processes of making with digital media. This was achieved by reviewing patterns of action related to digital video and film production in formal and non-formal school settings and the ways in which discursive tensions influence these practices.

Situated Stories in a Post-Analogue Age

Unlike some educational research my methodological choices were not driven by the need to prove hypotheses or measure learning effectiveness statistically (EEF—Education Endowment Foundation—2015; Hattie 2012; Hattie and Yates 2014; see also Bergeron 2017 for a statistician's critique of specific approaches that quantify), rather, educational experience is explored and interpreted using qualitative research methods. I weave into my account insights from years of experience in schools' creative media practices, adopting an autoethnographic approach informed by the principles of critical visual anthropology (Hammersley and Atkinson 2007; Pink 2013; Rose 2006). In line with other recent research activity in the field (Livingstone and Sefton-Green 2016; Parry 2013, 2014; Potter 2012; Potter and Bryer 2014, 2016), the observational and audiovisual capture of media-making and teaching methods in schools accounts for much of the empirical research material to be discussed.

My overall motivation to research digital media use in schools stems from my belief that the capacity to understand and participate in media production supports democracy and social justice (Buckingham 2003; Selwyn 2012; Selwyn et al. 2016). Schools are the agencies through which we make available representative forms to children and young people (Eisner 2005/1993, p. 153), and for policy makers to actively limit the expressive offer could be construed as discriminatory in this post-analogue age. This critical approach relates to naming the enabling and constraining forces influencing school media activities (Buckingham 2014; Rose 2006), and the ways in which literacy, and what counts as legitimate in terms of curriculum content, is socially determined (Rosen 2012; Yandell 2014).

Some may question founding film education advocate, Cary Bazalgette's claim that "film and the moving image is the richest and most complex art form and means of expression human beings have ever invented" (Reid 2017) but few could argue with her assertion that "it's the first one we learn" (Bazalgette 2018; Reid 2017). Is this not reason enough to be included in the school experience? Readers will be presented with evidence that explores the contours of Bazalgette's long held argument and fleshes out its provocative claim, now that the digital is unravelling old ideologies related to print literacy and shuffling the curricula deck with alternative modes of meaning-making.

Why Is Film and Media-Making in Schools Important?

Many would advance the timeliness of their research, but I can think of no other subject area more relevant to our historical and political moment, more academically worthy of study, nor more 'endangered' than the social structures, texts, tools and practices related to digital media in society (Buckingham 2017). This is significant not only in relation to evolving digital landscapes and the need for pedagogy and learning to adapt to digitisation, but also on account of patchy, partial and prescriptive trends in educational reform (Husbands 2015). This lack of holistic thinking is mirrored by a gap in the literature that fails to account for currently scattered and largely non-formal media production projects (Sefton-Green 2013b). The revelations of my research add to and enrich speculation over what Sefton-Green (2013a) has identified as a missing set of theoretical underpinning educational values—this research builds capacity around such a proposal.

Media Education Discourses and Debates

My account first situates the study in the context of prevailing educational discourse. I go on to locate the research in relation to current literacy practices and media education debates. Given the focus of my account, particular attention will be given to the positioning of media production in schools (McDougall and Berger 2012). For primary and early secondary children, the idea of making is often aligned with practical arts activities, with associated gains in cultural, critical and creative engagement (Sefton-Green 2008). I examine the claims made in support of these assumptions as they pertain to practical media work. Such work often takes place in the non-formal spaces of extracurricular programmes, thus necessitating a critical engagement with the practices of creative practitioners and the pedagogic climate in which such projects are conducted (Loveless 2012; Thomson et al. 2012).

Crucial to a comprehensive review is an account of how research in the field documents the relationship between formal segmented curricula and the fluid non-linear affordances of digital media that favour collaboration and plurality (Burn 2009; Fisher et al. 2006). Furthermore, some commentators claim that spaces of learning are no longer fixed geographic domains but distributed and porous—ones that benefit from processes of digital exchange and reciprocity (Potter 2011; McDougall and Potter 2015). In this view, normative roles and hierarchies are potentially upended and propelled instead by flatter structures and autonomous creative agency. Amid the mêlée of discourses jostling for position, my account reveals the attitudes and dispositions of young people, whose interests it is argued, are often sidelined in the service of other partial agendas (Bazalgette et al. 2011; Potter 2012).

There is an urgency to this research that advocates for educational experience to be made more relevant to young people and their everyday lives. A review of the literature seems to broadly reflect this recommendation, but points to a lack of empirical evidence with which to aggregate the good practice in scattered media projects (Sefton-Green 2013a). The main thrust then of this body of work interrogates the academic and social discourses relating to reconceptualisations of literacy, and the human skills and dispositions evinced whilst makers are engaged in digital manipulation. It is found that trust in the preferences and integrity of learners and in the judgement of teachers is what most erodes in the current climate.

Fictive Narrations

My narratives are 'versioned visions', they do not claim to be transparent transcriptions of events as they occurred, and are acknowledged as always-already interpreted accounts in a postmodern sense. As such these are composite descriptions of a 'fictive reality' (Clough 2002; Jones 2013) subject to critical and theoretical reflective commentaries that tease out possible explanations of relevance to current thinking on new literacies and pedagogies related to digital media production.

In Chap. 6, material is interpreted through a critical visual anthropological lens (Rose 2006) engaging with: the social and economic context of the sites of learning; observed human and non-human interactions in the making of digital artefacts (Dezuanni 2014); and the 'performance' of makers as they negotiate sense-making with material and symbolic resources (Burn 2009). Producing a coherent and faithful account of these strands of experience, whilst exposing any contradictory assumptions, allows us to move forward with debates on literacy, media composition practices, progressive pedagogies and the productive agency of young learners.

Reconciling the Binaries and Pedagogic Progression

The final Chapter draws together the evidence arguing for the accommodation of a range of expressive resources, modes and mediating platforms across the curriculum. In this way, there may start to be a sense of reconciliation between dimensions of literacy often conceived in binary ways: the digital and the analogue; the online the offline; the oral/aural and the written; the moving/still image and the word; the hand-wrought and the algorithmic; the page and the screen; and the material and the virtual. I argue that to be a literate social actor in a networked environment is as much about cultivating a confident productive disposition as it is about acquiring knowledge, skills and competences. Further, my account suggests that media composition practices open up specific pathways to conceptual learning involving a necessary oscillation between the above binaries to generate rich new meanings.

The way this research has been designed and implemented constitutes a stepping stone in a necessary cultural shift in pedagogic thinking. Its findings suggest the need to deliver relevant school experiences for young people across visual and filmic modes—as standard rather than extra. Using communicative art forms familiar to young people may encourage deeper critical engagement in civic participation and personally charged rhetorical performance. If so, the practical implications for change and additional research are legion, pointing to the development of hybrid digital pedagogies, an evolving curriculum, pertinent formative and summative assessments and sustained professional development for teachers.

Finally, before launching into an exploration of the literature, I will clarify some of the more slippery terms used throughout the book. In public and academic discourse, appending a learning domain with the word 'literacy' confers status (Potter 2012), a condition that goes beyond simply knowing how to read and write. Being literate traditionally assumes a grasp of a certain body of knowledge, and competence in a set of pertinent skills, so as to be able to demonstrate understanding and apply it productively. By using the term 'established literacy' I refer to the functional practices of meaning-making with print, to which substantial parts of the curriculum are committed and for which schools are held publicly accountable. At the same time, foundational pre-digital literacy theories (Street 1984, 2003) on which media literacy is predicated will be acknowledged (Gee 2004, 2015a, 2015b).

Throughout the book I also make reference to established pedagogy, by which I mean the largely paper-based procedures that form around the implementation of national curriculum content. Whilst there are many exceptions, this system may result in vertically designed pedagogy with little latitude for self-determined teacher or student agency. Preparing young people for adult life with rigid approaches is problematic considering the fluid digital aptitudes that many young people acquire informally.

It is a challenge to nail an all-encompassing definition of literacy, so politically useful, contextually sensitive and malleable are its contours. Given this slipperiness, literacies germane to this account are understood as follows:

- media literacy is an outcome achieved as a result of media education and assumes the ability to access, explore, critique, evaluate, enjoy, create and share media texts in all their forms, and engagement with the same on a variety of digital platforms (Buckingham 2003).

- still and moving image literacy is a subset of media literacy, understood as the ability to access, explore, critique, evaluate, enjoy, create and share digital audiovisual resources—specifically the photograph, and film, video and sound through time—also on a variety of digital platforms (Bazalgette et al. 2011; Burn and Durran 2006, 2007).
- the phrase new media literacies subsumes the previous two literacies, with an emphasis on the multimodal, productive, participative and social affordances of new media technologies and their use on a variety of digital platforms (Burnett and Bailey 2014; Gee 2004, 2015a, 2015b; Lankshear and Knobel 2003; Potter 2011; Street 1984, 2003).
- the phrase a wider literacy is borrowed from collaborative work between the Northern Ireland Film and Television Council and The British Film Institute (NIFTC/BFI 2004). The resultant paper details a holistic and cross-disciplinary view of communicative strategies in formal education, highlighting moving image literacy, which supports my proposition:

> Although print literacy is immensely important, it is no longer enough to ensure our full participation in the culture, social life and politics of the 21st century.
> (NIFTC/BFI 2004, p. 6)

Throughout my account reference is made to digital media production, media-making, digital and multimodal meaning-making—terms which encompass the creation of, and engagement with, a variety of media texts, assets and processes as outlined above. I also refer to media composition practices denoting the aesthetic and critical arrangement of symbolic resources in the act of textual development, while film-making is seen as a particular art form within this frame.

My research activities take place in formal and non-formal educational environments. Formal refers to those school spaces whose practices are accountable to institutional structures. Non-formal refers to less accountable school practices taking place beyond formal structures but still under the aegis of the school, such as after school clubs and extracurricular programmes (Sefton-Green 2013b). Informal educational activities are understood as those that take place externally, such as in the home, cultural institutions, cinemas, galleries and community spaces, that are unconstrained by regulatory school procedures. It is important to make the distinction between the latter two terms because a case is made supporting particular practices in the non-formal space between home and school, described as a 'third space' by Potter and McDougall (2017) and others (,,,). As a counterpoint to structured regimes, learning in these liminal zones is conceived as negotiated and contingent. Indeed, sites of learning, including spaces opened up through partnerships with external creative agencies, will be seen as salient facets of practical media work with young people.

This overview has lain the foundations on which this exploration can proceed in greater depth. The background to my personal interest in children's interactions with digital media production has been given, as has a sketch of the issues related to schools' interface with the audiovisual vernacular. The following Chapter explores the literature related to creative media production and moving image literacy in schools.

Bibliography

Ball, S. J. (2013). *The Education Debate* (2nd ed.). Bristol: Policy Press.

Banaji, S., Buckingham, D., & Burn, A. (2006). *The Rhetorics of Creativity: A Review of the Literature*. London: Institute of Education, Creative Partnerships, Arts Council England.

Bazalgette, C. (1989). *Primary Media Education: A Curriculum Statement*. London: British Film Institute.

Bazalgette, C. (2000). A stitch in time: Skills for the new literacy. *English in Education, 34*(1), 42–49.

Bazalgette, C. (2011). Rethinking text [online]. In *Empowerment Through Literacy: Literacy Shaping Futures—UKLA 47th International Conference*. Chester: UKLA, 20–31. Retrieved February 7, 2018, from http://www.ukla.org/downloads/UKLA_Chester_International_Conference_Papers_2011.pdf.

Bazalgette, C. (2018). *Some Secret Language: How Toddlers Learn to Understand Movies*. PhD Thesis, UCL, Institute of Education, University of London, London.

Bazalgette, C., & Bearne, E. (2010). *Beyond Words: Developing Children's Understanding of Multimodal Texts*. Leicester: UKLA.

Bazalgette, C., Parry, B., & Potter, J. (2011). Creative, cultural and critical: Media literacy theory in the primary classroom [online]. In *Creative Engagements: Thinking with Children*. Oxford: Inter-Disciplinary.net. Retrieved February 7, 2018, from http://www.inter-disciplinary.net/wp-content/uploads/2011/06/bazalgettecpaper.pdf.

Bergeron, P. J. (2017). *How to Engage in Pseudoscience with Real Data: A Criticism of John Hattie's Arguments in Visible Learning from the Perspective of a Statistician* [online]. Retrieved February 7, 2018, from http://mje.mcgill.ca/article/view/9475/7229.

Buckingham, D. (1986). Against demystification: A response to teaching the media. *Screen, 27,* 80–85.

Buckingham, D. (1990). *Watching Media Learning: Making Sense of Media Education*. London: The Falmer Press.

Buckingham, D. (2003). *Media Education: Literacy, Learning and Contemporary Culture*. Cambridge: Polity Press.

Buckingham, D. (2007). *Beyond Technology: Children's Learning in the Age of Digital Culture*. London: Routledge.

Buckingham, D., 2014. The Success and failure of media education [online]. *Media Education Research Journal, 4*(2), 5–17. Retrieved February 7, 2018, from http://merj.info/wp-content/uploads/2014/01/MERJ_4-2-Editorial.pdf.

Buckingham, D. (2017). *The Strangulation of Media Studies* [online]. Retrieved January 1, 2018, from https://ddbuckingham.files.wordpress.com/2017/08/strangulation-final-2.pdf.

Buckingham, D., & Sefton-Green, J. (1994). *Cultural Studies Goes to School*. London: Taylor & Francis.

Burn, A. (2009). *Making New Media: Creative Production and Digital Literacies*. New York: Peter Lang.

Burn, A., & Durran, J. (2006). Digital anatomies: Analysis as production in media education. In D. Buckingham & R. Willett (Eds.), *Digital Generations: Children, Young People, and the New Media* (pp. 273–293). London: Routledge.

Burn, A., & Durran, J. (2007). *Media Literacy in Schools: Practice, Production and Progression*. London: Paul Chapman.

Burnett, C. (2016). *The Digital Age and its Implications for Learning and Teaching in the Primary School*. York. Retrieved February 7, 2018, from http://cprtrust.org.uk/wp-content/uploads/2016/07/Burnett-report-20160720.pdf.

Burnett, C., & Bailey, C. (2014). Conceptualising collaboration hybrid sites: Playing *Minecraft* together and apart in a primary classroom. In J. Davies,

G. Merchant, & J. Rowsell (Eds.), *New Literacies around the Globe: Policy and Pedagogy (Routledge Research in Literacy)* (pp. 50–71). Abingdon: Routledge.

Burnett, C., & Merchant, G. (2015). The challenge of 21st-century literacies. *Journal of Adolescent & Adult Literacy, 59*(3), 271–274.

Clough, P. (2002). *Narratives and Fictions in Educational Research*. Maidenhead: Open University Press.

Curriculum Review Group. (2004). *A Curriculum for Excellence* [online]. Education Scotland. Retrieved February 7, 2018, from https://education.gov.scot/scottish-education-system/policy-for-scottish-education/policy-drivers/cfe-(building-from-the-statement-appendix-incl-btc1-5)/Experiences%20and%20outcomes#arts.

Dezuanni, M. (2011). *Media Education as a Basic Entitlement for all Children and Young People* [online]. Manifesto for Media Education. Retrieved February 7, 2018, from http://www.manifestoformediaeducation.co.uk/2011/06/michael-dezuanni/.

Dezuanni, M. (2014). The building blocks of digital media literacy, socio-material participation and the production of media knowledge. *Journal of Curriculum Studies, 1–24.*

Donaldson, G. (2015). *Successful Futures: Independent Review of Curriculum and Assessment Arrangements in Wales* [online]. Retrieved February 7, 2018, from http://gov.wales/docs/dcells/publications/150225-successful-futures-en.pdf.

EEF. (2015). *About the Education Endowment Foundation* [online]. Retrieved February 7, 2018, from https://educationendowmentfoundation.org.uk/about/.

Eisner, E. (2005/1993). Forms of understanding and the future of educational research. In E. Eisner (Ed.), *Reimagining Schools* (pp. 150–162). Abingdon: Routledge.

Fisher, T., Higgins, C., & Loveless, A. (2006). *Teachers Learning with Digital Technologies: A Review of Research and Projects* [online]. Bristol: Futurelab at NFER. Retrieved May 23, 2018, from https://www.nfer.ac.uk/teachers-learning-with-digital-technologies-a-review-of-research-and-projects/ .

FLAG (Film Literacy Advisory Group). (2015). *A Framework for Film Education* [online]. London: British Film Institute. Retrieved February 7, 2018, from http://www.bfi.org.uk/sites/bfi.org.uk/files/downloads/ bfi-a-framework-for-film-education-brochure-2015-06-12.pdf.

Gauntlett, D. (2007). Wide angle: Is it time for Media Studies 2.0? *Media Education Association Newsletter, 5,* 3–5.

Gauntlett, D. (2011). *Making is Connecting*. Cambridge: Polity Press.

Gee, J. P. (2004). *Situated Language and Learning: A Critique of Traditional Schooling*. New York: Routledge.

Gee, J. P. (2015a). The new literacy studies. In J. Rowsell & K. Pahl (Eds.), *The Routledge Handbook of Literacy Studies* (pp. 35–48). Abingdon: Routledge.

Gee, J. P. (2015b). *Literacy and Education*. New York: Routledge.

Gove, M. (2013). *Michael Gove Speaks at the SMF* [online]. Social Market Foundation. Retrieved February 7, 2018, from http://www.smf.co.uk/michael-gove-speaks-at-the-smf/.

Hagel, J., & Seely Brown, J. (2005). *From Push to Pull—Emerging Models for Mobilizing Resources* [online]. Retrieved February 7, 2018, from http://www.johnhagel.com/paper_pushpull.pdf.

Hammersley, M. & Atkinson, P., (2007). *Ethnography Principles in Practice* (3rd ed.). London: Routledge.

Hattie, J. (2012). *Visible Learning for Teachers: Maximizing Impact on Learning*. Abingdon: Routledge.

Hattie, J., & Yates, G. (2014). *Visible Learning and the Science of How We Learn*. Abingdon: Routledge.

Husbands, C. (2015). *Twenty-seven Years on From the National Curriculum* [online]. UCL, Institute of Education blog. Retrieved February 7, 2018, from https://ioelondonblog.wordpress.com/2015/06/22/twenty-seven-years-on-from-the-national-curriculum/.

Ito, M. (2009). *Hanging Out, Messing Around, and Geeking Out: Kids Living and Learning with New Media*. The John D. and Catherine T. MacArthur Foundation Series on Digital Media and Learning. Cambridge, MA: MIT Press.

Ito, M., Livingstone, S., Penuel, B., Rhodes, J., Salen, K., Schor, J., et al. (2013). *Connected Learning: An Agenda for Research and Design* [online]. Digital Media and Learning Research Hub. Retrieved February 7, 2018, from http://dmlhub.net/wp-content/uploads/files/Connected_Learning_report.pdf.

Jenkins, H., Ito, M., & boyd, d. (2016). *Participatory Culture in a Networked Era: A Conversation on Youth, Learning, Commerce, and Politics*. Cambridge: Polity Press.

Jenkins, H., Purushota, R., Clinton, K., & Robinson, A. J. (2006). *Confronting the Challenges of Participatory Culture: Media Education for the 21st Century* [online]. Chicago: The John D. & Catherine T. MacArthur Foundation. Retrieved February 7, 2018, from https://www.macfound.org/media/article_pdfs/JENKINS_WHITE_PAPER.PDF.

Jones, K. (2013). Infusing biography with the personal: Writing Rufus Stone. *Creative Approaches to Research, 6*(2), 4.

Kafai, Y. B., & Peppler, K. A. (2011). Youth, technology, and DIY: Developing participatory competencies in creative media production. *Review of Research in Education, 35*(1), 89–119.

Lankshear, C., & Knobel, M. (2003). *New Literacies: Changing Knowledge and Classroom Learning.* Buckingham: Open University Press.

Lankshear, C., & Knobel, M. (2011). *New Literacies: Everyday Practices and Social Learning.* Maidenhead: Open University Press.

Livingstone, S. (2009). *Children and the Internet.* Cambridge: Polity Press.

Livingstone, S., & Bulger, M. (2014). A global research agenda for children's rights in the digital age. *Journal of Children and Media,* 8(4), 317–335.

Livingstone, S., & Sefton-Green, J. (2016). *The Class: Living and Learning in the Digital Age.* New York: NYU Press. Retrieved February 7, 2018, from http:// connectedyouth.nyupress.org/book/9781479824243/.

Loveless, A. (2012). Body and soul: A study of narratives of learning lives of creative people who teach. In I. Goodson, A. Loveless, & D. Stephens (Eds.), *Explorations in Narrative Research: Studies in Professional Life and Work* (pp. 107–122). Rotterdam: Sense Publishers.

Marsh, J., & Bearne, E. (2008). *Moving Literacy On: Evaluation of the BFI Lead Practitioner Scheme for Moving Image Media Literacy.* UKLA, University of Sheffield.

McDougall, J., & Berger, R. (2012). What is media education for? *Media Education Research Journal, 3*(1), 5–20.

McDougall, J., & Potter, J. (2015). Curating media learning: Towards a porous expertise. *Journal of E-learning and Digital Media, 12*(2), 199–211.

Merrin, W. (2009). Media studies 2.0: Upgrading and open-sourcing the discipline [online]. *Interactions: Studies in Communication and Culture, 1*(1). Retrieved February 7, 2018, from http://mediastudies2point0.blogspot. co.uk/2010/03/studying-me-dia-problem-of-method-in.html.

Merrin, W. (2014). *Media Studies 2.0.* Abingdon: Routledge.

Mumford, S., Parry, B., & Walker, G. (2013). *Pockets of Excellence: Film Education in Yorkshire and the Humber* [online]. Leeds: IVE Creative (formerly CAPEUK). Retrieved February 7, 2018, from https://weareive.org/ impact/pockets-excellence-film-education-yorkshire-humber/.

NACCE, National Advisory Committee on Creative and Cultural Education. (1999). *All Our Futures: Creativity, Culture and Education* [online]. London: DCMS. Retrieved February 7, 2018, from http://sirkenrobinson.com/pdf/ allourfutures.pdf.

NI DOE, Northern Ireland Department of Education. (2010). *The Big Picture at Key Stages 1 and 2* [online]. Belfast: Northern Ireland. Retrieved February

7, 2018, from http://www.nicurriculum.org.uk/docs/key_stages_1_and_2/ Big-PicturePrimary-KS12.pdf.

NIFTC, Northern Ireland Film & Television Council, and BFI Education. (2004). *A Wider Literacy: The Case for Moving Image Media Education in Northern Ireland* [online]. Belfast: Northern Ireland Film & Television Council, BFI Education Policy Working Group. Retrieved February 7, 2018, fromhttp://www.bfi.org.uk/sites/bfi.org.uk/files/downloads/bfi-case-for-moving-image-media-education-in-northern-ireland.pdf.

Parry, B. (2013). *Children, Film and Literacy*. Basingstoke: Palgrave Macmillan.

Parry, B. (2014). Popular culture, participation and progression in the literacy classroom. *Literacy, 48*(1), 14–22.

Pink, S. (2013). *Doing Visual Ethnography* (3rd ed.). London: Sage.

Potter, J. (2011). New literacies, new practices and learner research: Across the semi-permeable membrane between home and school. *Lifelong Learning in Europe, 16*(3), 174–181.

Potter, J. (2012). *Digital Media and Learner Identity: The New Curatorship*. New York: Palgrave Macmillan.

Potter, J., & Bryer, T. (2014). *Out of the Box: A Project Evaluation Report for Shoot Smart*. London: DARE, Digital, Arts, Research, Education.

Potter, J., & Bryer, T. (2016). 'Finger flowment' and moving image language: Learning filmmaking with tablet devices. In B. Parry, C. Burnett, & G. Merchant (Eds.), *Literacy, Media, Technology: Past, Present and Future* (pp. 111–128). London: Bloomsbury.

Potter, J., & McDougall, J. (2017). *Digital Media, Culture and Education: Theorising Third Space Literacies*. London: Palgrave Macmillan.

Pring, R. (2004). *Philosophy of Educational Research* (2nd ed.). London: Continuum.

Readman, M. (2010). *What's in a Word? The Discursive Construction of 'Creativity'*. PhD Thesis, Centre for Excellence in Media Practice (CEMP), University of Bournemouth, Bournemouth.

Reid, M. (2009). Reframing literacy: A film pitch for the 21st century. *English Drama Media: The Professional Journal of the National Association for the Teaching of English, 14*, 19–23.

Reid, M. (2013). Film 21st century literacy: Re/defining film education—Notes towards a definition of film education. In *Film: 21st Century Literacy Strategy Seminar*. London. Retrieved February 7, 2018, from http://www.bfi.org.uk/sites/bfi.org.uk/files/downloads/film-21st-century-literacy-redefining-film-education.pdf.

Reid, M. (2014). Film, literacy and cultural participation. In S. Brindley & B. Marshall (Eds.), *Master Class in English Education: Transforming Teaching and Learning* (pp. 84–98). London: Bloomsbury.

Reid, M. (2017). Little Film about Cinema Cent Ans de Jeunesse (CCAJ). Retrieved February 7, 2018, from https://markreid1895.wordpress.com/2017/01/27/little-film-about-ccaj/.

Robinson, K. (2006). How schools kill creativity [online]. *TED.com.* Retrieved February 7, 2018, from http://www.ted.com/talks/ken_robinson_says_schools_kill_creativity.html.

Robinson, K. (2011). *Out of our Minds: Learning to be Creative* (2nd ed.). Chichester: Capstone.

Robinson, K. (2013). *Finding Your Element: How to Discover Your Talents and Passions and Transform Your Life.* London: Allen Lane.

Rose, G. (2006). *Visual Methodologies. An Introduction to the Interpretation of Visual Materials.* London: Sage.

Rosen, M. (2012). *Who Owns Literacy?* [online]. Michael Rosen's blog. Retrieved February 7, 2018, from http://michaelrosenblog.blogspot.co.uk/2012/02/who-owns-literacy.html.

Sefton-Green, J. (2008). *Creative Learning* [online]. London: Creative Partnerships, Arts Council England. Retrieved May 22, 2018, from https://www.sussex.ac.uk/webteam/gateway/file.php?name=creative-learning-sept-2008&site=45.

Sefton-Green, J. (2013a). *Mapping Digital Makers: A Review Exploring Everyday Creativity, Learning Lives and the Digital.* State of the Art Reviews. London: Nominet Trust.

Sefton-Green, J. (2013b). *Learning at Not-School: A Review of Study, Theory, and Advocacy for Education in Non-formal Settings.* The John D. and Catherine T. MacArthur Foundation Reports on Digital Media and Learning. Cambridge, MA: MIT & MITE.

Selwyn, N. (2012). Ten suggestions for improving academic research in education and technology. *Learning, Media and Technology, 37*(3), 213–219.

Selwyn, N., Bulfin, S., & Johnson, N. (2016). Toward a digital sociology of school. In J. Daniels, K. Gregory, & T. McMillan Cottom (Eds.), *Digital Sociologies.* Bristol: Policy Press.

Shirky, C. (2009). *Here Comes Everybody: How Change Happens When People Come Together.* London: Penguin.

Sinker, R. (2000). Making multimedia—Evaluating young people's creative multimedia production. In *Evaluating Creativity* (pp. 187–215). London: Routledge.

Street, B. (1984). *Literacy in Theory and Practice*. Cambridge: Cambridge University Press.

Street, B. (2003). What's 'new' in new literacy studies? Critical approaches to literacy in theory and practice. *Current Issues in Comparative Education, 5*(2), 77–91.

Thomson, P., Hall, C., Jones, K., & Sefton-Green, J. (2012). *The Signature Pedagogies Project: Final Report* [online]. London and Newcastle-upon-Tyne: Creativity, Culture and Education. Retrieved February 7, 2018, from http://cprtrust.org.uk/wp-content/uploads/2015/02/signature_pedagogies_report_final_version_11.3.12.pdf.

Yandell, J. (2014). Classrooms as sites of curriculum delivery or meaning-making: Whose knowledge counts? *Forum, 56*(1), 147–155.

2

Contexts, Practices and Pedagogies

This Chapter develops a theoretical framework that grounds debates on the value and practices of practical media work in schools in relation to both literacy theory and digital making trends. For a deeper understanding of the conditions that shape practices with digital media, I review media production processes in schools examining their positioning and status, I then follow this up with an assessment of schools' digital making environments and pedagogies. By detailing the relationships between production practices in schools and the ways in which possible benefits are framed in relation to literacy and evolving media technologies, I am able to examine the tensions that imbue these questions:

How does creative media work constitute a wider literacy in formal and non-formal school spaces?

What can established pedagogy learn from moving image production processes?

How do social discursive factors determine practical media work in schools?

© The Author(s) 2018
M. Cannon, *Digital Media in Education*,
https://doi.org/10.1007/978-3-319-78304-8_2

Contexts

Media-Making and 'Amorphous Skills'

Claims as to the social, educational and economic benefits of making and manual dexterity are on the increase in several social spheres. They are witnessed variously in discourses related to: creativity and the arts (Gauntlett 2011a; NACCE 1999; Robinson 2011, 2013; Shirky 2011), craft and the vocational (Crawford 2009; Sennett 2008), the global Maker Movement (Bennett and Doherty 2010), and the STEM[1] lobby (Gibb 2015a; Livingstone and Hope 2011; Morgan 2015; Truss 2013). Moreover, the skills and dispositions that practical activities are said to mobilise are considered valuable assets in the business world and in the make-up of a workforce for the so-called 'knowledge economy'. So if educational and economic value can be derived from the processes of making and experimentation, questions must be raised as to why the practice of such activities seems to be eroding in school curricula. Why is practical work, and practical media work in particular, often set in opposition to understandings achieved through academic thought and language? (Buckingham 2014a; Wolf 2011, p. 6). Why are the 'softer skills' often ascribed to collaborative making experiences, such as team work and the building of self-esteem, relatively undervalued? Why is it that students' critical consciousness and capacity for reflection are disregarded as 'amorphous skills' (Gibb 2015a) that dilute the 'rigour' and application of academic knowledge?

In order to address these questions and clarify the possible impediments to a more capacious conception of literacy which is inclusive of digital media and the audiovisual, I explore the dichotomies at play in relation to classical perspectives on the abstract, the visual and the

---

[1] STEM refers to the academic subjects Science, Technology, Engineering and Maths. Although a preferred acronym in some circles is STEAM, propelling the Arts back into the acceptable academic canon (Cultural Learning Alliance 2014; Maeda 2013; see also the EU funded Digital Learning Across Boundaries project—DLaB—whose aim is to promote digital learning in teacher education, curriculum subjects, languages and cultures, to facilitate collaborative learning and community approaches across national boundaries: http://dlaberasmus.eu/ [Accessed 7 January 2018].

material. This is followed by a review of the socio-cultural context of digital media-making practices, and of relevant discourses on craftsmanship and vocationalism.

The Empirical and the Mind

Recent educational policy reform (Bassey et al. 2013) has re-kindled debates on the perceived gulf between: the merits of academic knowledge acquisition on the one hand (Abrams 2012; Hirsch 2006; Willingham 2012) and those of social, cultural and aesthetic learning through the creative arts on the other (Bragg and Manchester 2011; Sefton-Green 2008; Thomson et al. n.d). Like many suspicious of binary modes of thinking (Pring 2004), in this instance between pedagogies that deliver knowledge and those that are more concerned with autonomous self-expression and sensorial experience, Eisner (2005/1985) suggests this is a misleading dichotomy.

The latter draws on the long-term legacies left by Plato's 'hierarchies of knowledge' (Eisner 2006), relating them to the present day and the ways we make sense of experience. Far from reinforcing the polarities referenced in C. P. Snow's 'Two Cultures' (1961),[2] Eisner draws attention to the continuities between the arts/sciences schism (as does Burn 2013, p. 60) seeing the practitioners of both as 'form-makers':

> Both scientists and artists ... are makers of order—the former through the relationships created between theoretical material and the other through the ordering of the qualitative. Our sense of rightness ... is rooted in that ineffable experience to which the word "aesthetic" is assigned.
> (Eisner 2005/1985, p. 100)

For Plato it seems there was no room for the ineffable in the pursuit of truth; the only dependable knowledge was that associated with the 'episteme', that is, with sustainable and enduring rationality and abstraction.

---

[2] This refers to British scientist, C. P. Snow's Cambridge lecture in 1959 (see C. P. Snow 1961), whose polarising perspective lives on in Western discourse via the separation between science and the humanities. Snow's thesis sought to favourably re-position science in intellectual circles.

Hence, concrete product and the visual were untrustworthy, finite and subject to contamination. Eisner reminds us of the Platonic view of sensory information, as:

> dependent on the stuff of which our universe is made, namely material things. Since material things are in a state of constant decay, any knowledge derived from them must, of necessity, be short term at best and misleading at worst.
> (Eisner 2005/1985, p. 100)

Equally the domain of feelings was thought to sully the purity of the mind which should function "unencumbered by emotion or by the misleading qualities of the empirical world" (Eisner 2005/1985, p. 101). By re-visiting these formulations we can begin to see how thinking from antiquity continues to inform modern educational agendas in terms of the ways in which the visual arts in particular, a discipline to which creative media is often annexed, are secondary in status to epistemic, propositional knowledge.

Eisner, in a critique of hierarchical Platonic values, and in the context of discourses on qualitative research methodology, welcomes more granular Aristotelian thinking. The latter concerns the derivation of knowledge from differentiated perspectives: from the theoretical (out of necessity or perceived inevitability, such as that found in the natural sciences), from the practical (taking into account local social contingencies) and from the productive (from considerations in relation to the processes of making):

> With Aristotle, we get an effort to draw distinctions in the service of conceptual clarity. This aim is wholly congruent with current efforts to make distinctions between types of research, even to redefine the meanings of research so that they are no longer singular, but multiple.
> (Eisner 2008, p. 4)

Eisner goes on to argue that this more discursive view of the formation of knowledge proposes that a greater understanding of the epistemological—the ways in which knowledge can be shaped rather than discovered—would enable a wider appreciation of the value of aesthetic forms of knowing implicit in creative acts across the disciplines. The next section addresses the challenges that are perceived as standing in the way of such a vision.

Instrumental Learning and the 'Digital Native' Discourse

Arguably education systems are devised to maximise the potential for leading a life this is personally fulfilling, socially rewarding, culturally enriching and economically beneficial whilst being of benefit to the wider community (Bruner 1990; Lave and Wenger 1991; Pring 2004). Working towards this and widening the parameters of experience, means aspiring towards a more integrated educational offer. This would enable young people not only to demonstrate their learning using all available means of expression—digital or otherwise (Bazalgette 2010, 2011; Bazalgette and Bearne 2010; Buckingham 2003; Potter 2012)—but also to conceptualise with, learn about, imagine in and create through different media.

The above commentators propose an alternative educational paradigm which is rich in productive engagement with media and learners' personal, cultural and social environment (Street 1995). Tensions arise when policy makers and interest groups champion specific curricular components with campaigns, interventions and assessment procedures. These effectively divert resources, privilege favoured 'useful' subjects and de-privilege others, as raised by Lord Aberdare (2015) in relation to the UK's EBacc[3] qualification, which includes English, Maths, Science, History or Geography and a language, and notably excludes Arts subjects as a core constituent.

By way of example, in 2014, the then Secretary of State for Education, Nicky Morgan, lauded an educational intervention (Morgan 2014, 2015) that functioned expressly in the service of workforce development and global competitiveness. Science, Technology, Engineering and Maths (STEM subjects) continue to be mobilised as 'facilitative' subjects (Adams 2013), with more perceived instrumental value than those of the arts and

---

[3] See http://www.baccforthefuture.com/ [Accessed 6 March 2018]—a campaign to reform the EBacc and 'save creativity in schools'.

humanities—the area in which creative media production, if it is present at all, is often located. In fact, it was claimed by Morgan, that choosing to pursue arts subjects could be detrimental to young people's career prospects:

> maths, as we all know, is the subject that employers value most, helping young people develop skills which are vital to almost any career. And you don't just have to take my word for it—studies show that pupils who study maths to A level will earn 10% more over their lifetime. These figures show us that too many young people are making choices aged 15, which will hold them back for the rest of their life.
> (Morgan 2014, my emphasis)

I cite this passage from a speech delivered by Morgan at the Google Offices, London (10 November 2014) as it exemplifies the managerial, means-to-an-end culture (Ball 2013; Pring 2004; Sinker 2000; Williamson 2017a, 2017b) that imbues education policy. The benefits of earnings-related education are expressed with a rhetorical modality of certainty.

Further contextualisation reveals an ironic twist related to my object of study. The speech was given at the launch of a three-year government-backed campaign, Your Life, sponsored by a group of global corporations to ensure young adults in the UK had the maths and science skills needed to 'succeed' in the current competitive global economy. Spearheading the campaign was a competition—Formula 100—aimed at eleven to eighteen year olds, for which entrants were asked to submit thirty seconds of video describing an imagined innovatory artefact.

In order to participate in this competition, there was an implicit assumption that teachers and students had access to and were proficient in a variety of media practices from authorship to social media distribution. In an appeal to schools the Powerpoint 'lesson plan' simply listed the competition rules and a series of STEM advocacy messages, with no guidance on the practices of film-making itself. This intervention was flawed in a number of ways: it extolled the winner-takes-all ideology; its reach was limited and appealed to certain types of schools with certain types of priorities and resources; and the home page explicitly targeted young people with global banking aspirations. It is a highly instrumental, government-backed initiative explicitly driven by corporate interests, and at the very least represented a lost opportunity to introduce editing as a new, relevant and inclusive literacy practice.

By inviting digital participation from 11 year olds, the Formula 100 organisers implicitly supported the discredited 'digital native' (Prensky 2001) discourse that assumes the innate competency of most young people in a range of digital production practices (Bennett et al. 2008; Selwyn 2009; Thomas 2011): this may be the case in certain well-resourced schools, but by no means all. The implication is that sufficient media expertise accumulates informally in young people's leisure time in neutral and automatic ways. Buckingham (2003) challenges the homogenisation of young people and characterises the assumptions about universal access and skills related to creative media practice, as nefarious. Indeed, the closing lines of his 2003 opus warn that market-led forces, with interests in profit rather than public service imperatives, could result in "a privatised educational dystopia … and the emergence of an educational 'underclass'" (Buckingham 2003, p. 203). He makes the point, supported by this account, that practical media education alone, is not the silver bullet that will lead to universal social participation. However, the need for a critical eye on the prioritisation of business interests in education is paramount, if social inequality is not to subtly proliferate (Selwyn 2006). This critical assessment of particular discursive digital making practices now moves further afield by exploring the international Maker Movement which promises to unsettle traditional learning paradigms in ambiguous ways.

Maker Faires and Human Pipelines

Whilst UK educational reform reinforces the primacy of intellectual 'rigour', the purpose of the Maker Movement (most prominent in the US, but global in scope and gaining momentum in the UK) is to stimulate technical, electronic and robotic maker activities in formal and informal educational settings. Attended by leaders in education, science, technology and the arts, it began as a 'Maker Workshop' in The New York

Hall of Science in 2010, attracting a panoply of hackers, crafters, coders and DIY enthusiasts. The Movement's principles and practices subsume a number of discourses pertinent to my questions: the STEM initiative, practical work with new technologies and the progressive principles of learning-by-doing (Cantrill et al. 2014; Dewey 1997/1938; Peppler and Kafai 2007).

Reports of events from the US and the UK (Bennett and Doherty 2010; Maker Media Inc 2014; Maker Faire NYC 2017; Maker Faire UK 2015) indicate enthusiastic public support for now global phenomena known as Maker Faires. Despite the family-friendly 'Greatest show (and tell) on earth' tag line, events under this 'carnivalesque' brand are another commercial wing of Maker Media Inc—owners of Maker Magazine and Maker Shed, and formerly a division of O'Reilly Media. Their values are hence more likely to be profit-driven, and less likely to be apolitical:

> Part science fair, part county fair, and part something entirely new, Maker Faire is an all-ages gathering of tech enthusiasts, crafters, educators, tinkerers, hobbyists, engineers, science clubs, authors, artists, students, and commercial exhibitors.
> (Maker Media Inc 2014)

The title of the New York Hall of Science (NYHS) 2012 report makes the aim of the movement explicit: Growing the Next Generation of Science Innovators, as well as establishing:

> a framework for assessing design, making and play as methodologies for reforming and improving STEM education as a first step toward meeting the need for a more plentiful and diverse STEM workforce. (NYHS, Maker Faire 2012, p. 1)

Investment in design, making and play is a laudable pursuit in the sphere of arts and science education, nevertheless the utilitarian economic agenda complicates any sense of intrinsic worth that might otherwise be attached to such activities.

Possibly as a function of its corporately-sanctioned inception, the document takes the liberty of referring to 'human capital' being squeezed through pipelines. The pipeline is assumed to represent the education system which is malfunctioning and not producing 'the right type of worker', due to human flow 'dropping out':

> Assuming that one outcome is engagement and persistence in STEM the STEM pipeline is leaking badly. Pipelines are about pressure and constriction, but we really don't know much about the junctures or the dynamics along the way. And we need a better sense of what the workforce needs to look like. Those are the levers that policymakers have to work with.
> (NYHS Maker Faire 2012, p. 15 my emphasis)

Along with references to tightening up the junctures to prevent leaks,[4] it should be noted that the Maker Movement conceives of curriculum reform as shifting from a transmission model, to one that attracts young people into certain areas perceived to be of interest to them. Or as they put it, "moving ... from 'pushing' what students need to know to 'pulling' them into innovative and engaging content that is personally relevant" (Hagel and Seely Brown 2005; NYHS Maker Faire 2012, p. 16). Both these motivations are based on values which leave little room for independent critical judgement. Whether 'human resources' are being pushed or pulled in certain curriculum directions, the implication is that young people, as they are making, are being systematically interpellated and objectified by pre-determined political ideologies, so as to mould 'the citizen-worker-of-the-future' (Kaplan 2008, p. 176, drawing on Williams 2004, p. 408).

This said, despite questionable allusions to growing, leaking and wasting human capital, paradoxically, other outcomes of the Maker Movement—such as their seven learning goals (NYHS 2012, p. 20) could be lifted directly from progressive accounts of connected learning and pro-social, media-making experiences. We see in the above referenced text, for example, support for interdisciplinary, intergenerational dialogue (Ito et al. 2013); community building (Sefton-Green 2013);

---

[4] The same industrial metaphor is used in NESTA's Next Gen report (Livingstone and Hope 2011, p. 7) in relation to keeping the 'talent pipeline' flowing. In addition, NESTA's Young Digital Makers report (Quinlan 2015), whilst being a comprehensive UK audit, seems in part, to have been conceived to address the perceived shortfall of technological skills.

agency, collaboration and experimentation (Burn and Durran 2006, 2007; Burnett and Bailey 2014; Potter 2012). Furthermore, an emphasis on learning through knowledge exchange is part of the Maker ethos, and this could be said to support a reconciliation between 'sage-on-the-stage', 'guide-on-the-side' pedagogies, and learning in 'third spaces' (Potter and McDougall 2017) to be discussed later in this chapter in relation to teaching and 'habitus'.

I have quoted at length from the Maker Faire document as it seems to rehearse the contradictions inherent in making practices with new technologies and ideological problematisation. It could be that the ways in which acts of design, making and play are framed in informal educational fora are becoming increasingly determined by external forces with interests beyond the ideals of public service and personal fulfilment.[5]

This subsection has addressed 'making trends' in informal making spaces, as a way of questioning the reification and marketisation of making, which, if it proceeds unchecked stands to 'naturally' align with government and corporate priorities. The instrumental positioning of the practical is now further examined in the formal school media-making environment, demonstrating the ways in which it is often delivered as a form of vocational training.

Schools, Computing and 'Growing the Workforce'

Sennett (2008) and Crawford (2009) have enjoyed success with publications extoling the benefits of manual work and craftsmanship (to be discussed in more depth in the next section). Their work reinforces the idea of individual, pragmatic maker-experts meeting the objective standards of their particular craft. Although they focus more on the personal and moral dimensions of pragmatism, it seems their respective exegeses fit, unintentionally perhaps, but readily within the parameters of cultures of competition and the neoliberal agenda (Monbiot 2016). So too did Livingstone and Hope's (2011) Next Gen report, which partly

---

[5] It is also worth noting that the Maker Movement has been supported by the research wing of the American military (DARPA—Defense Advanced Research Projects Agency), to the tune of over $13 million (Williamson 2014, p. 12), indicating alternative motives for its activities.

functioned as an entreaty for urgent government action to address a perceived skills deficit in the 'creative industries' (or perhaps more precisely in the video effects industry). The Department for Education conflated this dearth of talent with the idea that 'UK plc' could be losing the perceived 'global race' (Williamson 2014), which is so damagingly publicised in the triennial international OECD PISA[6] league tables:

> what really matters is how we're doing compared with our international competitors. That is what will define our economic growth and our country's future. The truth is, at the moment we are standing still while others race past. (DfE 2010, p. 3)

One of the consequences of the Next Gen report and other corporate appeals (Schmidt 2011) was the rapid reform of the UK ICT curriculum, which has mutated from competence in Microsoft software packages, to 'training' in coding and computer programming (DfE 2013).

The outcome is a mixed blessing: on the one hand, young learners can now experience computational thinking at primary level—a welcome intervention with implied opportunities for creative media engagement—on the other, it invites narrow and partial industry constituents into school programmes with unprecedented pace and penetration. Livingstone himself is the former Chairman and CEO of Eidos Interactive Ltd—a key global player in the video and special effects industry. There are also strong implications for school infrastructure and training, and given the speed with which this intervention was made, it remains to be seen how adequately the logistics, resources and success criteria have been thought through.

More socially framed responses to socio-economic change and advances in communicative media are emerging from such countries as New

---

[6] Starting in 2000, the OECD's (Organisation for Economic Cooperation and Development) PISA (Programme for International Student Assessment) survey tests over half a million fifteen-year-old students in '65 economies' for their reading, maths and science ability and publishes the results globally. Although the tests offer interesting data on global numeracy and literacy 'performance', some question the extent to which educational policies are determined by its outcomes, considering the absence of contextual information and its contested methods of testing, data and comparison (Ball 2013, p. 38; Sellar et al. 2017).

Zealand[7] and Finland (the New Zealand approach becomes more salient later in Chap. 6, as it informs one of my studies). Finnish education has become something of a talismanic touchstone globally, in terms of its regular appearance at or near the top of the PISA league tables mentioned earlier. There is no scope here to examine the premise of the international league tables, nor to account for Finnish achievements in any detail, except to say that their education system is perceived as successful at the same time as it professes an intrinsic commitment to equity, well-being, teacher professionalism and digital participation, imbued with cross-disciplinary, critical and creative media literacy.[8]

Routes to media learning which are less partially framed and more meaningful to the learner (Cantrill et al. 2014; Peppler 2013; Sefton-Green 2013, p. 45), particularly in relation to computer programming, may counter the potential for the reproduction and testing of grammar-like computer code to 'grow the workforce'. Of relevance here is Crawford's observation on the deleterious effects of learner commodification:

> If occasions for the exercise of judgment are diminished, the moral-cognitive virtue of attentiveness will atrophy.
> (Crawford 2009, p. 101)

For Crawford, attentiveness to interactions between elements and the capacity to make immediate material adjustments on the fly, are key characteristics of craftsmanship. Applying judgement and making open-ended choices are equally as important in the creative process, these are skills which would be adversely affected in the event of media-making in schools becoming narrowly conflated with right or wrong coding decisions.

Arguably, the current swing towards vocationalism (Wolf 2011) is a reaction against putative over-indulgence towards progressive learning strategies under the former Labour government (such as the intervention

---

[7] See the 2007 New Zealand curriculum's key competencies which are stipulated as both ends and means. Available from http://nzcurriculum.tki.org.nz/Key-competencies [Accessed 6 March 2018].

[8] The Finns produced a specific media education policy booklet: https://kavi.fi/sites/default/files/documents/mil_in_finland.pdf (KAVI 2013) [Accessed 22 May 2018] and further comment can be found in my MA Dissertation: https://fashioningandflow.wordpress.com/2011/11/09/international-perspective/ (Cannon 2011) [Accessed 6 March 2018].

known as SEAL—Social and Emotional Aspects of Learning, DfES 2005—and the expansive Creative Partnerships[9] programme) which for some are incompatible with knowledge and skills acquisition. This book however proposes that to narrow media-making down to the unambiguously functional needs of industry and the economy, is to forego opportunities for young people to engage with aesthetics, with critical thinking, and with the conceptually complex. The next section addresses factors affecting media-making in schools by offering a critique of the more populist portrayals of everyday media production that are seen to stall the progress of film and media presence in schools.

Cyber-Libertarianism and Creative Production

The subtitle of this section refers to an academic standpoint that rallies around the alignment of human development and democracy with technological advance. As there are powerful social and commercial forces that stand to gain from the promotion of such a view, and as schools are implicated in this nexus, the cyber-libertarian trajectory merits some interrogation. For commentators such as Gauntlett (2011a) and Shirky (2009, 2011) the performance of online 'show and tell', such as that displayed on many YouTube channels, is a cause mainly for celebration, whilst criticality and politically engaged commentary seem to be consciously bracketed. A certain democratised vision of web culture is promoted in which many willing crafters and media producers are growing in unprecedented numbers, possibly already equipped with Jenkins et al.'s (2006) twenty-first century skills (see the Pedagogies section later in this Chapter for more on these skills).

Some potential repercussions of this populist approach number as follows: determining forces go unquestioned, ideologies become entrenched, and monolithic 'self-evident' patterns of thought are given credence and built into the social firmament (Manovich 2001). Arguably, these

---

[9] From 2002–2011 the Creative Partnerships programme worked intensively with over 2700 schools across England, 90,000 teachers and over 1 million young people, building partnerships with creative workers, such as artists, scientists, architects, and cultural organisations, and generating numerous reports (Lord et al. 2007; Sefton-Green 2008).

rhetorical Web 2.0[10] discourses help to render media-making universal, inevitable and obvious. So much so, that studying media texts of any kind often equates to 'soft subject' fun and triviality in the wider public debate (Buckingham 2014a, Laughey 2012). One way of countering this damaging trend is to borrow a key formulation from Cultural Studies. Williams (1961) asserts that a cultural practice, text or artefact cannot be understood in isolation from the historically situated 'structure of feeling' from whence it emerges. The 'structure of feeling' describes the relationships between constantly shifting cultural production and the fixity of socio-cultural institutions. Discursive processes, Williams claims, are paradoxically both fugitive and defined within a framework: they encapsulate both the rigidity of institutionalised codes, "[whilst operating] in the most delicate and least tangible parts of our activity" (1961, p. 64). It is this elusiveness of discourse that makes its articulation an important part of intellectual work. 'The structure of feeling' will be revisited in Chap. 6 as a useful analogy with which to understand tensions in contemporary classroom practice.

In his book Making is Connecting (2011a), Gauntlett gives voice to both on and offline creative communities and celebrates social engagement through new technologies. His view, however, has been critiqued for neglecting socio-economic structures and conferring agency-giving powers on technology. Both sides of the argument are discussed in a conversation with contributors to the Media Education Research Journal (Gauntlett 2011b), during which Gauntlett claims to be redressing the imbalance caused by more sceptical colleagues' critique of Web 2.0 celebratory rhetoric (Buckingham 2010). My study argues that choosing to bracket a critical frame can create a layer of insulation between rhetoric and social change. As unalloyed optimism around digital 'creativity' takes hold in public consciousness, a perspective such as this could further devalue the function of media education and its place in schools.

While disagreeing with some of Gauntlett's arguments, McDougall offers a more conciliatory assessment by drawing out the ways in which

---

[10] 'Web 2.0' refers to the shift from user consumption of web content and directory searches (taxonomies) to user-generated content, tagging (folksonomies) and participatory practices, such as blogging and wiki development.

his perspective offers a welcome counterpoint to prevailing 'technological moral panics':

> [taking] us beyond instrumental notions of assessing creative practice or teaching with new media into a more far-reaching and political view of how human beings are finding new ways of making their mark on the world, contributing to culture and 'doing it for ourselves'.
> (McDougall in conversation with Gauntlett 2011b, p. 120)

Despite McDougall's affirmation that Making is Connecting is cogently argued essential reading for media educators, Buckingham (2010) critiques several aspects of its premise. For example, Buckingham re-affirms that: consumption as the primary pattern of digital media engagement; commercial gain is the main driver of 'loser-generated content' (2010, p. 7, drawing on Petersen 2008); levels of participation remain uneven; and finally, that it is the usual (middle class and resourced) suspects who are the primary digital content creators. Moreover, Buckingham questions the sophistication, ubiquity and creative potential of 'home-mode' outputs (2010, p. 6) and denounces 'populist cyber-libertarianism' (2010, p. 4) as a form of technological determinism: "a view of technology as somehow autonomously producing social change" (2010, p. 4). He goes on to suggest that contrary to 'digital native' rhetoric (Prensky 2001), access alone does not equate to aptitude in textual production, nor to social fulfilment, nor to the inevitable desire to share. According to Buckingham (2007) and from my own experience, it falls to schools to deliver the opportunities, competencies and motivation for media craft skills to be distributed more evenly, by furnishing opportunities that students may not otherwise encounter.

I have suggested that this enquiry takes its cue from Williams (1961) by unpacking both (civic and semiotic) structure and feeling. These are understood as interdependent elements in relation to the processes of media composition as well as the processes of researching social conditions of possibility. To this end, the following section examines school media production's contested relations with discourses on creativity and its relation to policy-making.

Media and Creativity Rhetoric

Media production's alignment with creativity is something of a poisoned chalice: whilst distancing it from utilitarian 'skills and training', the tendency is for media production to be re-assigned as an extracurricular marginal activity, estranged from core literacy strategy. Some headway was made during Creative Partnerships (Sefton-Green 2008), during which the idea of creativity blossomed as a transcendent theme, and school film and digital media projects began to develop. However, this diffuse and discursive concept, often aligned with practical media work, is not uncomplicated, as Banaji et al. (2006) have expounded. Creativity is commonly over-determined—either yoked into the service of specific interest groups (Readman 2010), or reified as an all-purpose, universally 'good' human trait with almost balm-like qualities.

Robinson's claims (2011, 2013) in support of creativity and the imagination in learning bemoan the antiquated Victorian nature of the UK education system, and his assertions now seem to have been absorbed into western public consciousness, if over fifty million views of his 2006 TED talk[11]—as at March 2018—are any reliable index. Indeed, in many respects, his seductive views are a welcome antidote to current narrow reforms, however it is questionable the extent to which the romantic and totalising appeals of "charismatic educationalists on the conference circuit" (Gibb 2015a) translate beyond the rhetorical in the political arena. As creativity rides high in popular discourses related to social and emotional well-being, the easier it is for it to be derailed and re-routed by neoliberal factions, and 'operationalised' (Readman 2010) into more 'useful' areas, like coding.

In contrast with the cultivation of "active, technical co-producers" (as critiqued by Williamson 2014), Robinson proclaims the potential for creative education to assist in the search for personal fulfilment (2013). Similarly other commentators such as (Claxton 2003; Gardner 2009) and Belshaw (2012) support the pro-social aspects of learning, by promoting the personal qualities said to be essential to digitally literate twenty-first century learners

---

[11] See https://www.ted.com/talks/ken_robinson_says_schools_kill_creativity?language=en [Accessed 6 March 2018].

(Belshaw 2012). There may well be a place in media production settings for Belshaw's (2011) Eight Essential Elements of Digital Literacies in pursuit of broader notions of literacy, and many of his scientifically styled elements pepper my account too.[12] Participants in my case studies demonstrate certain of the characteristics he lists, but as Loveless points out, in terms narratives of disposition, it is important to note that attributes are framed as preconditions as well as outcomes of creative processes (2012).

Other creative media research projects and interventions report similar findings (Bazalgette et al. 2011; Mumford et al. 2013; FLAG 2013, 2015; Potter and Bryer 2016; Scottish Screen 2006). So, if as the evidence suggests, the rewards are great, where does school media-making sit on the slippery continuum of cultural value? Some would like to see moving image inscription as commonplace and unassailable as the technology known as cursive writing (Bazalgette 2010; Burn and Parker 2001), by virtue of the complex social mediascapes inhabited by most western young people (boyd 2014; Ito 2009). However, because of the embattled status of the arts (Cultural Learning Alliance 2011; DfCMS 2013, paragraphs 117 and 118), the ambiguous relationship policy makers have with media education and the 'discourses of derision' (Barker 2001) aimed at Media Studies as a subject, creative media production in schools is tainted by association.[13]

Wider public debates seem to ignore the creative and critical potency of media education, seeing it as "a byword for triviality, for the dumbing down of education, for the degenerate, celebrity-obsessed, loser-take-all culture that modern Britain has (apparently) now become." (Buckingham 2014a, p. 7). But as Buckingham points out, it is perhaps time to be less defensive and more pro-active at school level. The summer of 2015 saw much activity on the part of the Media Education Association (MEA 2015)

---

[12] The elements are: Cultural, Cognitive, Constructive, Communicative, Confident, Creative, Critical and Civic. They are cited here as a welcome counterpoint to what might be described as the imperative for students' 'Conservative Compliance' with curriculum diktats.

[13] So hostile to the digital arts is the current administration that the line 'digital texts shall not be included' features in the English GCSE specification. See page 4 here: https://www.gov.uk/government/uploads/system/uploads/attachment_data/file/206143/GCSE_English_Language_final.pdf [Accessed 6 March 2018].

to re-write specifications and save GCSE and A' Level Media Studies from simple 'deletion' by the current Schools Minister. This is indicative of the status of creative and media-related educational activity in government circles, and the need for a concomitant shift in local strategy, if film and digital media production are to gain traction in the lower years of schooling.

Creativity, then, in the Robinsonian sense, is a part-time ally of media production, which, for any long term benefits to materialise, has to be viewed critically in conjunction with hegemonic forces and celebratory rhetoric. Reid et al. (2002) pragmatically observed in pioneering research on young people's DV editing in schools (supported too by BECTA's findings 2003), that without a mandate for inclusion in core curricula, unless they can be 're-branded' as a communicative craft, practices such as these will remain unevenly located around the country. On a more optimistic note, an investigation into the principles and processes of craftsmanship , a discipline that embraces cognitive, creative and functional dimensions (Frayling 1993), may illuminate current evaluations of digital media production and draw it closer to the social modes of literacy that this book supports.

Media-Making and Craft Principles

Discursive commentary on utilitarianism and its relation to personal absorption conflate in recent publications around the notion of craftsmanship. As video production and editing in particular have been distinguished as craft-like activities (Bordwell and Thompson 2010; Murch 2001) I contemplate related rhetorical claims. Notably Sennett (2008) and Crawford's (2009) accounts of the benefits of working with one's hands relate to centuries of stigma around craft (Frayling 1993). These writers re-assert positive pragmatic philosophies with respect to manual activity and the benefits and pleasures therein. Crawford—office worker-turned-academic-turned-mechanic—laments the obsolescence of 'shop class' in schools (the US equivalent of Woodwork, Textiles and Resistant Materials), and sets up a romantic dialectic between the economic imperative for 'mindless' clerical employment and the offices of 'mindful' fixing.

More helpfully, in terms of clarifying the principles of craft, Crawford conceives of his relationship with raw materials as dialogic. References to tinkering and iterative interaction are also useful in transposing these practices to the context of media production. There is however an overall sense in which Sennett and Crawford, in their recruitment of the traditional craft principles, are invoking discourses of authenticity that cleave questionably towards nostalgia and essentialism. Like Robinson (2013), both authors adopt a somewhat totalising tone in the manner in which they refer to all humans' capacity to develop a life-affirming manual skill—if only the conditions were right (Sennett 2008, p. 11).

This latter observation recalls Hall's sobering dictum on our historical 'situatedness', that: "Men and women make history but not under conditions of their own making." (Hall 1991, p. 11). This somewhat reductive assessment of human agency aggravates any sense of reassuring solutionism that can build up around a belief in universal giftedness (Selwyn 2006, 2016) or ed-tech panaceas (Morozov 2013; Watters 2015). Rather than addressing inequality, some argue that commentaries veering towards essentialism and techno-celebration paradoxically set up conditions that secure winners and losers. In other words, whilst individuals are busy honing personalised choices and unlocking their creativity, notions of improving understandings of social conditions are side-lined.

In light of Halls' related assertion that there are no values other than those constructed within discourse (Hall 1991), a connection can be made here with Eisner's critique of western hierarchical constructions of knowledge, which are played out in perceptions of talent versus intelligence (2005/2002a, p. 206). Talent is often associated with the corporeal and the affective, to the makers and the doers in art, craft and sport; whilst the cognitive implies intelligence, an attribute assigned to the 'superior' wielders of language and logic. The latter is accorded greater value scholastically with a sense of intelligence having been earned, whereas the former is often framed as intuitive or genetic in origin and thereby "not a function of thinking" (Eisner 2005/1985, p. 100).

Sennett would arguably align himself with Eisner's critique in that, for him, practical craftwork is an iterative cognitive process of problem-finding, problem-solving and Deweyan "flexible purposing" (Eisner 2005/2002a, p. 209). Assuming that such craft principles can be grafted onto the processes of media production, one might start to ponder on the nature of the talented media-maker and that of the intelligent media-maker. Do they share similar dispositions, skills and knowledge? Should such a distinction even be made?

In a shift to recruit the ideas of Sennett and Crawford, it is proposed in this account that attentive media-makers, focused on precision and qualitative refinement, may be compared with Sennett's apprentice violin makers or Crawford's mechanics. This analogy is made in recognition of the suspicion accorded digital raw materials such as numerically-derived, inorganic audiovisual assets (Burn 2009a, p. 18, 2011). Both theorists argue against perceptions of craftsmanship as an 'unthinking' occupation, by identifying an agility of mind which is alert to innovative syntheses, thus bolstering Eisner's support of aesthetic learning in order to improve cognition (Eisner 1986). Some scholars have also advanced the notion of 'critical making' (Maeda 2013; Somerson and Hermano 2013) so as to capture and critique what happens in the often tacit interstices of planned design and actual 'artistic' production—an idea to be unpacked in Chaps. 6 and 7.[14]

Craftwork and media-making share similar inward and outward perspectives: attention is given to: the material in hand in the mode of a dexterous expert; the product in the mode of an artist working with integrity; and the expectations of an intended user or recipient in the mode of performance (Craft Council 2014). The tension between these modes might serve as the locus for a more holistic conceptualisation of media composition and alternative literacy practices. These practices would be less vested with monitoring understanding of canonical texts, and more engaged with makers' vocal and reflective accounts of process and contextualised decision-making (Ross et al. 1993). Film and digital media production, like much creative practice, embraces experimentation and ambiguity, and expressing the ways in which these have been negotiated are key capacities in the proposed wider literacy advocated by this book (Lankshear and Knobel 2003; Reid 2009; Sefton-Green 2000, p. 228; Street 1995, p. 133).

---

[14] See Bergala et al. 2016, p. 92, where, in the context of film production, and drawing on Marcel Duchamp, he names this important schism in mathematical terms, as 'the personal art coefficient'.

Above I have articulated some thoughts from antiquity and their relation to contemporary debates around digital and video production in schools. Young makers seem caught in a traverse between cultures of technocratic and functional ideology at one end of the spectrum, and at the other rhetorical appeals to harnessing creative potential and fulfilling personal dreams. I have also introduced a practical craft dimension to the discussion of media production as a means of addressing polarised thinking and moving creativity debates forward. The next section sets out some challenges to established literacy practices, namely more practical ways of knowing and the bearing they have on a broader literacy offer. I then move on to detail recent media production research carried out in concrete school settings.

Literacy and Social Participation

Throughout the book I make reference to established school literacy and the intellectual work that contests what constitutes this pillar of the curriculum. Of relevance here is Street's thinking on The New Literacy Studies (NLS) and the social dimension of literacy (1984, 2003). He and others (Belshaw 2011; Gee 2004, 2015a, 2015b; Potter 2012) argue that literacy, in addition to the acquisition of cognitive skills, competency in grammar and the appreciation of canonical texts, is one's capacity to negotiate and participate in sets of social and cultural practices. Further, these practices need to be understood as interactions that bleed purposefully into situated relations of power. As such, Street's ideological model of literacy,[15] and the ways in which he invokes theorists such as Bourdieu, Dewey and Freire (Street 2003, pp. 81–84), grounds the wider literacy debate on which this account is based.

The premise is that literacy is not simply a mental phenomenon, but an achievement based on "changing patterns of participation" (Gee 2015, p. 36) that are:

---

[15] Street (1984) introduced two models of literacy: the 'autonomous' and the 'ideological'. The former remains relevant in schooled literacies of the moment and refers to the blanket teaching of decontextualised functional skills—such as phonic recognition—that are believed to be automatically empowering, 'inevitably' enhancing understanding and life chances. Whereas the 'ideological' model embodies a value system and is culturally sensitive to variable contexts. It takes into account the uses of multi-literacies and a large number of associated socio-economic factors.

always embedded in socially constructed epistemological principles. It is about knowledge: the ways in which people address reading and writing are themselves rooted in conceptions of knowledge, identity, and being ... It is not valid to suggest that "literacy" can be "given" neutrally and then its "social" effects only experienced afterwards.

(Street 2003, pp. 77–78)

Street observes that increased critical engagement with social theory and practical educational applications since the inception of NLS, have seeded debates across formal and non-formal learning contexts, and also within policy-making circles. Here lies the relevance of his theorising to my research, in that media-related literacy events and practices in the primary and early secondary years are largely confined to the non-formal, thus implicating understandings of the social, the contextual and alternative representational modes of address. The widespread use of digital media tools and technologies across contexts makes explicit NLS advocates' original insight that "literacy relates to more general issues of social theory regarding textuality, figured worlds, identity and power" (Street 2003, p. 87).

Another member of the original NLS group was Gee, who in 2015, reflected on its seminal work. He proposed that a new movement called 'The New Literacies Studies' might carry over the NLS argument about written language into the digital age. Rather than new ways of studying established literacy, it is about "studying new types of literacy beyond print literacy, especially 'digital literacies' and literacy practices embedded in popular culture" (Gee 2015, p. 44). Drawing on Scollon and Scollon (1981), Gee raises the problematic and garlanded dominance of 'essayist-prose style' and 'essay-text literacy' in contemporary schooling, and its constraining impact on modern consciousness. In brief, it is proposed that the insular focus on lexis and the relationships between sentences exacts a cost:

With the heightened emphasis on truth value, rather than social or rhetorical conditions, comes the necessity to be explicit about logical implications.

(Gee 2015, p. 39)

My account reasons that meaning-making with media, not least because of the audience factor and the material embodied nature of its tools and processes, goes some way to addressing the limitations that prose places on both perceptual intelligence (Gee 2015, p. 37, drawing on Hawkins and Blakeslee 2005), and the provocatively identified "effacement of individual and idiosyncratic identity" (Gee 2015, p. 39). Thus it would appear that just at the time when children and young people may be seeking to establish a sense of selfhood through outward-facing representations, the routes to experimenting fully therein are restricted in the school day. Multimodal production opportunities may well help diversify literacy portfolios, however, my analysis moves to complicate this proposition, by looking at approaches to media education itself that mirror divisions between perceived types of intelligence.

Practices

Media-Making, Phronesis and Rhetoric

Media education has defined sets of practices when it comes to theory and practice: rather than conceived as two facets of the same coin, they are more often taught with monocular vision. By and large, in current Secondary, Further and Higher education curricula, Media Studies concerns itself with the conceptual, and Media Production with practical industry training. This section of the book assumes a more holistic binocular view by looking at theories of practical media work in the lower school years, and how these could inform deeper understandings of junior multimodal capabilities and associated pedagogies.

Earlier I alluded to Eisner's commitment to plural ways of knowing, and in so doing a link between the Greek 'episteme'—the rational pursuit of 'true' and universal knowledge—and present-day 'scientistic' research was suggested. There are two other constructs from the classics that can be affiliated with media composition practices, namely rhetoric and the less familiar phronesis. The former relates to practices of outward expression, the latter to knowledge drawn from practical wisdom, and both relate to themes in current progressive and socially-oriented teaching and learning discourses. These approaches are largely based on social constructivist learning theory (Dewey 1997/1938; Freire 1993/1970; Vygotsky 1978) and the development of media-rich 'Connected Learning' programmes developing in the US[16] (Cantrill et al. 2014; Ito et al. 2013; Peppler 2013). By uniting old and new thought on teaching and learning, I hope to advance some sobering theoretical continuity with history, which may check the pendulum-like swing between fashionable or retrogressive ideologies.

Aristotelian thinking proposes that subject matter within practical life is contingent rather than necessary, and Eisner (2005/2002b, p. 193) uses this observation to argue the case for improved artistry in teaching, through deeper understandings of the workings of phronesis. The concept is also useful for articulating the kinds of knowledge gained in an aestheticised view of media production—a practical domain in which seeming audiovisual inevitabilities could in fact be otherwise:

> Practical reasoning is deliberative, it takes into account local circumstances, it weighs tradeoffs, it is riddled with uncertainties, it depends upon judgment, profits from wisdom, addresses particulars, it deals with contingencies, is iterative and shifts aims in process when necessary … It is not enduring and it is not foundational. Its aim is to arrive at good but imperfect decisions with respect to particular circumstances.
> (Eisner 2005/2002b, p. 193)

The passage rehearses the kinds of dispositions often exposed at the video editing interface, as decisions are made 'in flight' (Eisner 2005/2002b, p. 202). As Crawford (2009) and Sennett (2008) have argued in support of craft practices, practical knowledge is pragmatic and reflective: the to-ing and fro-ing between local and corrective action, and the exercise of judgment therein, are the defining qualities of phronetic knowing. As will be seen, the making and editing of short form video clips requires precisely this kind of negotiation and experimentation with

---

[16] The 'Connected Learning' programme is defined by three *Learning* Principles whereby activities are: (a) interest-powered, (b) academically-oriented and (c) peer-supported; and three *Design* Principles whereby curricula are: (a) openly-networked, (b) production-centred, and (c) involve shared purpose (Ito et al. 2013).

filmic materials, in order to achieve what Goodman describes as "the rightness of fit" (1978) between and amongst certain elements to produce particular meanings and effects.

Inspired by a prescient observation from Green (1995, p. 400), Burn (2009a, p. 9) recruits rhetoric as an enriching and politicising strand in the understanding of moving image (see also Robinson, M. 2013, on the study of rhetoric in modern curricula). To explore this further, it is worth noting that Greek philosophy was rooted in oral tradition which privileged language and demoted the status of the image as ephemeral (Eisner 2006). Forms of material making were then, and to an extent still are accorded the lower status of artistry, mimicry, craft or manual labour, categories which even amongst themselves are assigned sliding scales of cultural value (Frayling 2011). Writing, on the other hand, as a form of knowledge demonstration, has over centuries accrued academic value in contrast with the image. Burn (2009a), however, asserts that the technical and social affordances of digital media are set to unsettle the 'natural' order of cultural expression, claiming that oracy (or orality—Ong 2002/1982) and rhetoric are in the ascendant. If true, then a reassessment of literacy and its communicative tools and practices is overdue.

Burn argues for a mediating modality some way between reading modes of suspicion for 'factual and untruthful' media texts, and appreciation for 'fictional and truthful' literary texts (2009a; see also Burn 2011). A rhetorical approach seems to subsume both, and is rather:

> more even-handed. It allows us to recognise duplicity, exploitation, and misrepresentation ... but also the stylistic properties of a text or an oral performance: how an idea is conveyed with passion and conviction, how an audience believes in a representation with its head and its heart ... how a text makes a truth claim, and what a reader makes of this ... [it] invokes the immediacy, performance and context of speech ... [in fact] orality and oracy may often be better metaphors for the communicative processes of new media than literacy, with its associations of the fixity, abstraction and temporal deferral of print.
> (Burn 2009a, p. 9)

Burn's appeal for even-handedness is welcome and reflects the tone and purpose of this enquiry. This research aspires to influence educators from all sectors to engage with digital media production with 'head and heart': thinking beyond useful knowledge and skills agendas, and in more critical and imaginative ways about the nature of communication, audience and purpose.

Building more outward-facing educational experiences with media acknowledges a potential audience and the school could be a safe practice ground for un-simulated digital interactions with 'the outside world'. Clearly the presence of an audience is not always necessary for learning to take place, but offering opportunities to communicate understanding in more dialogic and 'participative' ways represents for many, a more personally engaging and memorable experience. As Jenkins observes:

> Media education needs to be framed for participants, a role distinct from yet closely related to both producers and consumers as they were classically conceived.
> (Jenkins 2011)

Burn and Durran sum up their understanding of the relevance of becoming a literate media practitioner and speculate on the nuts and bolts of stewarding this in the classroom:

> If media literacy allows us to engage in cultural practices through which we make sense of and take control of our world and ourselves, in expressive practices in which we represent ourselves and our ideas, and in critical practices in which we interpret what we read, view, play, then the final question is how does all this take place?
> (Burn and Durran 2007, p. 16)

Their question introduces the following section that offers theories on the more granular aspects of audiovisual inscription.

Media Composition and Multimodal Performance

Media production seen as a form of active cultural expression through the metaphor of writing is an established analogy in the field (Sefton-Green 1998), however media composition could be a more apt term for media inscription practices. The word is already strongly redolent of other art forms—music, painting, dance, photography and mise-en-scène in film production—and embraces the idea of the 'artful' combination and layering of audiovisual elements. Indeed, from a technological point of view, the recent conflation of expressive functionality into a tablet such as the iPad (used as a creative tool in mine and others' research studies—Cannon et al. 2014; Potter and Bryer 2014) could be seen to materially occasion "synaesthetic experience" (Sefton-Green 2005, p. 109) on a mobile "multimodal mixing desk" (Burn and Parker 2003, p. 23).

Burn and Durran (2007) claim that cultural, expressive and critical processes related to literacy are bound together through an understanding of social systems of signification and the use of semiotic tools. However, semioticians' preoccupation with the text, make it less of a useful analytical tool for my study, which is more concerned with people and processes. A more anthropological approach to 'writing' with media, inspired by Alexander Reid,[17] will be grafted onto my understanding of production processes. A. Reid's work on new media composition, digital rhetoric and the evolution of writing (2007) are relevant to my research in so far as they help to advance literacy as a socially rooted practice. Not only this, but cross-disciplinary perspectives alleviate the potential for educational instrumentalism and narrow technologically deterministic practices to dominate.

Inspired by Massumi (2002) and poaching from other disciplines, A. Reid, develops correlations between cognition, 'behaviour with symbols' and social hierarchy dating back to Paleolithic times. He claims that:

> the adaptation of symbolic behaviour was largely about being able to gain a social, competitive advantage—both individually and socially (for one's kin group). In short, symbolic behaviour has always been discursive and rhetorical … it is our ability to store and process information in spaces outside our body that allows us to engage in the complex thoughts on which consciousness is founded.
> (A. Reid 2007, p. 25)

---

[17] For clarity from here on, I refer to the American Professor, Alexander Reid, as A. Reid and Mark Reid at BFI Education simply as, Reid.

Importantly, for this author and for the purposes of this study, it is claimed that "modern consciousness and symbolic behaviour emerged together … and that consciousness is indeed a product of the exteriorization of embodied mental processes" (A. Reid 2007, p. 25), rather than a product of the private rumination of the individual.

This is not the arena for further discussion on consciousness but I include these deliberations here as they not only entwine cognition and making, they also re-locate the compositional process into "a material-historical-cultural-space" (A. Reid 2007, p. 25). In this view, technologies become actors in these processes (along with human actors), neither reified nor objects of suspicion, but regarded "as elements in a distributed network of cognition" (A. Reid 2007, p. 26). These ideas will be expanded in Chap. 6, congruent as they are with Jenkins et al.'s twenty-first century skills (2006) to be discussed shortly (most notably those that connect with Distributed Cognition and Collective Intelligence). They help to frame the processes of media composition and literacy in a networked environment, as illustrated in my theoretical framework to follow.

Before concluding this section I would like to explain an adaptation of A. Reid's terminology—instead of describing human expressive acts as 'symbolic behaviour', I call this 'rhetorical performance'. The word 'performance' is free from 'scientistic' associations of insular animalistic behaviour, conveying rather the conscious public enactment of identity through mediated representation and rhetorical expression. To be clear, I invoke the kinds of 'situated identity performances' related to Goffman's (1990/1959) dramaturgical front stage/back stage selves, rather than performativity in the delivery of results. Rhetorical performance embraces the critical agency of the maker, and the enabling and constraining factors related to: process, raw materials, hardware, software, textual conventions, audience, sites of production and sites of reception. The next section addresses these very performances with new technologies, and the ways in which learners negotiate DV editing with digital resources.

Digital Video (DV) Editing and 'Decorous Trickery'

Of the various forms of media production, my study focuses on DV and film, chiefly because the manipulation of time, image and sound is a levelling pursuit whose production processes function without bias towards any particular social group—apart perhaps from those with certain sensory impairments. One of the defining creative acts in the production of moving image is the editing of a film's 'assets' into a coherent text, or as Potter describes it: "the organisation of intertextual space" (2012, p. 141). Most Western individuals from infancy to adulthood, assuming they have access and resources, possess an accumulated repertoire of implicit moving image expertise from years of media viewing and interpreting (Bazalgette 2010, p. 7). In my experience, most learners can draw on this knowledge to make simple still and moving image montages, but the seeming simplicity of unscrambling and cutting clips belies the visual eloquence it is possible to achieve as skills develop.

Potter notes, drawing on Fisher et al. (2006), the provisional always unfinished nature of the digital draft is an enticing draw for children, and it is this very elasticity and reversibility that becomes a source of fascination:

> This process is more than the simple act of placing things in the right order and joining them together; it is an act of authorship and marshalling of key meaning-making resources into a cohesive whole.
> (Potter 2012, p. 141)

Iterative doing, undoing and redoing is routine in DV editing but young people's experience of the same in writing is, for many, a cause for shame, a visible reminder of irreducible binaries: competence and incompetence, rightness and wrongness, followed by finite procedures to rectify that wrongness. Potter's young participants identify that even DV editing is a frustrating process, the difference being that it is largely seen as a series of open-ended improvements made by makers themselves.

Potter's experiences of DV editing with young children mirror my own, in that the grasping of even the most minor functionality produces quasi-euphoric feelings of creative control, at least initially. Indeed 'mistakes' in this environment are formative and more often experienced as compelling play—as fun not failure. Indeed for those inclined to lock on to the 'possibility thinking' (Craft 2013) and guesswork inherent in audiovisual editing, it is a practice that allows for processes of finessing, and for oscillation between textual modalities and modes of thought.

One of the distinguishing characteristics of DV editing is that its practitioners are liminally positioned, in active negotiation with their raw materials. In other words, they occupy an 'in-between state', located amongst: the made/unmade, the complete/incomplete, the familiar/strange, play/work, determination/improvisation, fantasy/reality, front stage/back stage, and intuitive/conscious reckoning. Lanham, in a percipient text, expresses this interstitial tension as 'bi-stable oscillation' (1994, p. 81). He holds that digitisation destabilises texts, which more easily enables Western culture's predisposition for shuttling between looking AT texts, and THROUGH them to meanings. Looking AT relates to the stylistic surface of texts, while THROUGH them relates to the world of abstraction that lies beyond them.

For Lanham printed texts make these oscillatory processes separate, controllable, finite, and for some, obscure. He claims that they "interfere with our integrative powers" (Lanham 1994, p. 81), whereas 'electronic texts' combine and blur symbols and meanings with rhetorical effect:

> Rhetoric as a method of literary education aimed to train its students to toggle back and forth between AT and THROUGH vision, alternately to realise how the illusion is created and then to fool oneself with it again.... To feel that characteristic oscillation is to understand the decorum of that work … from the inside. Such dynamic knowledge puts us inside the work looking out. (Lanham 1994, p. 81, original emphasis)

My study transposes Lanham's "decorous trickery" (1994, p. 81) of the 'electronic word' to the realm of the audiovisual, and re-casts production of this nature as a form of education in audiovisual rhetoric. It offers a hands-on inside out perspective, a position that some might construe as advantageous, so that INTERACT/THROUGH becomes a more apposite frame for understanding digital meaning-making. In the act of DV editing on tablets, it is entirely possible for Key Stage 1 children (5 to 7 years old) to experience the forging of meaning through this irresistible oscillation—arguably in ways that learning to write first can delay, obscure, or at worst, obstruct.[18] Commentators in the field of film and

---

[18] Burnett et al. (2012) introduce the concept of '(im)materiality' in relation to digital meaning-making that may be helpful in this context. The term conveys: the recursive relationship between

media education have already embraced dynamic motion between modes as strong components of literacy (Burn and Durran 2006; Cannon et al. 2018; Reid 2003), so as digital tools develop, should we not then be investigating the "integrative powers" of children and young people?

I have discussed ways of conceptualising media composition and highlighted some possible frames for deeper understandings of DV editing: the practical reasoning in phronesis, the affective potential of rhetorical expression, the modern relevance of performance with symbols and the 'oscillating ontologies' of Western perception. By articulating these frames, I hope to suggest improved learning experiences for young people as they negotiate their relationship with the world, and the media in which most of them bathe.

Pedagogies

Alternative Approaches to Literacy with 'New' Media[19]

With technological innovation comes a reconfiguration of social arrangements, especially concerning new technologies related to the visual (Jewitt 2008). New communicative media enable us to perceive, assimilate, embody, transform and publish our understandings and identities in complex ways, ways that include and extend reading and writing. In terms of understanding the production and circulation of texts, theoretical frameworks drawn from Media and Cultural Studies (such as that described by Buckingham 2003, p. 53), remain relevant. Buckingham's model comprises four concepts: Production, Language, Representation and Audience which are comprehensive as regards understanding the codes, conventions and political economies of the media landscape. This

---

the physical and the representational; the importance of 'siting' in literacy practices as an ongoing fluid negotiation (p. 8); and the salience to literacy of human situatedness (p. 10)—all of which becomes significant in later discussions in Chap. 6 on spaces for the translation of meanings (see also Burnett 2011a).

[19] I describe media production as 'new' with some hesitation, as it inadequately describes communicative tools and practices that have been quotidian for many for more than a decade; only in the sense that they are continually in renewal is the term useful.

said, more theoretical development is necessary for engagements with the affective, the aesthetic and the participative dimensions of digital media and the pedagogies therein (Burn 2009a, p. 6; Jenkins et al. 2006, 2016; Reid 2009). In order to explore the misalignment between established literacy practices and those attuned to the digital, I look at facets of the standard approach and then at alternatives addressing play, collectivity, the social and the nurturing of engagement in a connected world.

Some literacy research pivots around measuring cognitive skills such as pupils' ability to read words. To facilitate this, phonics testing is now mandatory—they are also relatively easy to teach and unquestionably easy to test (DfE 2015; EEF 2015), producing statistics that purport to show improvements in literacy standards. Gibb's (2015b) supportive statement on phonics demonstrates the managerial ways in which such literacy interventions are implemented and researched, suggesting a blinkered interdependence between the two that forsakes the present needs of the child. See Rosen (2013) and Alexander (2014, p. 16) for critiques that condemn the whole premise of phonics testing, and Grundin who positions these screenings as "the product of policy-based evidence, rather than evidence-based policy-making" (2018, p. 39). This book seeks to loosen literacy from the grip of imposed schemes and "unambitious" literacy definitions (Potter and McDougall 2017), and to locate it firmly within the dynamics of inclusive everyday experience. This is an approach supported by Potter, who champions:

> the ideological nature of literacy [with] its roots in lived culture, and in what people actually do and say as part of their daily existence … which has unrecognised value and worth in narrow systems of education.
> (Potter 2012, p. 3, drawing on Street 1995)

The view that "cultural practices are also literacy practices" (Potter 2012, p. 3) points to a re-examination of the purpose of education in our particular historical 'conjuncture' (Grossberg 2013) and a re-configuration of the classical hierarchies of knowledge alluded to earlier.

The entanglement of everyday digital media uses, lived experience and the structures of mainstream education is problematic, creating tension between teachers, students and stakeholders with other interests. Having said this, it could be that regulatory systems such as: the National Curriculum, SATS (Standard Assessment Tests), SPAG (Spelling, Punctuation and Grammar) and phonics testing, print-based examinations, analogue assessment procedures, and related industries such as textbook publishing, may start to destabilise via grassroots local initiatives and digital innovatory practices (Cannon et al. 2014; Pendleton-Jullian 2009; Waugh 2015). In short, exclusive and measurable directives often stemming from 'common-sense' ideologies (Abrams 2012) look to become increasingly irrelevant in flatter, connected educational environments. In these spaces, teachers and learners collaborate on 'literacy events' and digital portfolios of achievement, many of which are rooted in personal interests and the aesthetics of popular culture (Buckingham 2014b; Burnett and Bailey 2014; Marsh 2010; Parry 2014; Potter 2012, p. 22).

Jenkins et al.'s influential paper Confronting the Challenges of Participatory Culture: Media Education for the twenty-first Century (2006) lists the social skills and cultural competencies with which the literate citizen, it is claimed, should be equipped to understand, engage with and produce media texts.[20] I absorb some of these concepts for use in my theoretical model to follow, as they chime with a more sophisticated and inclusive form of literacy, relevant to young people's lived lives. Jenkins et al.'s report elevates human capacity for:

Play*—experimenting with one's surroundings as a form of imaginative problem-solving

Performance*—adopting alternative subjectivities for the purpose of improvisation and discovery

Simulation—interpreting and constructing dynamic models of real-world processes

Appropriation*—meaningfully sampling and remixing media content

Multitasking—scanning the environment and shifting focus onto salient details

Distributed cognition*—interacting with tools and media that expand mental capacities

---

[20] There's an allure to creating and citing lists, and media education specialists are not immune to their putative power to sum up and simplify. I include them here as I am struck by the accumulative potential of these capacities to improve the life chances of many young people.

Collective Intelligence*—pooling knowledge and consulting with others toward a common goal
Judgment—evaluating the reliability and credibility of different information sources
Transmedia Navigation—following the flow of stories and information across multiple platforms and modalities
Networking—searching for, synthesizing and disseminating information between agents
Negotiation—travelling across diverse communities, discerning and respecting multiple perspectives, and grasping and following alternative norms
(adapted from Jenkins et al. 2006, p. xiv)

There is no scope in this volume to fully account for each of these capacities but some dimensions (marked thus*) have particular resonance with my field of study. The capacity for: **Play** (Koh 2014; Marsh 2009; Vygotsky 2002/1933; Wohlwend and Peppler 2015), **Performance** (Merchant 2006; Potter and Gilje 2015), **Appropriation** (Knobel and Lankshear 2008, 2010; Manovich 2001), **Distributed Cognition** (Fisher et al. 2006, p. 7; A. Reid 2007) and **Collective Intelligence** (Burn 2009a, p. 20; Ito et al. 2013; Kafai and Peppler 2011) all foster dispositions for social, material and virtual interactions with local and wider communities, suggesting the need for radical shifts in thinking in relation to literacy, pedagogy and associated practices of consumption and production.

Jenkins and others (Merchant 2010; Potter 2012, p. 29) urge that alternative learning paradigms and pedagogies be sought to cultivate engagement, in addition to skills, in order to secure full participation as transmedia social actors. Furthermore, Merchant (2010) asserts that media literate practitioners rely on cross-platform competencies and "the spirit, habit and skills of inquiry" in equal measure (Merchant 2010, p. 105, citing Qian 2009). Literacy then constitutes far more than just the ability to mechanically read and write, it is a condition and a disposition to engage with a range of social and digital environments. Later, in Chap. 6, will examine the ways in which pedagogy might develop so as to manage the necessary 'climate change' in the classroom, precisely to propagate such a spirit. Before this, I look at the importance of 'signal' discrimination amongst the 'white noise' overload of digital information.

Curating Order Out of Chaos

This research embraces the above capacities and links them specifically to media production. Participants were offered the freedom to experiment with the digital tools and the software at hand, and encouraged to use audiovisual language to shape and order form out of a perceived chaos of possibility (Eisner 2005/1985, p. 100; Potter 2012, p. 43). Potter sums up the form-making processes of selection, composition and distribution of media texts both as an important emerging literacy practice and as an act of personal curation. For him "the new Curatorship" is the fourth C, after the Cultural, Critical and Creative[21] social functions identified by various agents and commentators (Bazalgette et al. 2011; BFI 2008; Burn and Durran 2006, 2007, p. 11; Potter 2012, p. 38). The idea of curation attends to the iterative and performance aspects of digital media-making, as well as to the impermanence and fragility of the digital identities formed in online spaces:

> It is a new form of cultural production that is pitched part way between making and sharing, creating temporary collections for specific purposes, and then dismantling them again.
> (Potter 2012, p. 181)

My account does not pretend to engage with relationships between identity formation and media-making, but there are two dimensions appended to curatorship with relevance to my study, namely the critical and the affective. This is on the basis that the practice of creating and assembling digital resources often involves making specific critical choices for specific emotional or narrative effects.

The DV editing process in particular teems with tiny judgements based on ill-defined emotional, aesthetic and cultural sensitivities, and these unite to offer a sense of what 'feels right'. Learners can be encouraged to

---

[21] The 3 C's framework is deployed in ongoing EU-funded research into ways of supporting film literacy in various film education settings (FLAG 2013, 2015).

articulate these choices and make explicit these sentiments, to bring about a reflexive, social and embodied learning experience. Audiovisual manipulation can play an important role in this kind of inclusive approach to literacy and pedagogy, whereby making new texts and adapting archetypal ones become concrete and personally-involving activities (Blum-Ross 2013; Berger and Zezulkova 2018).

The Affective 'Poetics' of Media Education

This narrative suggests that the plasticity of digital media promotes enhanced meaning-making opportunities in terms of revising and remixing content (Knobel and Lankshear 2008; Kress and Van Leeuwen 2001). Leander and Franks (2006), however, in their study of young people's online practices with images, question a primarily semiotic orientation to learning with media texts. Firstly, they claim that multimodality as a discipline tends to elide particular expressive resources (linguistic, visual, audio, gestural and spatial). They argue that multimodality focusses on meaning-making at the expense of cultural and aesthetic attachment, thus producing a deficit model:

> The relations of persons to texts are strategic and rational, involved in 'design' and 'work', including the 'design' of 'social futures' (New London Group 1996), rather than embodied, sensual, and involved in personal attachments and cultural affiliation.
> (Leander and Franks 2006, p. 186)

So Leander and Franks call for a uniting of media texts with a differentiated aesthetic dimension, that is, with the sensorial, the affective and the corporeal. An additional observation supports what has already been argued above in relation to the dynamics and constitution of sociocultural phenomena:

> Greater attention to aesthetic attachments helps us understand how imaging practices, in addition to expanding the canon of traditional literacy constitute social relations and social capital.
> (Leander and Franks 2006, p. 185)

Arguments that relate 'imaging practices' to social equality are supported by Potter (2012, p. 28), and are reflected in Burn's call for an inclusive 'poetics of media education' (2009b). For these commentators, as one makes media there is a need for a balanced understanding between the semiotic, the multimodal, the aesthetic, the ludic (the playful), the popular and the critical dimensions of the work in hand (Bazalgette and Buckingham 2013).

Further, some scholars (Burnett 2011a; Dezuanni 2014) are developing a related and possibly overlooked aspect of media production which foregrounds the affective and the physical relationships between the human and non-human (but notably man-made and commercially driven) elements within digital making settings. Whilst Dezuanni (2014) regards digital makers as 'actors in a network', which could seem constrained and sterile, he is mindful of agentic relations between the affective and the haptic (related to touch) in the networked teaching environment. For this study these become important factors in consideration of the optimum conditions for reaching new complex, literate states of being that include (im)material relations (Burnett et al. 2012).

It does appear then, that digital making engages with various aspects of everyday living and social phenomena from the creative and the cultural, to the affective, the cognitive and the material. My account suggests that a combination of these factors comes into play in the construction of film and media texts, and occasions the exercise of critical thinking. Moreover, any marginalising of this more abstract strand of media education makes for less personally meaningful, and perhaps more re-productive practical work. Similarly, on the academic circuit, less critically-oriented commentary on media function, use and production in society stands to hinder traction of the same, in core school curricula.

Over the past few pages I have explained some of the characteristics that distinguish digital making as a new literacy practice, singling out specific aspects—the compositional, the affective, and the critical—for more detailed commentary. The next section engages with the work of teachers in digital spaces. I look at the ways in which pedagogy might benefit from more fluid and dynamic relationships in epistemological, ontological and axiological terms (Thomson et al. 2012, p. 9).

Scattered Sites of Learning

In the introduction to an early text on media teaching and learning, media education was identified as an embattled practice straddling the disciplines (Buckingham 1990, p. 14), an observation as applicable now as it was in the 1990's. Media production is variously housed within Computer Programming/Information and Communication technologies (ICT), Film and Media Studies, English, Drama and Art & Design, often down to randomly situated teacher-film/media-enthusiasts. This discursive positioning, and indeed the earlier conflation of aesthetic dimensions of learning with social capital (Leander and Franks 2006), animate debates over the value and function of media production. This section investigates the ways in which this very reach is both problematic and generative, by looking at the nature of production spaces and possible philosophical paths to new pedagogies.

A central issue twenty-five years ago that still inheres, was how to manage media learning's relation to other curriculum areas, and to 'subject English' in particular (Bull 2012). Freedman, recognised that reading texts is a context-bound social activity for which:

> we need to offer a greater plurality of possible forms of response. What is needed is an area in which students can transform texts without an externally imposed gulf between reading and responding.
> (Freedman 1990, p. 211)

Personal subjective response, Freedman lamented at the time, was deemed as something to be recognised but moved beyond, so as to reproduce more 'valued' prescribed readings, often of the kind required to pass exams.

Freedman's misgivings were grounded in a pre-digital pedagogy, but now that textual responses can be mediated in multiple modes, the 'area' in which young people can 'transform texts' with 'plural responses' is tangibly realised through the composition and distribution of digital media on virtual platforms (Potter 2009). Here lies the tension with the ways in which teaching and learning are traditionally managed. Orthodox pedagogy revolves around individual, linear and mono-modally realised 'progression' towards imposed standards. These stringent practices are at odds with living the rest of one's life in a social, rhizomic 'networked public' (boyd 2008; Ito 2009) and many teachers live with the repercussions of this 'ontological schizophrenia'[22] on a daily basis.

Habitus and Ecotonal Borderlands

Burn and Durran's (2006, 2007) research based on classroom production practices with secondary students, asserts the potency of interstitial space that is, the space between primary objectives and actual practices (Bergala et al. 2016, p. 92). They posit that it is in these transitional spaces that student knowledge and aspiration can be mobilised to encourage social participation through the processes of digital making. These fertile interstices, it is claimed, are "exactly the space education is best suited to occupy" (Burn and Durran 2006, p. 274). At the time, the authors referred to virtual space as the zone located between domestic and professional video camera usage, but with the mushrooming of amateur recording devices, 'the interstitial' could now accurately describe the space between home and school. Some children and young people become familiar with media production in informal out-of-school contexts, practices which are largely ignored by school systems (Parry and Hill Bulman 2017).

As Burn and Durran's research indicates, the need to draw on this implicit knowledge and expertise is now more pressing, as the differential between what matters in statutory school literacy and the repertoires acquired informally is widening (Instrell 2011). Scholars in the field argue that it is time to harness digital connectivity and to see that arguments have moved on even beyond the 'the home-school mismatch hypothesis', to debates grounded in multiply-situated literacy practices stretching across domains in tactical ways (Bulfin and Koutsogannis 2012).

The fact that development of new technologies is constantly in a state of flux means those teachers interested in the liminal zones of learning

---

[22] The phrase 'ontological schizophrenia' comes from Lanham (1994, p. 81) who uses it to describe the ironic tension between Plato's 'rant' against writing as an expressive output, and—his prose output.

might be the professionals in the social sphere most suited to engage with what Sennett has described as "a live edge, a porous membrane" (2008, p. 234). The analogy is developed by Potter (2011) who suggest that established top down pedagogies—where teachers are positioned as experts—may need to adapt to contingent shifting terrain (see also McDougall and Potter 2015). Their proposal is that edge conditions could be made more supple and permeable to the media skills, dispositions and consumption and production habits many young learners acquire beyond school parameters.

The current fixed boundaries between school, home and the outside world, could be re-conceived as a series of borders, with all the generative ambiguities that permeability introduces. For Sennett, both are 'sites of resistance': whereas boundaries "resist contamination, exclude and deaden … borders [are] a site of exchange as well as of separation" (2008, p. 231). For example, a Cultural Studies emphasis would invite and value popular culture into media composition and pedagogic practice, in ways that critically integrate what students have assimilated from public discourse (Buckingham 2014b; Buckingham and Sefton-Green 1994). An Arts and Humanities emphasis would invite aesthetic and cultural affiliations into media composition in ways that creatively integrate students' personal interests (Burn 2009b, 2013).

An additional example of the ways in which sites of learning with media can be imagined is offered by Professor of Architecture, Ann Pendleton-Jullian (2009), who adumbrates the design of a network of technical innovation hubs, and the manner in which they might interact with traditional social institutions. She uses a metaphor from the natural world—the ecotone—to describe juxtapositions of disparate cultures. The ecotone is a fertile edge-zone where different eco-systems collide, such as estuarine deltas or the borders between rivers and mangroves. Organic life at these junctures is said to be rich in biodiversity, a zone where organisms adapt in order to sustain and/or create new life. The metaphor is a useful analogy for explaining the potential at the intersection between media ecologies of everyday life and the often ponderous workings of education systems. Could it be that the ecotone is nature's equivalent of Bourdieu's (1984) habitus?

Burn (2009a) recoups habitus to describe the school territory in which media texts—especially those drawn from popular aesthetics—meet educational experience. This is a zone where objective procedures:

> meet, merge, collide with subjective, embodied experience, aspiration, desire … In Bourdieu's scheme [habitus] is the system of dispositions in which objective structures meet subjective thoughts, actions and perceptions.
> (Burn 2009a, p. 11)

Following Buckingham and Sefton-Green (2003), he adds a simple suggestion that a route through the complexity of this environment might be facilitated through the agile guidance and intuitive sense of a teacher:

> A mediating force in an otherwise endless speculation about the determining effects of structure or agency is pedagogy, conceived broadly here as an intervention to promote critical understanding.
> (Burn 2009a, p. 11, my emphasis)

The learners' dispositions referred to above are those that embrace creative possibility in relation to the criticality, aesthetics and pleasures of media production. Rather than servile clerks (Crawford 2009) or technicians (Ball 1995) delivering approved versions of literacy, Burn conceives of English teachers in particular, as dynamic facilitators whose embrace of media's potential fosters flexible and responsive formal learning environments. In non-formal 'third spaces' (Bhabha 1994; Gutierrez 2008; McDougall and Potter 2015; Potter and McDougall 2017; Soja 1999) the 'semi-permeable membrane' (Potter 2011, p. 175) between school, home and other sites of learning, is a space for the transmedia 'translation' of cultural sensibilities. The protagonists in the field cited in this section are proponents of an inclusive and critical media education that 'levels the playing field' in terms of social and cultural participation.

Mobilisation and Participation

Consistent with McDougall and Potter's 'verbs of pedagogy' and in contrast with the prevailing 'nouns of the curriculum' (2015, p. 206) some suggest that 'doing text' is a more appropriate way of describing pedagogy with digital media and (subject) English (Waugh 2016), which raises the issue of place and context. Spaces of learning are no longer necessarily fixed in geographic domains structured with hierarchies of expertise, but they are variously located sites of exchange and reciprocity, more akin to Wenger's 'community of practice' (1998) or Sennett's 'joined skill in community' (2008, p. 51).

The after school club could and often does offer a valuable site for discovering "relations between different patterns of thought" (Sefton-Green 1990, p. 150) through the mobilisation of home-spun media expertise, creative experimentation, play and display. Non-formal 'third spaces' of learning offer more opportunities to make new and tentative connections, and to accumulate and express tacit knowledge (Eisner 2005/2002a, p. 210; Polanyi 2009/1967). Such knowledge can be construed as a form of incremental intuitive wisdom—cited as valuable in craft processes (Sennett 2008, p. 51) and reminiscent of Eisner's practical phronesis—forms of knowing which are routinely denied value in academic systems of education.

Earlier I alluded to three dimensions in the teacher habitus that might help articulate a climate conducive to the development of learners' intuitive or tacit knowledge. I refer to Thomson et al.'s Signature Pedagogies (2012), which reports on teaching strategies in the Creative Partnerships programme. According to the report, creative practitioners were found to combine the epistemological—the building of new knowledge and know-how; the ontological—our orientation to being and sense-making in the world; and the axiological—an intrinsic commitment to the value of collaboration and co-operation (2012, p. 9). To underpin a report on pedagogy by drawing on wide interdependent dimensions of human experience—or 'life-worlds'—is a bold and necessary step to restrain instrumentalist trajectories and to anchor our understanding of ethical and successful learning environments.

As the report acknowledges, it is difficult to separate the three dimensions in practice, but it is important to spell out the theoretical relevance of this approach to my research. Signature Pedagogies' findings resonate with media learning pedagogies, as they are understood in this book, in a number of ways:

- teaching and learning are seen as both participative and acquisitive, presenting a challenge to 'default pedagogies'
- the authors acknowledge the parts played by history, tradition and policy regimes in the makeup of 'schooling spaces'
- they stress the importance of 'sociality' (Bragg and Manchester 2011) and 'collegial' practice
- mobility, hybridity and permeability (Haas Dyson 1997) are prerequisite elements in an inclusive creative learning space
- there is a dual commitment to present and future 'horizons of possibility'

    (Thomson et al. 2012, p. 9)

The report took much of its analytical inspiration from Delors's 'four pillars of learning' (1996)—summarised here as learning how to know, to do, to live together and to be—fundamental aspects of living which invoke "in–the-moment-ness" (Thomson et al. 2012, p. 32). This key finding is salient to my account as it brings to mind the focussed, tacit present-ness of shooting film and DV editing. These activities sit in stark contrast with many school priorities, such as curriculum compliance, future-oriented tests and inspections—experienced by some as punitive, and by many as impersonal "arid and removed technical exercises" (see Potter 2012, p. 13 and p. 171).

In an earlier section I drew on the duality of Williams' metaphor for cultural experience—the 'structure of feeling'—in relation to the critical and affective aspects of media education. I suggested that these were two sides of the same coin which were difficult to analyse in isolation. Signature Pedagogies extracts similar significance from Williams' articulation (1977, p. 132), citing it at length and using it to explain:

presentism through art forms: "meanings and values as they are actively lived and felt, and the relations... characteristic elements of impulse restraint, and tone; specifically affective elements of consciousness and relationships: not feeling against thought, but thought as felt and feeling as thought: practical consciousness of a present kind, in a living and interrelating continuity" ... It is this newness, Williams suggested, that makes activities meaningful on an affective as well as an intellectual level.

    (Thomson et al. 2012, p. 32)

There is an 'in solution' (Williams 1977, p. 133) quality to the nexus of practice and structure, and thought and feeling, described here that invites comparison with Lanham's AT (INTERACT)/THROUGH meaning-making construct explained earlier (1994). Oscillation between the elements in spaces of learning relies on fluid, permeable relations. The feeling of being alert to present patterns of thought, sensitive to the material environment, and competent with the digital tools in hand, is a potent mix for the advance of new thinking about literacy and the link with media expertise (Burnett et al. 2012).

Media composition pedagogies and practices can be traced back to the 'learning-by-doing' and 'reflection and action' principles of the progressive movement (Dewey 1997/1938; Freire 1993/1970), and these persist in the post-analogue age. However, commentary from the field suggests that the time is ripe to enable more sophisticated mutual engagements between teachers and learners than those for which even early progressivists advocated.[23]

We have seen that the advent of digital media and associated technologies diversifies concepts of literacy, fragments learning spaces and hybridises tools:

> There is more to be literate about and, because of the connection with pedagogy, more to educate about and more to be educated by.
>   (Potter 2009, p. 64)

The attendant implications for pedagogy require leaps of faith from all stakeholders—teachers, young people and families—to support an environment less driven by adherence to standards and outcomes, and more by choice, agency, and opportunities for learners to take responsibility for their own learning (Waugh 2017). What follows is a strategy for organising these discursive constructs into an intelligible frame with digital media participation as a central component. In addition, the model

---

[23] A network of educators, academics and youth workers in the US called the Connected Learning Alliance (2015), supported by public/private partnerships and the MacArthur Foundation, work with these very principles to create a network of 'Cities of Learning'—"a world where all young people have access to participatory, interest-driven learning that connects to educational, civic, and career opportunities." Available at: http://clalliance.org/why-connected-learning/ (Connected Learning Alliance 2015) [Accessed 7 February 2018] (see also, Ito et al. 2013).

clarifies how media-making in schools connects with broader social cycles of cultural production.

Theoretical Framework

This section elaborates a theoretical model for viewing contemporary understandings of literacy and pedagogy underpinned by digital making and sharing practices. In the first instance I was inspired by Ross et al.'s (1993) theoretical model—which was in fact a reprisal of psychologist Rom Harré's Social Reality Matrix (1983). Harré's original matrix details stages of 'personal development' as a sequence of unceasing 'identity projects' (Ross et al. 1993, p. 51), akin to Giddens' 'reflexive project of the self' (1991, p. 5), that coupled personal development with the expressive dimension of human activity. More currently, links between identity 'performance' and digital media production have also been made by Potter (2012), to wit, the contemporary usefulness of Harré's model. The axes recall familiar paradigms for understanding the media landscape—Private/Public display (boyd 2008; Goffman 1990/1959), Individual/Collective Realisation (Gauntlett 2011a) and Active/Passive Agency (Buckingham 2003; Buckingham and Sefton-Green 2003). It is proposed here that with some adjustment, the matrix may help interpret the processes of digital making and eventually point to the ways in which literacy and pedagogy might be re-conceived for the digital age.

Before describing this, I explain an important interim adjustment: with a prescient leap Ross et al. (1993) deployed Harré's matrix as the basis on which to improve the assessment of artistic achievement in schools (Fig. 2.1). A similarly embattled domain, the perceived ambiguities in measuring 'artistic merit' in the visual arts correspond with those in assessing media texts (Sefton-Green 2000, p. 228). For Ross et al. the appeal of Harré's matrix lay in "his emphasis on the processes of individual growth rather than the outcomes" (1983, p. 51, original emphasis) which chimed with their mutual interest in aesthetic education and "the development of the pupil and not the fate of the product" (1983, p. 51, original emphasis).

Crucially, Ross et al. incorporated Harré's understanding of the cyclical phases of personal development, and their association with the life of circulating cultural products:

conventionalisation > appropriation > transformation
> publication > conventionalisation

Ross et al. lay this formulation over their 'arts curriculum cycle' and dispensed with the transversal describing Agency. This resulted in a two-dimensional matrix (Fig. 2.1), with arrows representing interaction between and amongst the quadrants. They argued that this provided "a means of mapping both productive and contemplative aesthetic activities" (Ross et al. 1993, p. 52) through teacher-pupil dialogue.

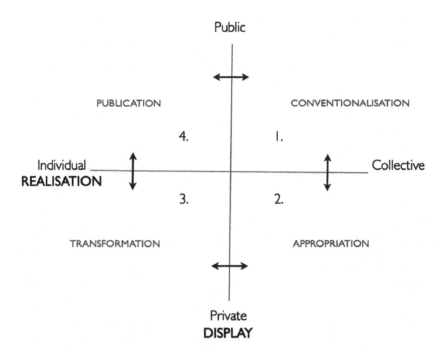

Fig. 2.1 Assessing achievement in the Arts. Adapted from Ross et al. (1993, p. 52), based on Harré's (1983) Social Reality Matrix

Ross et al.'s cycle mirrors the now more visible processes of digital production, and their statement above emphasises the importance of pedagogy in heightening states of awareness and articulating processes of analysis, dialogue, reflection and action. In addition, there is a political and emancipatory inflection to Ross et al.'s model recalling Freire's (1993/1970) concept of consciousness-raising (conscientização), a pedagogic approach supporting reflection and action—which is congruent with aspects of my research methodology to be discussed in Chap. 3.

Cycle of Digital Making

Figure 2.2 is my adaptation of Ross et al.'s model reflecting the changes that digitisation has wrought on cultural production. One of the main differences locates the learner at the centre of the cycle. Before interpreting the diagram any further, it is worth noting that matrices can seem overly rigid or enticingly unproblematic, however its subdivisions merely serve to contextualise this study. The schema is not intended as an infallible representation of a fixed and natural order or sequence; it is rather a heuristic onto which social processes might be provisionally mapped for the purposes of a considered 'version of events' in relation to the function of digital making.

As a consequence of converging participative digital technologies (Jenkins et al. 2006, 2016; Merchant 2009) there has been a lowering of barriers to the production and dispersal of media texts, hence the removal of Realisation on the horizontal axis and the re-insertion of Harré's Agency. This reflects, for some social actors, the increased level of social participation that could result from opportunities to contribute to flows of culture. Extra detailing such as dotted lines denote non-linear cross-pollination of domains and the porosity of social and pedagogic boundaries.

Participants' actions whilst making with digital media are socially and publicly embedded in discourses associated with:

- Consumption—which replaces Ross et al.'s Conventionalisation, the latter being textually-oriented and the former process-oriented (Buckingham 2003)

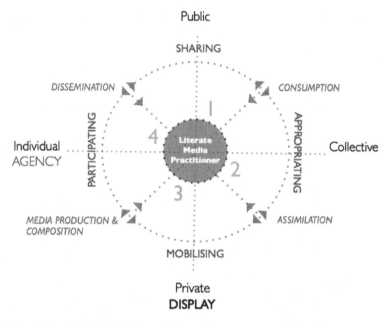

Fig. 2.2   Cycle of Digital Making. Adapted from Ross et al. (1993)

- Assimilation—understood as a process of internalisation (Fisher et al 2006; Peppler 2013; Vygotsky 1978) and a perceived progression from selective acts of Appropriation (Jenkins 1992)
- Production/Composition—a key dimension of this account in which symbolic resources are selected, assembled, remixed, composed and curated on makers' own terms for public display (Burn and Durran 2007; Knobel and Lankshear 2008; Potter 2012; Potter and McDougall 2017)
- Dissemination—replaces Publication as more apt terminology to describe the seed-like scatter of digital modalities on multiple platforms (Gauntlett 2011a; Manovich 2001)

In this view, media practitioners—both teachers and learners—are perceived as active stakeholders operating along lines of continua, engaged in social iterative processes in the messy realm of actual practice. In line with the previously mentioned 'verbs of pedagogy', and in order to link the discourses, I have added gerunds that help to explain activities in the transitional spaces between quadrants, which correspond with agentic literacy and pedagogic practices and dispositions:

* Sharing—of symbolic resources in active engagement with texts and social practices in the public realm (Gauntlett 2011a; Jenkins et al. 2006, 2016; Merchant 2009)
* Appropriating—or 'poaching' of texts and practices in public discourse with which 'affinity' is felt by individuals or groups (Gee 2004; Jenkins 1992; Lévi-Strauss 1966)
* Mobilising—of a disposition for experimentation and action with multi-sensory modes, guided and coaxed by facilitative mentors (Burn et al. 2001; Burn and Durran 2006, 2007; Cope and Kalantzis 2000; New London Group 1996; Vygotsky 1978)
* Participating—in ways that augment social interaction and create diverse meanings and identities across different contexts (Bazalgette 2011; Burnett 2011a, 2011b; Merchant 2009; Potter 2012; Reid 2014)

The Cycle of Digital Making names the dimensions of a culturally situated conceptual framework and builds on the work of many different scholars over decades. Although it is anticipated that all of these dimensions will to some extent inform this study, I largely limit the scope of this research to Quadrant 3 (Media Production and Composition) and its boundary spaces (Mobilising and Participating) as seen in Fig. 2.3. These transitional areas represent the interstitial, ecotonal spaces (as described by Burn and Durran 2007, and Pendleton-Jullian 2009, respectively), where dynamic literacy practices and pedagogies are best placed to flourish (Cannon et al. 2018).

One of my guiding intellectual impulses draws on Burn's 'critical utopian' standpoint (2009a), and this study aspires to maintain the same oxymoronic tension.[24] This means steering a middle course between

---

[24] Delors' introduction to UNESCO's 'Learning—the treasure within' (1996) is entitled 'A necessary Utopia' which he conceives as a vital imaginary "if we are to escape from a dangerous cycle sustained by cynicism or resignation" (1996, p. 20).

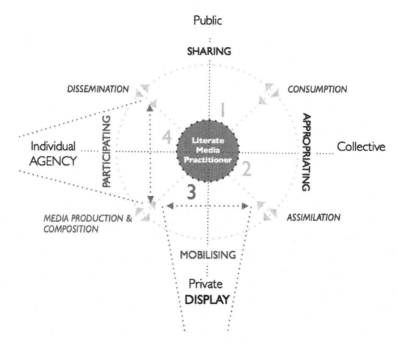

Fig. 2.3 Cycle of Digital Making: pedagogic perspective. Adapted from Ross et al. (1993)

cautionary scepticism towards "the extremes of cyber-optimism and Luddite denial … [and] a world of technological determinism" (2009a, 2009b, p. 23) and guarded optimism towards a groundswell of teacher empowerment and innovation (Teachmeet Wiki 2018; NUT 2014; Waugh 2016, 2017).

In this Chapter, I have sought to examine the mêlée of discourses and theories related to pre-digital and moving image literacies, media composition and new pedagogic practices. I have taken into consideration the positioning of media production in schools, academic commentary on craft, creativity and vocationalism, and the ways in which the socioeconomic context affects the function of literacy. I have also foregrounded aspects of making with digital symbols that distinguish it from traditional writing practices, and counselled approaches to learning relevant to expertise in media-making. Finally, I have offered a reconceptualisation of the teaching and learning habitus and put forward suggestions as to how it might become more attuned to rhythms within the digital landscape.

Sefton-Green's Mapping Digital Makers (2013) makes the case for developing:

> an overarching conceptual framework to underpin curriculum thinking and innovation across discrete fields of action … and creative production disciplines.
> (Sefton-Green 2013, p. 60)

My research seeks to address this and others' accounts that signal an absence of empirical evidence (Burnett 2009, 2016). The suggestion is that:

> there is a real problem of collecting evidence about learning in the cutting-edge projects, of securing the status of such research, and of building up a broad-based, theoretically informed body of knowledge in this field.
> (Sefton-Green 2013, p. 60)

The next Chapter lays out the philosophical thinking that girds my contribution to that 'body of knowledge', along with a rationale for the manner in which I have chosen to conduct my research.

Bibliography

Aberdare, (Lord). (2015). *Parliamentlive.tv* [online]. *House of Lords debate* [online]. Retrieved February 7, 2018, from http://www.parliamentlive.tv/Event/Index/8ae0f3a3-e276-48e1-b921-b6b6e7a148d8 (Time code: 11:14:22–11:23:00).

Abrams, F. (2012). Cultural literacy Michael Gove's school of hard facts. *BBC Radio 4's Analysis* [online]. Retrieved February 7, 2018, from http://www.bbc.co.uk/news/education-20041597.

Adams, J. (2013). The English baccalaureate: A new Philistinism? *International Journal of Art & Design Education, 32*(1), 2–5.

Alexander, R. (2014). The best that has been thought and said. *Forum, 56*(1) [online]. Retrieved February 7, 2018, from http://www.robinalexander.org. uk/wp-content/uploads/2014/02/19_Alexander_FORUM_56_1_web.pdf.

Ball, S. J. (1995). Intellectuals or technicians? The urgent role of theory in educational studies. *British Journal of Educational Studies, 43*(3), 255–271.

Ball, S. J. (2013). *The Education Debate* (2nd ed.). Bristol: Policy Press.

Banaji, S., Buckingham, D., & Burn, A. (2006). *The Rhetorics of Creativity: A Review of the Literature.* London: Institute of Education, Creative Partnerships, Arts Council England.

Barker, M. (2001). On the problems of being a 'trendy travesty'. In M. Barker & J. Petley (Eds.), *Ill Effects: The Media/Violence Debate* (pp. 202–224). London: Routledge.

Bassey, M., Wrigley, T., Maguire, M., & Pring, R. (2013, March 19). Gove will bury pupils in facts and rules. *The Independent* [online]. Retrieved February 7, 2018, from http://www.independent.co.uk/voices/letters/letters-gove-will-bury-pupils-in-facts-and-rules-8540741.html.

Bazalgette, C. (2010). *Teaching Media in Primary Schools.* London: Sage.

Bazalgette, C. (2011). Rethinking text [online]. In *Empowerment Through Literacy: Literacy Shaping Futures—UKLA 47th International Conference.* Chester: UKLA, 20–31. Retrieved February 7, 2018, from http://www.ukla.org/downloads/UKLA_Chester_International_Conference_Papers_2011.pdf.

Bazalgette, C., & Bearne, E. (2010). *Beyond Words: Developing Children's Understanding of Multimodal Texts.* Leicester: UKLA.

Bazalgette, C., & Buckingham, D. (2013). Literacy, media and multimodality: A critical response. *Literacy, 47*(2), 95–102.

Bazalgette, C., Parry, B., & Potter, J. (2011). Creative, cultural and critical: Media literacy theory in the primary classroom [online]. In *Creative Engagements: Thinking with Children.* Oxford: Inter-Disciplinary.net. Retrieved February 7, 2018, from http://www.inter-disciplinary.net/wp-content/uploads/2011/06/bazalgettecpaper.pdf.

BECTA. (2003). *What the Research Says About Digital Video in Teaching and Learning* [online]. Coventry: BECTA ICT Research. Retrieved February 7, 2018, from http://www.nsead.org/ict/resources/downloads/Research15_DigitalVideo.pdf.

Belshaw, D. (2011). *The Essential Elements of Digital Literacies* [online]. Presentation to the Association of Independent Schools of New South Wales (Australia) ICT Managers Conference. Retrieved February 7, 2018, from http://www.slideshare.net/dajbelshaw/the-essential-elements-of-digital-literacies.

Belshaw, D. (2012). *What is Digital Literacy? A Pragmatic Investigation* [online]. PhD Thesis, Durham University, Durham. Retrieved February 7, 2018, from http://neverendingthesis.com.

Bennett, D., & Doherty, D. (2010). Innovation, education, and the maker movement [online]. In *Innovation, Education, and the Maker Movement*. New York: New York Hall of Science. Retrieved February 7, 2018, from http://nysci.org/wp-content/uploads/Maker-Faire-Report-Final.pdf.

Bennett, S., Maton, K., & Kervin, L. (2008). The 'digital natives' debate: A critical review of the evidence. *British Journal of Educational Technology, 39*(5), 775–786.

Bergala, A., Whittle, M., & Bachmann, A. (2016). *The Cinema Hypothesis—Teaching Cinema in the Classroom and Beyond*. Vienna: Austrian Film Institute.

Berger, R., & Zezulkova, M. (2018). A remaking pedagogy: Adaptation and archetypes in the child's multimodal reading and writing. *Education 3–13, 46*(1), 64–75.

BFI Education. (2008). *Reframing Literacy* [online]. London: British Film Institute. Retrieved February 7, 2018, from http://www.bfi.org.uk/sites/bfi.org.uk/files/downloads/bfi-education-reframing-literacy-2013-04.pdf.

Bhabha, H. K. (1994). *The Location of Culture*. London: Routledge.

Blum-Ross, A. (2013). 'It made our eyes get bigger': Youth film-making and place-making in East London. *Visual Anthropology Review, 29*(2), 89–106.

Bordwell, D., & Thompson, K. (2010). *Film Art: An Introduction* (9th ed.). New York: McGraw-Hill.

Bourdieu, P. (1984). *Distinction: A Social Critique of the Judgement of Taste*. London: Routledge.

boyd, d. (2008). Why youth (♥) youth social network sites: The role of networked publics in teenage social life. In D. Buckingham (Ed.), *Youth, Identity, and Digital Media*. The John D. and Catherine T. MacArthur Foundation Series on Digital Media and Learning (pp. 119–142). Cambridge, MA: MIT Press.

boyd, d. (2014). *It's Complicated—The Social Lives of Networked Teens* [online]. New Haven, CT: Yale University Press. Retrieved February 7, 2018, from http://www.danah.org/books/ItsComplicated.pdf.

Bragg, S., & Manchester, H. (2011). *Creativity, School Ethos and the Creative Partnerships Programme* [online]. Newcastle upon Tyne. Retrieved May 22, 2018, from https://www.creativitycultureeducation.org/publication/creativity-school-ethos-and-the-creative-partnerships-programme/.

Bruner, J. S. (1990). *Acts of Meaning*. Cambridge, MA: Harvard University Press.

Buckingham, D. (1990). *Watching Media Learning: Making Sense of Media Education*. London: The Falmer Press.

Buckingham, D. (2003). *Media Education: Literacy, Learning and Contemporary Culture*. Cambridge: Polity Press.

Buckingham, D. (2007). *Beyond Technology: Children's Learning in the Age of Digital Culture*. London: Routledge.

Buckingham, D. (2010). Do we really need media education 2.0? Teaching in the age of participatory media. In K. Drotner & K. Schroder (Eds.), *Digital Content Creation: Perceptions, Practices and Perspectives* (pp. 287–304). New York: Peter Lang.

Buckingham, D., 2014a. The Success and failure of media education [online]. *Media Education Research Journal, 4*(2), 5–17. Retrieved February 7, 2018, from http://merj.info/wp-content/uploads/2014/01/MERJ_4-2-Editorial.pdf.

Buckingham, D. (2014b). The (re-)making of media educators: Teacher identities in changing times. In P. Benson & A. Chik (Eds.), *Popular Culture, Pedagogy and Teacher Education: International Perspectives* (pp. 125–137). London: Routledge.

Buckingham, D., & Sefton-Green, J. (1994). *Cultural Studies Goes to School*. London: Taylor & Francis.

Buckingham, D., & Sefton-Green, J. (2003). Gotta catch 'em all: Structure, agency and pedagogy in children's media culture. *Media, Culture & Society, 25*(3), 379–399.

Bulfin, S., & Koutsogiannis, D. (2012). New literacies as multiply placed practices: Expanding perspectives on young people's literacies across home and school. *Language and Education, 26*(4), 331–346.

Bull, E. (2012). *Rationales for Film in Secondary English: Subject Identity, Situated Practice and Professional Histories*. Masters Dissertation, UCL, Institute of Education, University of London, London.

Burn, A. (2009a). *Making New Media: Creative Production and Digital Literacies*. New York: Peter Lang.

Burn, A. (2009b, December). Culture, art, technology: Towards a poetics of media education [online]. *Cultuur + Educatie, 26*. Retrieved February 7, 2018, from http://aburn2012.files.wordpress.com/2014/04/burn-towards-a-poetic-of-media-education.pdf.

Burn, A. (2011). Beyond the heuristic of suspicion: The value of media literacy [online]. In A. Goodwyn & C. Fuller (Eds.), *The Great Literacy Debate: A Critical Response to the Literacy Strategy and the Framework for English* (pp. 8–27).

London: Routledge. Retrieved February 7, 2018, from http://aburn2012.files. wordpress.com/2014/04/beyond-the-heuristic-of-suspicion.pdf.

Burn, A. (2013, June). Six arguments for the media arts: Screen education in the 21st century [online]. *NATE: Teaching English, 2*, 55–60. Retrieved May 22, 2018, from https://aburn2012.files.wordpress.com/2014/04/six-arguments-for-the-media-arts.pdf.

Burn, A., Brindley, S., Durran, J., Kelsall, C., Sweetlove, J., & Tuohey, C. (2001). The rush of images: A research report into digital editing and the moving image. *English in Education, 35*(2), 34–47.

Burn, A., & Durran, J. (2006). Digital anatomies: Analysis as production in media education. In D. Buckingham & R. Willett (Eds.), *Digital Generations: Children, Young People, and the New Media* (pp. 273–293). London: Routledge.

Burn, A., & Durran, J. (2007). *Media Literacy in Schools: Practice, Production and Progression*. London: Paul Chapman.

Burn, A., & Parker, D. (2001). Making your mark: Digital inscription, animation and a new visual semiotic. *Education, Communication and Information, 1*(2), 155–179.

Burn, A., & Parker, D. (2003). *Analysing Media Texts*. Continuum Research Methods. London: Continuum.

Burnett, C. (2009). Research into literacy and technology in primary classrooms: An exploration of understandings generated by recent studies. *Journal of Research in Reading (Special Issue: New Developments in Literacy and Technology), 31*(1), 22–37.

Burnett, C. (2011a). The (im)materiality of educational space: Interactions between material, connected and textual dimensions of networked technology use in schools. *E-Learning and Digital Media, 8*(3), 214.

Burnett, C. (2011b). Shifting multiple spaces in classrooms: An argument for investigating learners' boundary-making around digital networked texts [online]. *Journal of Literacy and Technology, 12*(3). Retrieved February 7, 2018, from http://www.literacyandtechnology.org/uploads/1/3/6/8/136889/jlt_v12_3_burnett.pdf.

Burnett, C. (2016). *The Digital Age and its Implications for Learning and Teaching in the Primary School*. York. Retrieved February 7, 2018, from http://cprtrust. org.uk/wp-content/uploads/2016/07/Burnett-report-20160720.pdf.

Burnett, C., & Bailey, C. (2014). Conceptualising collaboration hybrid sites: Playing *Minecraft* together and apart in a primary classroom. In J. Davies, G. Merchant, & J. Rowsell (Eds.), *New Literacies around the Globe: Policy and Pedagogy (Routledge Research in Literacy)* (pp. 50–71). Abingdon: Routledge.

Burnett, C., Merchant, G., Pahl, K., & Rowsell, J. (2012). The (im)materiality of literacy: The significance of subjectivity to new literacies research. *Discourse: Studies in the Cultural Politics of Education, 35*(1), 90–103.

Cannon, M. (2011). *Fashioning and Flow* [online]. MA Dissertation, Institute of Education, London. Retrieved February 7, 2018, from https://fashioningandflow.wordpress.com/.

Cannon, M., Bryer, T., & Lindsey, M. (2014). Media production and disruptive innovation: Exploring the interrelations between children, tablets, teachers and texts in subject English settings. *Media Education Research Journal, 5*(1), 16–31.

Cannon, M., Potter, J., & Burn, A. (2018). Dynamic, playful and productive literacies. *Changing English, 25*(2).

Cantrill, C., Filipiak, D., Antero, G., Bud, H., Lee, C., Mirra, N., et al. (2014). Teaching in the connected learning classroom [online]. In A. Garcia (Ed.), *Report Series on Connected Learning*. Irvine, CA: The Digital Media and Learning Research Hub. Retrieved February 7, 2018, from http://dmlhub.net/wp-content/uploads/files/teaching-in-the-CL-classroom.pdf.

Connected Learning Alliance. (2015). *Why Connected Learning?* [online]. Retrieved February 7, 2018, from http://clalliance.org/why-connected-learning/.

Cope, B., & Kalantzis, M. (2000). *Multiliteracies: Literacy Learning and the Design of Social Futures*. New York: Routledge.

Craft, A. (2013). Childhood, possibility thinking and wise, humanising educational futures. *International Journal of Educational Research, 61*, 126–134.

Crafts Council. (2014). *Our Future is in the Making* [online]. London. Retrieved February 7, 2018, from http://www.craftscouncil.org.uk/content/files/7822_Education_manifesto%4014FINAL.PDF.

Crawford, M. (2009). *The Case for Working with your Hands: Or Why Office Work is Bad for Us and Fixing Things Feels Good*. London: Penguin.

Cultural Learning Alliance. (2011). *ImagineNation—The Case for Cultural Learning* [online]. London. Retrieved May 20, 2018, from https://culturallearningalliance.org.uk/imaginenation-the-case-for-cultural-learning-published-today/.

Cultural Learning Alliance. (2014). *STEM + ARTS = STEAM* [online]. Retrieved May 20, 2018, from https://culturallearningalliance.org.uk/stem-to-steam-debated-in-westminster-hall/.

Delors, J. (1996). *Learning: The Treasure Within*. The International Commission on Education for the 21st Century. Paris: UNESCO.

Dewey, J. (1997/1938). *Experience and Education*. New York: Touchstone.

Dezuanni, M. (2014). The building blocks of digital media literacy, socio-material participation and the production of media knowledge. *Journal of Curriculum Studies*, 1–24.

DfCMS, Department for Culture, Media and Sport. (2013). *Culture, Media and Sport: Commons Select Committee—Third Report* [online]. Paragraphs 117 and 118. Retrieved February 7, 2018, from http://www.publications. parliament.uk/pa/cm201314/cmselect/cmcumeds/674/67409.htm.

DfE, Department for Education. (2010). *Foreword to The Importance of Teaching* [online]. London. Retrieved February 7, 2018, from https://www.gov.uk/government/uploads/system/uploads/attachment_data/file/175429/CM-7980.pdf.

DfE, Department for Education. (2013). *National Curriculum in England: Computing Programmes of Study* [online]. London. Retrieved February 7, 2018, from https://www.gov.uk/government/publications/national-curriculum-in-england-computing-programmes-of-study.

DfE, Department for Education. (2015). *Reading: The Next Steps* [online]. London. Retrieved February 7, 2018, from https://www.gov.uk/government/uploads/system/uploads/attachment_data/file/409409/Reading_the_next_steps.pdf.

DfES, Department for Education and Skills. (2005). *Primary National Strategy: Excellence and Enjoyment—Social and Emotional Aspects of Learning* [online]. Retrieved February 7, 2018, from http://webarchive.nationalarchives.gov. uk/20130401151715/http://www.education.gov.uk/publications/eOrderingDownload/DFES0110200MIG2122.pdf.

EEF. (2015). *Phonics | Teaching and Learning Toolkit* [online]. Phonics Teaching and Learning Toolkit. Retrieved February 7, 2018, from https://educationendowmentfoundation.org.uk/resources/teaching-learning-toolkit/phonics/.

Eisner, E. (1986). The role of the arts in cognition and curriculum. *Journal of Art & Design Education, 5*(1–2), 57–67.

Eisner, E. (2005/1985). Aesthetic modes of knowing. In E. Eisner (Ed.), *Reimagining Schools* (pp. 95–104). Abingdon: Routledge.

Eisner, E. (2005/2002a). What can education learn from the arts about the practice of education? [online]. In E. Eisner (Ed.), *Reimagining Schools* (pp. 205–214). Abingdon: Routledge. Retrieved February 7, 2018, from http://www.infed.org/biblio/eisner_arts_and_the_practice_of_education.htm.

Eisner, E. (2005/2002b). From episteme to phronesis to artistry in the study and improvement of teaching. In E. Eisner (Ed.), *Reimagining Schools* (pp. 193–204). Abingdon: Routledge.

Eisner, E. (2006). *What Do the Arts Teach?* [online]. Chancellors Lecture Series, Vanderbilt University, Nashville, TN. Retrieved February 7, 2018, from http://www.youtube.com/watch?v=h12MGuhQH9E.

Eisner, E. (2008). Art and knowledge. In J. G. Knowles & A. L. Cole (Eds.), *Handbook of the Arts in Qualitative Research: Perspectives, Methodologies, Examples, Issues* (pp. 3–12). Thousand Oaks, CA: Sage Publications, Inc.

Fisher, T., Higgins, C., & Loveless, A. (2006). *Teachers Learning with Digital Technologies: A Review of Research and Projects.* [online] Bristol: Futurelab at NFER. Retrieved May 20 2018, from https://www.nfer.ac.uk/teachers-learning-with-digital-technologies-a-review-of-research-and-projects/.

FLAG (Film Literacy Advisory Group). (2013). *Screening Literacy* [online]. London: British Film Institute, Institute of Education, Film Education. Retrieved February 7, 2018, from http://www.bfi.org.uk/screening-literacy-film-education-europe.

FLAG (Film Literacy Advisory Group). (2015). *A Framework for Film Education* [online]. London: British Film Institute. Retrieved February 7, 2018, from http://www.bfi.org.uk/sites/bfi.org.uk/files/downloads/bfi-a-framework-for-film-education-brochure-2015-06-12.pdf.

Frayling, C. (1993). Research in art and design [online]. *Royal College of Art Research Papers, 1*(1), 1–5. Retrieved May 20, 2018, from http://researchonline.rca.ac.uk/384/3/frayling_research_in_art_and_design_1993.pdf.

Frayling, C. (2011). *On Craftsmanship Towards a New Bauhaus.* London: Oberon Books.

Freedman, A. (1990). Teaching the text: English and media studies. In *Watching Media Learning: Making Sense of Media Education* (pp. 194–211). London: The Falmer Press.

Freire, P. (1993/1970). *Pedagogy of the Oppressed.* London: Penguin.

Gardner, H. (2009). *Five Minds for the Future.* Boston, MA: Harvard Business School Press.

Gauntlett, D. (2011a). *Making is Connecting.* Cambridge: Polity Press.

Gauntlett, D. (2011b). Extended book review: Making is connecting: The social meaning of creativity, from DIY and knitting to You Tube and Web 2.0 (A Conversation with McDougall, J., Readman, M., Trotman, D.) [online]. *Media Education Research Journal, 2*(1). Retrieved February 7, 2018, from http://merj.info/wp-content/uploads/2011/08/Gauntlett-review.pdf.

Gee, J. P. (2004). *Situated Language and Learning: A Critique of Traditional Schooling.* New York: Routledge.

Gee, J. P. (2015). The new literacy studies. In J. Rowsell & K. Pahl (Eds.), *The Routledge Handbook of Literacy Studies* (pp. 35–48). Abingdon: Routledge.

Gibb, N. (2015a, January 7). Schools minister Nick Gibb sets out his timetable for educational reform in Britain 2015 [online]. *The Independent*. Retrieved February 7, 2018, from http://www.independent.co.uk/news/education/schools/schools-minister-nick-gibb-sets-out-his-timetable-for-educational-reform-in-2015-9963751.html.

Gibb, N. (2015b). *The Purpose of Education* [online]. Department for Education, London. Retrieved February 7, 2018, from https://www.gov.uk/government/speeches/the-purpose-of-education.

Giddens, A. (1991). *Modernity and Self-identity: Self and Society in the Late Modern Age*. Cambridge: Polity Press.

Goffman, E. (1990). *The Presentation of Self in Everyday Life*. London: Penguin.

Goodman, N. (1978). *Ways of Worldmaking*. Indianapolis: Hackett Publishing.

Green, B. (1995). Post-curriculum possibilities: English teaching, cultural politics, and the postmodern turn. *Journal of Curriculum Studies, 27*(4), 391–409.

Grossberg, L. (2013). *Cultural Studies in the Future Tense*. Durham, NC: Duke University Press.

Grundin, H. (2018). Policy and evidence: A critical analysis of the year 1 phonics screening check in England. *Literacy, 52*(1), 39–46.

Gutiérrez, K. D. (2008). Developing a sociocritical literacy in the third space. *Reading Research Quarterly, 43*(2), 148–164.

Haas Dyson, A. (1997). *Writing Superheroes: Contemporary Childhood, Popular Culture, and Classroom Literacy*. New York: Teachers College Press.

Hagel, J., & Seely Brown, J. (2005). *From Push to Pull—Emerging Models for Mobilizing Resources* [online]. Retrieved February 7, 2018, from http://www.johnhagel.com/paper_pushpull.pdf.

Hall, S. (1991). Ethnicity: Identity and difference. *Radical America, 23*(4), 9–20.

Harré, R. (1983). *Personal Being—A Theory for Individual Psychology*. Oxford: Basil Blackwell.

Hawkins, J., & Blakeslee, S. (2005). *On Intelligence*. New York, NY: Henry Holt.

Hirsch, E. D. (2006). *The Knowledge Deficit: Closing the Shocking Education Gap for American Children*. Boston, MA: Houghton Mifflin Company.

Instrell, M. (2011). Breaking barriers: Multimodal and media literacy in the curriculum for excellence. *Media Education Journal, 49*, 4–11.

Ito, M. (2009). *Hanging Out, Messing Around, and Geeking Out: Kids Living and Learning with New Media*. The John D. and Catherine T. MacArthur Foundation Series on Digital Media and Learning. Cambridge, MA: MIT Press.

Ito, M., Livingstone, S., Penuel, B., Rhodes, J., Salen, K., Schor, J., et al. (2013). *Connected Learning: An Agenda for Research and Design* [online]. Digital Media and Learning Research Hub. Retrieved February 7, 2018, from http://dmlhub.net/wp-content/uploads/files/Connected_Learning_report.pdf.

Jenkins, H. (1992). *Textual Poachers: Television Fans and Participatory Culture*. New York: Routledge.

Jenkins, H., Ito, M., & boyd, d. (2016). *Participatory Culture in a Networked Era: A Conversation on Youth, Learning, Commerce, and Politics*. Cambridge: Polity Press.

Jenkins, H., Purushota, R., Clinton, K., & Robinson, A. J. (2006). *Confronting the Challenges of Participatory Culture: Media Education for the 21st Century* [online]. Chicago: The John D. & Catherine T. MacArthur Foundation. Retrieved February 7, 2018, from https://www.macfound.org/media/article_pdfs/JENKINS_WHITE_PAPER.PDF.

Jewitt, C. (2008). *The Visual in Learning and Creativity: A Review of the Literature* [online]. Creative Partnership Series, Institute of Education, University of London. Retrieved May 20, 2018, from https://www.creativitycultureeducation.org/publication/the-visual-in-learning-and-creativity-a-review-of-the-literature/.

Kafai, Y. B., & Peppler, K. A. (2011). Youth, technology, and DIY: Developing participatory competencies in creative media production. *Review of Research in Education, 35*(1), 89–119.

Kaplan, I. (2008). Being 'seen', being 'heard': Engaging with students on the margins of education through participatory photography. In P. Thomson (Ed.), *Doing Visual Research with Children and Young People* (pp. 175–191). Abingdon: Routledge.

KAVI, Finnish Media Education Authority. (2013). Finnish Media Education [online]. Helsinki: National Audiovisual Institute. Retrieved from https://kavi.fi/sites/default/files/documents/mil_in_finland.pdf

Knobel, M., & Lankshear, C. (2008). Remix: The art and craft of endless hybridization. *Journal of Adolescent & Adult Literacy, 52*(1), 22–33.

Knobel, M., & Lankshear, C. (2010). *DIY Media: Creating, Sharing and Learning with New Technologies*. New York: Peter Lang.

Koh, A. (2014). *The Political Power of Play* [online]. Hybrid Pedagogies. Retrieved February 7, 2018, from http://www.hybridpedagogy.com/journal/political-power-of-play/.

Kress, G., & Van Leeuwen, T. (2001). *Multimodal Discourse: The Modes and Media of Contemporary Communication*. London: Hodder Arnold.

Lanham, R. A. (1994). *The Electronic Word: Democracy, Technology, and the Arts*. Chicago: University of Chicago Press.

Lankshear, C., & Knobel, M. (2003). *New Literacies: Changing Knowledge and Classroom Learning*. Buckingham: Open University Press.

Laughey, D. (2012). Media Studies 1.0: Back to basics. *Media Education Research Journal*, *2*(2), 57–64.

Lave, J., & Wenger, E. (1991). *Situated Learning: Legitimate Peripheral Participation*. Cambridge, UK: Cambridge University Press.

Leander, K., & Frank, A. (2006). The aesthetic production and distribution of image/subjects among online youth. *E-Learning*, *3*(2), 185–206.

Lévi-Strauss, C. (1966). *The Savage Mind*. Chicago: University of Chicago Press.

Livingstone, I., & Hope, A. (2011). *Next Gen Report*. London: NESTA.

Lord, P., Jones, M., Harland, J., Bazalgette, C., Reid, M., Potter, J., et al. (2007). *Special Effects: The Distinctiveness of Learning Outcomes in Relation to Moving Image Education Projects: Final Report* [online]. London: Creative Partnerships. Retrieved May 20, 2018, from https://www.nfer.ac.uk/special-effects-the-distinctiveness-of-learning-outcomes-in-relation-to-moving-image-education-projects-final-report/.

Maeda, J. (2013). Foreword to. In R. Somerson & M. L. Hermano (Eds.), *The Art of Critical Making: Rhode Island School of Design on Creative Practice* (pp. 5–9). Hoboken, NJ: Wiley.

Maker Faire. (2017). *World Maker Faire | New York 2017* [online]. Retrieved February 7, 2018, from http://makerfaire.com/.

Maker Faire UK. (2015). *Brighton Mini Maker Faire* [online]. Retrieved February 7, 2018, from http://makerfairebrighton.com/.

Maker Media Inc. (2014). *Maker Faire: A Bit of History* [online]. Retrieved February 7, 2018, from http://makerfaire.com/makerfairehistory/.

Manovich, L. (2001). *The Language of New Media*. Cambridge, MA: MIT Press.

Marsh, J. (2009). Play, creativity and digital cultures. In R. Willett, M. Robinson, & J. Marsh (Eds.), *Play, Creativity and Digital Cultures* (pp. 216–218). Abingdon: Routledge.

Marsh, J. (2010). *Childhood, Culture and Creativity: A Literature Review* [online]. Newcastle. Retrieved May 20, 2018, from https://www.creativitycultureeducation.org/publication/childhood-culture-and-creativity-a-literature-review/.

Massumi, B. (2002). *Parables for the Virtual: Movement, Affect, Sensation*. Durham, NC: Duke University Press.

McDougall, J., & Potter, J. (2015). Curating media learning: Towards a porous expertise. *Journal of E-learning and Digital Media, 12*(2), 199–211.

MEA, Media Education Association. (2015). *MEA Response to the Consultations* [online]. Retrieved February 7, 2018, from http://www.themea.org. uk/2015/09/mea-response-to-the-consultations/.

Merchant, G. (2006). Identity, social networks and online communication. *E-Learning and Digital Media, 3*(2), 235–244.

Merchant, G. (2009). Web 2.0, new literacies, and the idea of learning through participation [online]. *English Teaching: Practice and Critique, 8*(3), 8–20. Retrieved February 7, 2018, from http://shura.shu.ac.uk/1102/1/Merchant_draft2.pdf.

Merchant, G. (2010). 3D virtual worlds as environments for literacy learning [online]. *Educational Research, 52*(2), 135–150. Retrieved February 7, 2018, from http://shura.shu.ac.uk/1206/1/Final_GM_Ed_Res.pdf.

Monbiot, G. (2016). *Neoliberalism—The Ideology at the Root of All Our Problems* [online]. Retrieved February 7, 2018, from http://www.theguardian.com/books/2016/apr/15/neoliberalism-ideology-problem-george-monbiot.

Morgan, N. (2014, November 10). *Nicky Morgan Speaks at Launch of Your Life Campaign* [online]. Retrieved February 7, 2018, from https://www.gov.uk/government/speeches/nicky-morgan-speaks-at-launch-of-your-life-campaign.

Morgan, N. (2015). Education secretary Nicky Morgan: 'Arts subjects limit career choices' [online]. *The Stage News*. Retrieved February 7, 2018, from http://www.thestage.co.uk/news/2014/11/education-secretary-nicky-morgan-arts-subjects-limit-career-choices/.

Morozov, E. (2013). *To Save Everything, Click Here: Technology, Solutionism, and the Urge to Fix Problems That Don't Exist*. London: Allen Lane.

Mumford, S., Parry, B., & Walker, G. (2013). *Pockets of Excellence: Film Education in Yorkshire and the Humber* [online]. Leeds: IVE Creative(formerly CAPEUK). Retrieved February 7, 2018, from https://weareive.org/impact/pockets-excellence-film-education-yorkshire-humber/.

Murch, W. (2001). *In the Blink of an Eye: A Perspective on Film Editing*. Los Angeles: Silman-James Press.

NACCE, National Advisory Committee on Creative and Cultural Education. (1999). *All Our Futures: Creativity, Culture and Education* [online]. London: DCMS. Retrieved February 7, 2018, from http://sirkenrobinson.com/pdf/allourfutures.pdf.

New London Group. (1996). A pedagogy of multiliteracies: Designing social futures. *Harvard Educational Review, 66*(1), 60–92.

NUT, National Union of Teachers. (2014). *Reclaiming Schools—The Evidence and the Arguments* [online]. National Union of Teachers. Retrieved February 7, 2018, from https://radicaled.files.wordpress.com/2015/03/reclaiming-schools.pdf.

NYHS, New York Hall of Science, Maker Faire. (2012). Design-make-play conference: Growing the next generation of science innovators [online]. In *Design-Make-Play Conference: Growing the Next Generation of Science Innovators*. New York: New York Hall of Science. Retrieved February 7, 2018, from http://www.yingtrsef.org/wp-content/uploads/DesignMakePlay_Report-2012.pdf.

Ong, W. (2002/1982). *Orality and Literacy: The Technologizing of the Word* [online]. London: Routledge. Retrieved February 7, 2018, from http://dss-edit.com/prof-anon/sound/library/Ong_orality_and_literacy.pdf.

Parry, B. (2014). Popular culture, participation and progression in the literacy classroom. *Literacy, 48*(1), 14–22.

Parry, B., & Hill Bulman, J. (2017). *Film Education, Literacy and Learning*. Leicester: UKLA.

Pendleton-Jullian, A. (2009). *Design Education and Innovation Ecotones* [online]. Retrieved February 7, 2018, from https://fourplusone.files.wordpress.com/2010/03/apj_paper_14.pdf.

Peppler, K. (2013). *New Opportunities for Interest-Driven Arts Learning in a Digital Age*. New York: The Wallace Foundation.

Peppler, K., & Kafai, Y. (2007). From Supergoo to Scratch: Exploring creative digital media production in informal learning. *Learning, Media and Technology, 32*(2), 149–166.

Petersen, S. M. (2008). Loser generated content: From participation to exploitation [online]. *First Monday*. Retrieved February 7, 2018, from http://journals.uic.edu/ojs/index.php/fm/article/view/2141/1948.

Polanyi, M. (2009/1967). *The Tacit Dimension*. Chicago: University of Chicago Press.

Potter, J. (2009). *Curating the Self: Media Literacy and Identity in Digital Video Production by Young Learners*. PhD Thesis, Institute of Education, University of London, London.

Potter, J. (2011). New literacies, new practices and learner research: Across the semi-permeable membrane between home and school. *Lifelong Learning in Europe, 16*(3), 174–181.

Potter, J. (2012). *Digital Media and Learner Identity: The New Curatorship*. New York: Palgrave Macmillan.

Potter, J. (2015). *Forward to the New Age of STEAM(M)! Digital Media, Education and Computing* [online]. Media Literacy, Learning and Curating. Retrieved February 7, 2018, from http://digitalcurationandlearning.com/2015/02/25/forward-to-the-new-age-of-steamm-digital-media-education-and-computing/.

Potter, J., & Bryer, T. (2014). *Out of the Box: A Project Evaluation Report for Shoot Smart*. London: DARE, Digital, Arts, Research, Education.

Potter, J., & Bryer, T. (2016). 'Finger flowment' and moving image language: Learning filmmaking with tablet devices. In B. Parry, C. Burnett, & G. Merchant (Eds.), *Literacy, Media, Technology: Past, Present and Future* (pp. 111–128). London: Bloomsbury.

Potter, J., & Gilje, Ø. (2015). Curation as a new literacy practice. *E-Learning and Digital Media, 12*(2), 123–127.

Potter, J., & McDougall, J. (2017). *Digital Media, Culture and Education: Theorising Third Space Literacies*. London: Palgrave Macmillan.

Prensky, M. (2001). Digital natives, digital immigrants part 1. *On the Horizon, 9*(5), 1–6.

Pring, R. (2004). *Philosophy of Educational Research* (2nd ed.). London: Continuum.

Qian, Y. (2009). New media literacy in 3-D virtual learning environments. In L. Hin & R. Subramaniam (Eds.), *Handbook of Research on New Media Literacy at the K-12 Level: Issues and Challenges* (pp. 257–270). New York: IGI Global.

Quinlan, O. (2015). *Young Digital Makers: Surveying Attitudes and Opportunities for Digital Creativity Across the UK* [online]. London. Retrieved February 7, 2018, from http://www.nesta.org.uk/sites/default/files/youngdigmakers.pdf.

Readman, M. (2010). *What's in a Word? The Discursive Construction of 'Creativity'*. PhD Thesis, Centre for Excellence in Media Practice (CEMP), University of Bournemouth, Bournemouth.

Reid, A. (2007). *The Two Virtuals: New Media and Composition*. West Lafayette, IN: Parlor Press.

Reid, M. (2003). Writing film: Making inferences when viewing and reading. *Literacy (formerly Reading), 37*(3), 111–115.

Reid, M. (2009). Reframing literacy: A film pitch for the 21st century. *English Drama Media: The Professional Journal of the National Association for the Teaching of English, 14*, 19–23.

Reid, M. (2014). Film, literacy and cultural participation. In S. Brindley & B. Marshall (Eds.), *Master Class in English Education: Transforming Teaching and Learning* (pp. 84–98). London: Bloomsbury.

Reid, M., Burn, A., & Parker, D. (2002). *Evaluation Report of the BECTA Digital Video Pilot* [online]. BECTA/BFI. Retrieved February 7, 2018, from http://archive.teachfind.com/becta/research.becta.org.uk/index9a09.html.

Robinson, K. (2011). *Out of our Minds: Learning to be Creative* (2nd ed.). Chichester: Capstone.

Robinson, K. (2013). *Finding Your Element: How to Discover Your Talents and Passions and Transform Your Life.* London: Allen Lane.

Rosen, M. (2013). Michael Rosen: Phonics: A summary of my views. Retrieved February 7, 2018, from http://michaelrosenblog.blogspot.co.uk/2013/01/phonics-summary-of-my-views.html.

Ross, M., Mitchell, S., Bierton, C., & Radnor, H. (1993). *Assessing Achievement in the Arts.* Buckingham; Philadelphia: Open University Press.

Schmidt, E. (2011). *MacTaggart Lecture, Edinburgh TV Festival* [online]. Edinburgh TV Festival. Retrieved February 7, 2018, from http://www.theguardian.com/media/interactive/2011/aug/26/eric-schmidt-mactaggart-lecture-full-text.

Scollon, R., & Scollon, S. B. K. (1981). *Narrative, Literacy, and Face in Interethnic Communication.* Norwood, NJ: Ablex.

Scottish Screen. (2006). *Moving Image Education & a Curriculum for Excellence* [online]. Glasgow. Retrieved February 7, 2018, from http://www.movingimageeducation.org/files/pdfs/mie-and-a-curriculum-for-excellence-2006-booklet.pdf.

Sefton-Green, J. (1990). Teaching and learning about representation: Culture and The Cosby Show in a North London comprehensive. In D. Buckingham (Ed.), *Watching Media Learning: Making Sense of Media Education* (pp. 127–150). London: The Falmer Press.

Sefton-Green, J. (1998). *'Writing' Media: An Investigation of Practical Production in Media Education by Secondary School Students.* PhD Thesis, Institute of Education, University of London, London.

Sefton-Green, J. (2000). From creativity to cultural production. In J. Sefton-Green & R. Sinker (Eds.), *Evaluating Creativity: Making and Learning by Young People* (pp. 216–231). London: Routledge.

Sefton-Green, J. (2005). Timelines, timeframes and special effects: Software and creative media production. *Education, Communication & Information, 5*(1), 99–103.

Sefton-Green, J. (2008). *Creative Learning* [online]. London: Creative Partnerships, Arts Council England. Retrieved February 7, 2018, from http://www.creativitycultureeducation.org/wp-content/uploads/creative-learning-booklet-26-233.pdf.

Sefton-Green, J. (2013). *Mapping Digital Makers: A Review Exploring Everyday Creativity, Learning Lives and the Digital.* State of the Art Reviews. London: Nominet Trust.

Sellar, S., Rutkowski, D., & Thompson, G. (2017). *The Global Education Race: Taking the Measure of PISA and International Testing.* Edmonton, Canada: Brush Education Inc..

Selwyn, N. (2006). Dealing with digital inequality: Rethinking young people, technology and social Inclusion. Conference paper: *Cyberworld Unlimited? Digital Inequality and New Spaces of Informal Education for Young People*, Bielefeld, Germany, 9 February 2006.

Selwyn, N. (2009). The digital native—Myth and reality. *Aslib Proceedings, 61*(4), 364–379.

Selwyn, N. (2016). *Is Technology Good for Education?* Cambridge: Polity Press.

Sennett, R. (2008). *The Craftsman.* London: Penguin.

Shirky, C. (2009). *Here Comes Everybody: How Change Happens When People Come Together.* London: Penguin.

Shirky, C. (2011). *Cognitive Surplus: Creativity and Generosity in a Connected Age.* London: Penguin.

Sinker, R. (2000). Making multimedia—Evaluating young people's creative multimedia production. In *Evaluating Creativity* (pp. 187–215). London: Routledge.

Snow, C. P. (1961). *The Two Cultures and the Scientific Revolution* [online]. New York: Cambridge University Press. Retrieved February 7, 2018, from http://sciencepolicy.colorado.edu/students/envs_5110/snow_1959.pdf.

Soja, E. (1999). Third space: Expanding the scope of the geographical imagination. In D. Massey, J. Allen, & P. Sarre (Eds.), *Human Geography Today* (pp. 260–278). Cambridge: Polity Press.

Somerson, R., & Hermano, M. L. (2013). *The Art of Critical Making: Rhode Island School of Design on Creative Practice.* Hoboken, NJ: Wiley.

Street, B. (1984). *Literacy in Theory and Practice.* Cambridge: Cambridge University Press.

Street, B. (1995). *Social Literacies: Critical Approaches to Literacy in Development, Ethnography and Education.* London: Longman.

Street, B. (2003). What's 'new' in new literacy studies? Critical approaches to literacy in theory and practice. *Current Issues in Comparative Education, 5*(2), 77–91.

Teachmeet Wiki. (2018). TeachMeet/FrontPage [online]. Retrieved May 20, 2018, from http://teachmeet.pbworks.com/w/page/19975349/FrontPage

Thomas, M. (Ed.). (2011). *Deconstructing Digital Natives: Young People, Technology, and the New Literacies.* New York: Routledge.

Thomson, P., Hall, C., Jones, K., & Sefton-Green, J. (2012). *The Signature Pedagogies Project: Final Report* [online]. London and Newcastle-upon-Tyne: Creativity, Culture and Education. Retrieved February 7, 2018, from http://www.creativitycultureeducation.org/wp-content/uploads/Signature_Pedagogies_Final_Report_April_2012.pdf.

Truss, E. (2013). *Elizabeth Truss Speaks about Curriculum Reform* [online]. Retrieved February 7, 2018, from https://www.gov.uk/government/speeches/elizabeth-truss-speaks-about-curriculum-reform.

Vygotsky, L. (1978). *Mind in Society: The Development of Higher Psychological Processes.* Cambridge, MA: Harvard University Press.

Vygotsky, L. (2002/1933). *Play and its Role in the Mental Development of the Child* [online]. Psychology and Marxism Internet Archive. Retrieved February 7, 2018, from https://www.marxists.org/archive/vygotsky/works/1933/play.htm.

Watters, A. (2015). *Ed-Tech Guide: What Should You Know About Education Technology?* [online]. Retrieved February 7, 2018, from http://guide.hackeducation.com.

Waugh, C. (2015). *The Edutronic* [online]. Retrieved February 7, 2018, from http://www.edutronic.net/.

Waugh, C. (2016). Connecting text. In J. McDougall & P. Bennett (Eds.), *Doing Text: Teaching Media After the Subject.* Leighton Buzzard: Auteur.

Waugh, C. (2017). *Rebel Education: Pick Your Teacher—Democratic Schooling in the UK.* Aljazeera website. Retrieved March 12, 2017, from http://www.aljazeera.com/programmes/rebel-education/2016/12/pick-teacher-democratic-schooling-uk-161220141451434.html.

Wenger, E. (1998). *Communities of Practice: Learning, Meaning, and Identity. Systems Thinker.* Cambridge: Cambridge University Press.

Williams, F. (2004). What matters is who works: Why every child matters to new labour. Commentary on the DfES Green Paper *Every Child Matters. Critical Social Policy, 24*(3), 406–427.

Williams, R. (1961). *The Long Revolution.* London: Chatto and Windus.

Williams, R. (1977). *Marxism and Literature.* Oxford: Oxford University Press.

Williamson, B. (2014). Political computational thinking: Cross-sector policy networks in the construction of learning to code in the new computing curriculum. In *British Educational Research Association Annual Conference,* Institute of Education, University of London, 23–25 September 2014.

Williamson, B. (2017a). *Big Data in Education The Digital Future of Learning, Policy and Practice*. London: Sage Publications.

Williamson, B. (2017b). Learning in the "platform society": Disassembling an educational data assemblage. *Research in Education, 98*(1), 59–82.

Willingham, D. T. (2012). *When Can You Trust the Experts? How to Tell Good Science from Bad in Education*. San Francisco, CA: Jossey Bass.

Wohlwend, K., & Peppler K. (2015). All rigor and no play is no way to improve learning [online]. *Phi Delta Kappan, 96*(8), 22–26. Retrieved February 7, 2018, from http://kpeppler.com/Docs/2015_Peppler_All-Rigor-No-Play.pdf.

Wolf, A. (2011). *Review of Vocational Education: The Wolf Report* [online]. London. Retrieved February 7, 2018, from https://www.gov.uk/government/publications/review-of-vocational-education-the-wolf-report.

3

Research Principles and Educational Values

This Chapter begins with some reflections on my overall research approach and on formative scholarly influences. I focus here on method choices and offer an overview of current trends in educational research, because my questions very much concern the construction of mediated knowledge, with implications for the nature and development of research methods at particular historical moments. In pursuit of more clarity on what happens when young people engage in DV and film production in schools and the circumstances in which it takes place, I chose to conduct a qualitative ethnographic study using insights from critical visual anthropology. My research principles rest on a belief in interpretive multiplicity and imaginative reflection, rather than on a belief in a single re-presentable objective reality (Lather 2006; Law and Urry 2003; Pring 2004). This conflation of the reflexive and the interpretive links with Hall's writing on open-ended research practice. He refers to it as "wrestling with conundra" (1992, p. 280) which expresses for him the intractability of intellectual work, involving:

> contested, localized, conjunctural knowledges, which have to be debated in a dialogical way… a practice which always thinks about its intervention in

© The Author(s) 2018
M. Cannon, *Digital Media in Education*,
https://doi.org/10.1007/978-3-319-78304-8_3

a world in which it would make some difference, in which it would have some effect. Finally, a practice which understands the need for intellectual modesty.
(Hall 1992, p. 286)

I position my research, then, at the intersection between explorations of action-oriented praxis (Freire 1970/1993; Lather 1991; Mäkelä 2007) and contextual understanding. This entails identifying my methods in such a way that other researcher-educators might respond to or adapt the actions taken (Bassey 1998), and deploying a reflexive stance to help counter researcher bias and "permit criticism" (Pring 2004, p. 134). Both these measures are consonant with Hall's dynamic epistemology whose precepts throw into question current research trends, many of which seek effective solutions for improved school 'performance'. The following section offers a philosophical rationale and then situates the study within current research trajectories.

Human Flourishing and Flexible Modes of Knowing

One might expect research whose object of study concerns the processes through which we build 'mediated realities' to be conducted with a constructionist worldview, and indeed it is the case with this study, though it need not necessarily be so. A constructionist ontology is allied to an interpretivist epistemology, that is, it rejects deductive approaches to research that test theory, in favour of inductive strategies that tend towards its generation. Social 'reality' is thus viewed as a "constantly shifting emergent property of individuals' creation" (Bryman 2008, p. 20), as further explained by Pring:

The world researched is affected by the research itself; our knowledge is a 'construction', reflecting the world, not as independent of our deliberations, but as something constructed by them.
(Pring 2004, p. 44)

As attested in the Cycle of Digital Making (see Fig. 2.2), my research predominantly concerns the tools, practices and human dimensions related to mediated meanings through which social phenomena are interpreted and understood. I therefore subscribe to the above view that our apprehension of the social is an "ongoing accomplishment by social actors" (Bryman 2008, p. 20) rather than an external objective entity to be 'acted upon'.

Particular world views affect research design. Some media education research is quantitative in nature, for example, it might set out to statistically prove that development of film and moving image literacy improves writing (Bradford City of Film 2010–2015) or can be aligned with progression in reading (Hill Bulman 2014). Approaches of this nature raise the issue of the intrinsic worth of film and media education: is gaining moving image literacy a valuable exercise in and of itself, in the pursuit of 'human flourishing'? (Heron and Reason 1997, p. 275); or must it, to gain status and funding, be rather more instrumentally positioned? There are benefits to the latter type of research in the short term, but it is not a good ontological fit with my study whose purpose is to reach a rich understanding of interactions between young people, and the teachers, tools and texts of media production.

Further, my researcher stance is shaped by a tripartite paradigm based on constructionism, a participatory worldview, and a critical perspective. This is supported by accounts already mentioned—Thomson et al.'s (2012) commitment to a more transactional pedagogy, Jenkins et al.'s (2006) observations on participatory culture and Pring's (2004) critique of dominant structures, respectively. Each of these scholars support values-driven educational enquiry which ethnography is well suited to explore as a function of its concern with social relationships. This is acknowledged by Conteh et al. where they describe ethnography as a "cultural grammar" of a social group (Conteh et al. 2005, p. xxi, following Heath 1983).

The participatory paradigm, presented by Lincoln and Guba (2000, p. 168, drawing on Heron and Reason 1997), is of particular significance ontologically speaking, as it questions constructionism's perceived sidelining of the experiential, of practical knowing and relations within the learning environment (Heron and Reason 1997, p. 275). This is relevant to my study in so far as media production is collaborative and has to do with the interface between material tools, practical skills, co-constructive assembly, and the in-the-moment-ness of everyday living:

> The participatory worldview allows us as human persons to know that we are part of the whole, rather than separated as mind over and against matter ... It allows us to join with fellow humans in collaborative forms of inquiry. It places us back in relation with the living world—and we note that to be in relation means that we live with the rest of creation as relatives, with all the rights and obligations that implies.
> (Heron and Reason 1997, p. 277)

This is analogous with the more recent theories on practice brought by Dall'Alba and Barnacle (2007), whose research in higher education supports an emphasis on the ontological, on 'being' and 'becoming'. They claim an over-emphasis on epistemology, that is, on ways of developing "unproblematic knowledge transfer" (Dall'Alba and Barnacle 2007, p. 680), a strategy that questionably leaves the student to work out how best to integrate this knowledge into skillful practice. Their observation resonates with my account of the narrowing effect of current curriculum reform, and reflects the ways in which teachers' 'skillfulness' in the digital media enabled classroom remains under-theorised. Ethnography helps to uncover the contradictions and common-sense assumptions associated with school practices as well as to determine the habitus of the social actors involved.

Dall'Alba and Barnacle reclaim what they consider to be a lost sense of wonder, passion and responsiveness in education (Loveless 2008), in ways which conflate knowing, being, and acting (Dall'Alba and Barnacle 2007, p. 686). This social, generative orientation parallels the mood of the media production environment and could revitalise pedagogical research agendas:

> we do not primarily access things conceptually or intellectually, but, instead, through being constantly immersed in activities, projects and practices with things and others.
> (Dall'Alba and Barnacle 2007, p. 681)

Law and Urry also note a shift in emphasis in research practice:

from epistemology (where what is known depends on perspective) to ontology (what is known is also being made differently). It is a shift that moves us from a single world to the idea that the world is multiply produced in diverse and contested social and material relations.
(Law and Urry 2003, p. 6, original emphasis)

They reflect on the political implications for research methods of social world enactments that can be made, unmade and re-made. Arguing that social inquiry is performative in nature, Law and Urry claim that it produces, at least partially, the object of which it speaks. This creates the conditions through which it is possible for social 'reality' to be manifold and flowing: a shape-shifting 'pluriverse' (Law and Urry 2003, p. 8, cited as attributable to William James) in which movement, texture and the visual become part of the sense-making process. Such arguments imply:

the possible need to imagine a fluid and decentred social science, with fluid and decentred modes of knowing the world allegorically, indirectly, perhaps pictorially, sensuously, poetically, a social science of partial connections. (Law and Urry 2003, p. 8)

The implications for formal, and particularly non-formal, school environments of a view of meanings as hybrid and workable are substantive. Lending formal ballast to the importance of different ways of making the known world, suggests that we are doing young people a disservice by underexposing them to wider, more dynamic epistemologies. These philosophical reflections on the liquid composition of social life point to more arts-based methods with which to represent and understand it (Jones and Fenge 2017).

Creative Methods

Law and Urry's support for a rapprochement with the arts suggests a sense in which enquiries are becoming un-tethered from traditional methodological moorings. This is reflected in the affirmations of Denzin (2001) via Roberts (2008). The latter recalls the former who likens:

the role [of] researcher/ethnographer to a "literary and intimate" public journalist—a view … that strengthens the idea of ethnography "as a performer-centred form of storytelling" and adds that "a shared public consciousness is shaped by a form of writing that merges the personal, the biographical, with the public".
(Roberts 2008, p. 99, citing Denzin 2001, p. 11)

Appeals to ethnography as constitutive of social life and to the blurring of the public and the private are evident here in Denzin's formulation. Such discourses feature in the field of media education in relation to issues of technological convergence, participatory social practices and increasingly, the public mediated curation of identity (Potter 2012). For my purposes, a more flexible approach to method adds breathing space to my role as participant-observer-practitioner-educator, and in turn offers a fresh diverse perspective.

Just as Jones sees sociologists as artist-narrativists, "collage-makers, narrators of narrations, dream weavers … natural allies of the arts and humanities" (2006, p. 67), there is latitude for media education researchers to follow a similar path by incorporating and interpreting the moving image in their research. Not simply "because the method should follow the object" (Buckingham 2009, p. 634), but because tools for the rich and varied representation of material associated with young people's media learning, remain largely print-bound or in academic penumbra. It is time for media education researchers in particular to push the boundaries of the interpretivist paradigm and offer arts-based 'versioned meanings' not only of interview data, but of still and moving images. Research would thus include more visceral and embodied dissemination practices, with the audiovisual moving beyond the merely illustrative (Prosser and Loxley 2008), towards a more reflexive modality into which performance might be incorporated (Orr 2013).

The argument that there is a proliferation of overlapping 'realities' to be explained (Lather 2006), suggests it is incumbent on researchers to make an axiological commitment, in other words, to ground their interpretation in an ethical framework of educational values (Pring 2004, p. 134). Indeed, intrinsic guiding principles are often missing from utilitarian educational research whose methods are frequently geared towards conclusions decided a priori, rather than towards interpretations open to contingency. With the conspicuous exception of the Cambridge Primary Review (Alexander 2010), the values and assumptions on which research questions are premised often remain unchallenged.

Educational Research Trends

Some educational research (EEF 2015[1]; Hattie 2012; Hattie and Yates 2014) is concerned with determining the effectiveness of interventions on learners' progress and schools' performance, some of which is used to foster economic success on national and international stages (Ball 2013, p. 57; Barone 2007; Kaplan 2008, p. 176; Pring 2004, p. 115, drawing on Lyotard 1984). In terms of educational policy, in 2010, £110 million was diverted from the Free School Meals fund to set up The Education Endowment Fund (EEF). This independent grant-making charity is designed to distribute money to those who claim to be able to raise standards in underperforming schools and reduce the attainment gap.[2] The EEF (2015) makes use of Randomised Controlled Tests (RCTs) to gather evidence for improved academic results in which consensus on the ends of the research are often presupposed.[3]

The culture of blanket metrics inherent in RCTs and the ideological narrative of performativity that they seem to sponsor, are at odds with the open-ended 'intellectual modesty' advocated by Hall (1992), and with the public-facing principles for educational research urged by Selwyn (2012, p. 213). Arguably, more ethical, socially-grounded research practice would go some way towards "addressing questions about the qualities which constitute or lead to a worthwhile form of life" (Pring 2004, p. 15). Pring goes on to challenge what he considers to be myopic trends, such

---

[1] The EEF is also part of the government's 'What Works Network' whose remit is to "enable policy makers, commissioners and practitioners to make decisions based upon strong evidence of what works and to provide costefficient, useful services." (What Works Network 2015).

[2] The EEF is also part of the government's 'What Works Network' whose remit is to "enable policy makers, commissioners and practitioners to make decisions based upon strong evidence of what works and to provide cost-efficient, useful services." (What Works Network 2015).

[3] I attended Frank Furedi's session at the first ResearchED Conference in 2013. He went against the grain of the conference—which supported evidence-based strategies—by calling into question scientistic procedures that frame children as 'patients', which is language he sees as misplaced (Furedi 2013).

as targeted managerial interventions (2004, p. 55) that fail to tackle the purpose of education, a pursuit he claims that requires:

> careful examination of what it means to be a person and to be so more fully. It is one of the absurdities of much research into the 'effective school' that these issues are ignored. 'Effective schools' are those which produce specific outcomes. But there is rarely any explanation why these outcomes are constituents of a worthwhile form of life, or whether the process through which the outcomes are produced transforms the learner in a significant way. (Pring 2004, p. 15, original emphasis)

Pring calls for more values-oriented research in contrast with short term utilitarian approaches. My research is more long term in scope in that it seeks an in depth understanding of primary and early secondary school environments that participate in digital video production, in order to generate credible theory. Rather than quantifying the effects of research interventions, I am researching educational media experiences of 'worthwhile' pertinence to young people and their visceral engagement therein. That is to say, I am interested in the ways in which an integrated sense of being, knowing and acting in the classroom can, at least partly, be facilitated through digital media production (Dall'Alba and Barnacle 2007, p. 686).

If social research methods produce reality, as Law and Urry (2003) claim, then social enquiry participates in 'ontological politics' from which no researcher can escape with a pristine account (Benedict 1934; Scott and Usher 2011, p. 101). In brief, doing research is an 'intentional state' (Bruner 1996, p. 136): however local and provisional, the responsibility to produce multiple truthful accounts of school practices (analogous with Heron and Reason's 'rights and obligations' with relatives above) necessitates ethical underpinning that goes deeper than the advantages of short term gain.

Research Principles and Educational Values

The following five conceptual tools were devised by Finnish academics Heikkinen et al. (2007, 2016) to assess the validity of Action Research in ethical ways. The Finnish criteria could function in alternative scenarios as foundations for both a set of research principles and educational values, which in turn underpin both the methodology and data interpretation. Heikkinen et al.'s account acknowledges the importance of:

- historical continuity: or temporal context, and the ways in which knowledge accretes and spirals within specific local conditions (Bruner 2009/1960; Hall 1992).
  When the specifics of our lived moment are articulated in terms of powerful forces in a context, this can lead to deeper social understandings. Developing an awareness of social configurations as patterned and permeable, helps learners to identify how their lives are culturally situated. This brings to mind the often cyclical nature of social phenomena and the ways in which discursive learning and media representations are implicated in this cycle.
- reflexivity: or personal critical response through reflection on situatedness, and the ways in which texts are constructed both in research and in everyday social practices (Le Gallais 2008).
  Holistic and reflexive approaches to learning encourage the questioning of assumptions and the analysis of power relations. One of the ways in which criticality can be enhanced is through the creation and anatomising of media texts, conceived as a new strand of literacy (Buckingham 2003; Ito et al. 2013; Potter and Gilje 2015).
- dialectics: the recognition that meaning is made through social transactions and the sharing of experiences (Bakhtin 1981; Dewey 1997/1938).
  This study positions researchers, teachers and learners as latent and capable multimodal meaning-makers with sensitivity towards their audiences. The significance of this educationally relates to the many modes and platforms available for this form of social participation, which in turn raises questions of 'literacy legitimacy' and how exactly modern literacy is constituted. Such issues relate to the dialogic activities in the third quadrant of the Cycle of Digital Making (Fig. 2.3) and the transitional spaces that bound it.
- workability: or what may or may not transpire through interactions brought about by researchers' and participants' engagement with tools, practices and environments.

- A sense of pragmatism imbues this study in relation to its emancipatory roots, as explained in Chap. 1 (Anyon 2009; Conteh et al. 2005, p. ix; Freire 1993). Nevertheless, workability is a term that carries with it a tension between potentiality and practicability: in order to effect change one has to work within the constraints of what is possible, whilst testing the boundaries. Educationally speaking, whether something is workable or not, is played out in situations where there is tension between the elements, for example: learners' negotiation of meandering creative processes and the constraints of aesthetic possibility; innovative pedagogies rubbing up against glacial institutional practices; or, school interventions that help shape the "citizen-worker-of-the-future" (Williams 2004, p. 408) and friction between these and more autonomous practices.

- evocativeness: the impact of aesthetic design and the use of appropriate rhetorical devices to provoke particular emotional responses.
Research wise, arts-based presentation of data invites a sense of pluralism and inspires connections with other disciplines. From the point of view of learning with digital media, evocativeness refers to the crafting of symbolic resources in purposeful ways that complement existing reading and writing practices. I go on to suggest that everyday artistry might be a more suitable term for the purposes of this study as it evokes creative practices that retrieve a sense of the ordinary from the rarified patterns of thought that 'art' can often summon.

To this list I add a sixth principle, not present in Heikkinen et al.'s original text (2007), that informs the values propelling my research:

- *equitability*: the adherence to democratic principles of fairness, inclusivity and flattened hierarchical structures.
As regards research, this concerns the extent to which sensitivity is extended to participants' input and fidelity to the material. In parallel with ethics of equality, my creative practice as researcher and practitioner embraces a spirit of cooperation and empathy, both of which sit well within an epistemology of co-construction and the collaborative composition work outlined in my theoretical framework.

An ethnographic approach to research is cognisant of the above foundational values based on human interests as well as being a form of enquiry that embraces contradiction and complexity. The next section outlines why this approach is appropriate for exploring issues related to digital making in school spaces.

Ethnography: Winks Upon Winks Upon Winks

Geertz's (1973) model of ethnography as 'thick description' has become axiomatic in the ethnographic lexicon. However, ethnographies do not just depend on evocative descriptive language for their 'thickness' but on the recognition:

> that what we call our data are really our own constructions of other people's constructions of what they and their compatriots are up to … [we are] explicating explications. Winks upon winks upon winks.
> (Geertz 1973, p. 9)

The idea of accumulative 'truthful' winks projects the discursive importance of the narrative approach, to be discussed in the next section. Geertz suggests that participants' and ethnographers' accounts emerging from social observation are stories then, that ought to be mutually, if tacitly, recognised as such for accounts to be made with integrity.

Not only is there an element of collusion in presentation and reception, but Geertz offers a vertiginous definition of the muddled phenomena the ethnographer is faced with, one that might put off all but the most resilient of researchers in search of coherent 'truth claims':

> [the researcher negotiates] a multiplicity of complex conceptual structures, many of them superimposed upon or knotted into one another, which are at once strange, irregular, and inexplicit, and which he must contrive somehow first to grasp and then to render. And this is true at the most down-to-earth, jungle field work levels of his activity: interviewing informants, observing rituals, eliciting kin terms, … Doing ethnography is like trying to read (in the sense of "construct a reading of") a manuscript—foreign, faded, full of ellipses, incoherencies, suspicious emendations, and tenden-

tious commentaries, but written not in conventionalized graphs of sound but in transient examples of shaped behavior.(Geertz 1973, p. 10)

The school environment is indeed 'knotted' and 'shaped' with discursive structures and personal trajectories, that the ethnographer must first make strange and unravel, and then render explicit and comprehensible. Of relevance to this study in particular is Geertz's reference to the fleeting and shaped nature of behaviour which I aimed to capture in my fieldwork through close observation, photography and film. Schools are among the most institutionalised of social settings, barely is there anything of the 'natural' in it, so prescribed and contingent are its standards and regulations. To enter this overbearing realm as a critically and visually attuned ethnographer is both a privilege and a necessity which brings to mind Hymes' (1981) statement that ethnography is the methodological approach "most compatible with a democratic way of life" (cited in Conteh et al. 2005, p. 97). Hence my ethnography, although only a partial exposé of young people's implicit understandings of the moving image, throws light on the harsher contradictory ideologies that tend to obscure them. To de-mist the discursive smoke-screen then, a critical visual anthropological approach was considered an appropriate way of forging new understandings of the media interests and skills of children and young people, and building capacity around them.

Throughout my research I have been conscious of materiality within social contexts (Dezuanni 2014; Dezuanni and Woods 2014), and also the material quality of digital texts themselves. I prefer to think of these as temporary assemblages of the stuff of culture, situated 'thought-things' as Arendt (1981/1971) might have put it, rather than virtual ephemera (Burnett 2011; Burnett et al. 2012). Reflecting on concrete textual qualities has helped me concentrate on young people's interactions with audiovisual texts and the making of them. Rose paraphrases Gell (1998) who writes of visual anthropology's interest "in the practical mediatory role of visual objects in the social process" (Rose 2007, p. 217); indeed, it is what is done and felt during audiovisual production, the manner and circumstance of digital fabrication, that is the focus of my ethnography. It is argued that this strategy prioritises digital making practices rather than the texts themselves, as Pink counsels in her appraisal of participatory video work:

it is not simply the final film document that is important, but rather the collaborative processes by which it is produced, and it is through these processes that both new levels of engagement in thematic issues and of self-awareness are achieved by participants and ethnographic knowledge is produced.

(Pink 2013, p. 118)

A Critical Visual Anthropological Approach

Choosing methods often relates to life experience as much as to 'rightness of fit' (Goodman 1978) with research questions: if these two dimensions mesh, then arguably the output is more persuasive. The ways in which my life experiences have influenced my choice of critical visual anthropology as a method relate to lengths of time spent teaching English abroad in Europe and South America. Living on the edge of different cultures as both a non-native observer and quasi-participant, meant continually negotiating shifts between my English identity and that which emerged within other cultural codes. This may have created a sensitivity towards the insider/outsider researcher status, identified by Le Gallais (2008, p. 148), and my study of liminal space.

The use of still and moving image in anthropological fieldwork has a long history, chiefly as a tool of reinforcement. I distinguish my approach to gathering visual research materials by claiming for them not only a supportive role but also a constitutive capacity; that is, they "conjure up synaesthetic and kinaesthetic effects" (following Edensor in Rose 2007, p. 248) through which some images create a unique visual agency. Rose articulates how those researchers' interested in:

precisely how the practices within which the materiality of social life is embedded can exceed their spoken or written expression, have turned to photography as a means of evoking such excess.

(Rose 2007, p. 248)

During the course of my own fieldwork certain photos and movies seemed to fit into this 'excessive' category in useful and surprising ways— some captured by participants, arguably exemplifying new cultural forms of literacy 'in action', and others taken by myself, offering a dynamic portrait of creative digital media learning.

Some commentators extend the agency of visual material inscribing them with 'a social life' of their own. Rose points out (drawing on Appadurai 1986) that images, like people and cultural artefacts, have a biography (2007, p. 217)—digital images even more so, in terms of the relative ease with which they are disseminated, re-contextualised and re-interpreted. The fourth quadrant of the Cycle of Digital Making (Fig. 2.2) becomes more salient here, as it is in the dispersal and exchange of still and moving image 'objects', that their materiality, mobility and translatability are brought to light. These are characteristics of digital texts as much as they are anthropological empirical touchstones. Rose (2007, p. 223) cites Appadurai who explains further:

> It is only through the analysis of [artefacts'] trajectories that we can interpret the human transactions and calculations that enliven things. Thus, even though from a theoretical point of view human actors encode things with significance, from a methodological point of view it is the things-in-motion that illuminate their human and social context.
> (Appadurai 1986, p. 5, original emphasis)

This signals that the anthropologically sanctioned capture of texts, people and processes 'in motion' are conduits to an illuminated understanding of young people's film and DV production. In practice this means photographing and videoing the interactive processes of production, and examining the social embeddedness of these and participant-generated texts (their 'social life'), so as to be able to theorise about distinct forms of digital meaning-making. Furthermore, the 'biographies' of my research 'objects' gain traction and meaning as they locate themselves within this body of work, within media education scholarship, and ultimately within discursive digital making cycles.

The photographic was a key communicative dimension of one of my case studies—The Clip Club, as it was the preferred medium through which one child expressed his identity. This democratic perspective is corroborated by Burke:

An important, and overlooked, levelling dimension of photography as a research tool is that, unlike traditional forms of literacy, it captures perspectives on experience in a format that adults and children can produce with similar levels of technical skill.

(Burke 2008, p. 25)

to which I would add, similar levels of observational skill. These two techniques arose from an effort to lessen the need for children to be verbally articulate in order to express themselves, and to prompt expression of feelings and attitudes in ways more associative than propositional.

In terms of analysis, strict attention ought to be paid to the point of view of the maker in the making of texts about texts. To productively participate in this cycle, in whatever role, capacity or medium, is to experience some form of empowerment, which is why scrupulously reflexive practices should underlie critical visual anthropological methods (Rose 2007, p. 262). Historically anthropology has been associated with practices of objective 'othering' in the context of colonial exploration, an academic practice in which the everyday routines of 'exotic others' would be observed and reported (Benedict 1934). Adults' othering of children in research is a phenomenon I tried to mitigate, by being mindful of power imbalances along the way. In practice this meant neutralising any assumed adult superiority which, if exercised, risked skewed findings and a loss of "specific and unique insights ... which can easily slip below the horizons of older inquirers" (Thomson 2008, p. 1). This is particularly true of research exploring the non-formal media ecology of young people and the ways in which this can be incorporated into educational practice.

Whenever possible, child participants were afforded opportunities to engage in activities ordinarily framed as adult territory: filming in the 'forbidden zones' of school or beyond the school gates; being handed the camera to record events; being interviewed by a group of professionals seeking their advice on film-making with tablets; contributing to a Q and A session in a public arena about their work; or simply having their personal responses listened to regularly and attentively. Rose advocates that attention be paid during fieldwork to the discursive relations of power that saturate all research texts and processes; visual texts being no different in this respect from the words emitted by participants and interpreted by researchers (Rose 2007, p. 262). Above all if a visual and anthropo-logically infused ethnography is to support emergent understanding, it is "the relationship between the subjectivities of the researcher and research participants that produces a negotiated version of reality" (Pink 2013, p. 37)—and the evocative construction of the same, that remains the researcher's challenge to communicate.

This observation is corroborated by Buckingham who cautions against "naïve empiricism" (2009, p. 633) and the so-called 'empowerment' experienced by participants who indulge in creative visual methods. Buckingham is sceptical about a recourse to the expressive arts that mines participants' depths and reveals notional seams of hitherto unreachable 'real data'. For him, this is a deficit approach signalling the need "to understand how research itself establishes positions from which it becomes possible for participants to 'speak'" (2009, p. 635). In other words, systematic reflexivity must be built into visual methodology spe-cifically in relation to researcher identity and responsibility, participants' briefing and the nature of the technology being used.

I have some sympathy with Buckingham's critique, in that young par-ticipants can tend to 'perform' responses they know will 'please the adult', but I also have faith in visual methods' capacity to shape the mood of research encounters. Given time for mutual trust to develop, young par-ticipants' familiarity with film and moving image can support a willing-ness to make sincere contributions. Moreover, a knowingness accrues on the part of the researcher to be able to detect signs of "empty verbalism … covering a vacuum" (Vygotsky 2012/1934, p. 159; see also Cannon et al. 2014, p. 26) and to respond with sensitivity.

Pragmatising the Imaginary

Eisner (1997) has written extensively on the virtues of arts practice in relation to qualitative research:

> The arts teach students to act and to judge in the absence of rule, to rely on feel, to pay attention to nuance, to act and appraise the consequences of one's choices and to revise and then to make other choices … Artists and

all who work with the composition of qualities try to achieve a "rightness of fit."
(Eisner 2005/2002, p. 208)

To present, or rather 'curate', ethnographic data is to qualitatively compose a compelling argument, and much of this relies on a creative as well as a critical orientation. Pursuing this line of thinking and in the context of encouraging new reporting mechanisms, Eisner elaborates a metaphor in which scientific verification (instrumental research) is perceived as a process of recording the temperature of phenomena, in contrast with the examination of experience (ethnographic narrative research) which corresponds to the exploration of the underlying heat:

> ... we report the temperature even when we are interested in the heat; we expect a reader to be able to transform the numbers representing the former into the experience that constitutes the latter. New forms of data representation signify our growing interest in inventing ways to represent the heat.
> (Eisner 1997, p. 7)

So the representation of 'heat' in my study equates to the embodied, human and non-human interactions that constitute the teaching and learning environment related to media-making, such as: pedagogic and pupil trial and error, participants' vexations and celebrations, and undulating creative acts in constrained spaces. Reporting on the texture of messy educational terrain does come with caveats, as researchers struggle to:

> represent the fluid, changing, multiple, necessarily incomplete, always partial, "for now" nature of experience.
> (Clandinin and Murphy 2009, p. 601)

In line with this provisionality, Barone talks of 'pragmatising the imaginary', by which he means embellishing researchers' capacity to lift the veil of conventionality from an audience's eyes in order to question familiar, comfortable discourses (2001, 2007, p. 465). To address this Clandinin and Murphy endorse narrative methodology as a means of questioning dominant narratives:

(in order to) change how we imagine and live out the storied structures, such as schools, that shape our lives ... narrative research offers the possibility of prompting "new imaginings of the ideal and the possible".
(Clandinin and Murphy 2009, p. 601, drawing on Barone 2001, p. 736)

Challenging assumptions related to digital media practices in schools is indeed one of the proposed aims of my research. Whilst exploring the dislocation between young people's media worlds in and beyond school, a simultaneous objective is to neutralise discourses forming around ed-tech 'evangelism' and technological determinism (Shirky 2009; Prensky 2001, 2012; Anderson 2012; O'Reilly 2017). 'Pragmatising the imaginary' is fitting for my mode of narration, as it encapsulates an interpretivist approach to 'chalk-face realities' and political critique. This is a methodological standpoint supported by Van Manen's wide-ranging treatise on curriculum design, where he calls for a still "higher level of deliberative rationality" (1977, p. 226, see also p. 214) in relation to interpretive work and practical action, than that manifested by the supporters of quantified learning.

Storying Children's Lives

Researchers' principled deliberation, to which Van Manen alludes above, is all the more important when producing representations of children. Some might question the premise on which research with children is based and the validity of its findings, and in answer I would emphasise the transparency with which this research was undertaken. For example, in the Clip Club setting each child is fleshed out in a 'pen portrait' as advocated by Hollway and Jefferson (2000).[4] A short crafted portrait is cognisant of the personal relationships between club members, and presents the reader with a series of sensitive summaries which are faithful to the wholeness of the children's subjectivities. These are open-ended ren-

---

[4] This approach was also adopted by renowned anthropologist Daniel Miller in his evocative account of residents on a particular London street (2008). From his observations on the belongings on display in their homes and his interview data, he constructed sensitive and compelling tales of their past and present lives.

derings that often remain unaccounted for in public discourse, but the sustained nature of the Clip Club enabled a storied "sense of truth" (Miller 2008, p. 24) for each participant.

Some may question the authenticity of the story but perhaps a more pressing concern is the cost of not representing or listening to the marginalised voices of children, a point forcefully asserted by both Kaplan (2008, p. 190) and Burke (2008). The latter links Freirian thinking, visual methodologies and the multiple "layering of re-interpretation" (Burke 2008. p. 34), concluding that:

> without a recognised political voice and presence, children will continue to be seen as less than equal to the adult in participatory projects.
> (Burke 2008, p. 34)

Nevertheless, it is difficult to defuse the tension between research perceived as carried out on and with participants, especially on and with those who are deemed vulnerable. Thomson and Gunter (2007, 2011) recognise this and embrace the fluid identities of researchers and the researched. They propose a 'standpoint' for research with children that resonates with my own, namely one which:

- addresses issues of importance to students and is thus in their collective interests
- works with students' subjugated knowledges about the way in which the school works
- allows marginalized perspectives and voices to come centre stage
- uses students' subjectivities and experiences to develop approaches, tools, representations and validities
- interrupts the power relations in schools including, but not confined to, those which are age related, and
- is geared to making a difference
  (Thomson and Gunter 2007, p. 331)

These are the precepts on which my narratives concerning children's media interactions are based, and many of the concluding recommendations towards the end of Chap. 7 issue from this critical standpoint.

Alasuutari (1995, cited in Conteh et al. 2005, p. 108) spoke of 'unriddling' ethnographic data rather than seeking certitude. So bearing in mind Hall's modest approach (1992) to enquiry, I explain how tentative meanings can be drawn from contexts in which there is a playful merging of 'school-not-school life-worlds' (Sefton-Green 2013).

A Möbius Strip and an Interpretive Rationale

Earlier I built on the principles of validation devised by Finnish academics (Heikkinen et al. 2007, 2016) to construct an ethical framework for research.[5] I suggested that these principles would inform my interpretations as part of a holistic methodology. To this end, I present the protocols through which I convey the 'occasioned' meanings in my research material. Figure 3.1 is a visual representation of how the settings might be framed for interpretation based on inductively inspired reflection and years of immersion in creative media practice.

I begin by invoking Merleau-Ponty's view of embodied vision being 'caught in things' (Furstenau and MacKenzie 2009, p. 18). He thought of the body as:

> Visible and mobile … a thing among things; it is caught in the fabric of the world and its cohesion is that of a thing. But because it moves itself and sees, it holds things in a circle around itself.(Merleau-Ponty 1964, p. 163)

I came to visualise my research data as arrested moments held notionally within a circular structure—like a Möbius strip.[6] This is a band whose peculiarities are its twist and seamless surface. With no discernible inner or outer side there is one surface that maps one topological space, whilst

---

[5] These principles are also referenced by Bold (2012, p. 175) in her endorsement of narrative and the validity of 'representative constructions' (2012, p. 162).

[6] The twist, the circularity and elasticity of the Möbius form articulate dynamic tensions in social formation and possible distortions as ideas circulate. The seamless surface offers robustness, while flexibility discourages any impulse to pin down one interpretation as 'truth'. I imagine it to be made of translucent man-made substance: man-made denotes the socially constructed nature of the interpretive process, while translucence invokes permeability and sensitivity to light. So there is a porosity to sense-making that invites alternative frames and interpretations.

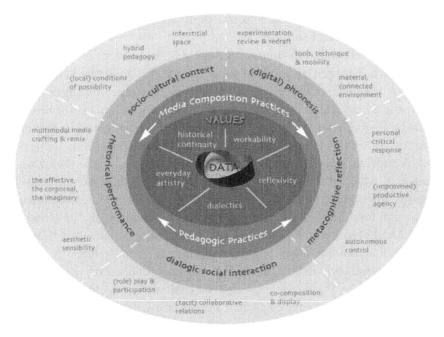

Fig. 3.1 Model for interpreting digital media composition practices and pedagogy. Drawing on Heikkinen et al. (2007)

retaining its capacity to form endless shapes. To me these characteristics lend themselves to accounts of related but contradictory phenomena, such as the role of the ethnographer as a situated observer/participant/ narrativist, and the ways in which textuality and context are in continuously unfolding dialogue with each other, as illustrated in the Cycle of Digital Making (Fig. 2.3). The data are visualised as remixable bundles of meaning (Knobel and Lankshear 2008; Manovich 2001) encircled by a malleable porous structure.

I propose that two overarching dimensions frame my material for the purposes of interpretation: our historical conditions of possibility (Scott and Usher 2011) and participants' symbolic performance—adapted from A. Reid's (2007) anthropologically rooted theories of media composition. These dimensions are interdependent, as rendered visually by the Möbius strip, and will be linked conceptually with Heikkinen et al.'s (2007) principles following these frames: workability, reflexivity, dialectics and everyday artistry, with historical continuity providing an underlying critical perspective on social context.

Earlier I referred to the tensions inherent in the concept of workability in research, between the kinds of social change that are desired and those that are feasible in the prevailing circumstances. I relate this to phronesis—the Greek notion of practical contingent wisdom mentioned in Chap. 2—and the to-ing and fro-ing involved in fixing and improving text or performance in some way. Composing with media, from planning to filming and editing, entails negotiating a tooled and peopled environment in which physical and digital materials are recursively assembled and disassembled, offering a more textured and dynamic environment than that found in orthodox literacy practices (Cannon et al. 2018; Potter and MacDougall 2017). For this reason, during my research I became aware of conditions that nurtured experiences and feelings of 'flow' (Csikszentmihalyi 1990), iteration and experimentation (Burn and Durran 2007). These concepts relate to challenge, judgement and feelings of mastery, and they combine to connect digital media-making to a wider conception of what it means to be literate.

I have suggested that digital media production is an activity that encourages metacognitive reflection—or reflexivity—in that it unpacks hitherto implicit visual understandings and renders them concrete in the act of making. Watching and then making moving image texts and articulating the process through specific typologies, nourishes a critical personal response and a disposition for (re-)productive action. This creative and questioning frame of mind is embodied in the term praxis which unites thought and action with purpose. As already suggested, finding alternative points of access for reflexive thinking develops children and young people's autonomous critical responses. My research explores how young people borrow and curate what is of interest to them in the 'cultural stock', to then 'mod' it and reflect their own interests and identities.

Moving on to dialectics, the term is viewed in this context as an exchange of social meaning. The extent to which dialogic interaction is instantiated through digital media in and beyond the classroom, makes explicit a disposition to co-design, build and externalise meanings socially. Examining young people's apparent willingness to engage in these types of collaborative and reciprocal activities is an additional interpretive protocol with which to embellish understandings of the media production environment in school spaces and related pedagogies.

Finally, evocativeness is a concept readily associated with the humanities and rhetorical performance. It is rooted in the idea of 'calling forth' associative images, memories and feelings (from the Latin evocat). As such it encapsulates much that is ambiguous and unquantifiable, those sensibilities related to the body, the affective and the imagination. In other words, the term evokes the 'quality' constituents of qualitative relations, whose aesthetic arrangement aspires to the creation of coherent patterns. For this study, I replace evocativeness, which is more textually-oriented, with everyday artistry, which suggests acts of routine non-expert production, whilst still retaining a textual element and a sense of audience.

There is a synergy in everyday artistry with film-making and editing, activities that require sensitivity towards the creation of mood. Similarly, mood in media production pedagogy is manipulated through continual adjustments on the part of teacher-facilitator, taking into account learners' feelings of autonomy, mastery and purpose (Pink 2009). The climate of the classroom is such that learners' are disposed to transition between the here-and-now and the ambiguity of 'that which isn't yet'. These movements are redolent of Lanham's (1984) oscillating AT (INTERACT)/THROUGH construct, where learners work with symbols and shuttle between inscriptions and projected meanings. Burnett (2011) recoups this notion in her thesis on the complex '(im)material relations' related to literacy practices in virtual and embodied worlds. Data are examined with reference to iterative movements between online/offline spaces, people, creative media tools, apps and software—all of which are recurring phenomena in the processes of film-making and DV production. I resolve to interpret data and transcripts attentive to dynamics and practices that involve oscillation between social spaces, courses of action and frames of mind.

A Turning of the Wheels

These are storied accounts then, with potentially wide-reaching implications, rather than a 'what works' project valued for its workability at scale. I would like these materials to be judged "by their aesthetic standard, their emotive force, their verisimilitude, and criteria of authenticity or integrity to the people they portray" (Bold 2012, p. 144, drawing on Clough 2002). On this basis, it is at grassroots level that I believe this book to be most practicable. It is hoped that a pragmatic approach might impact on readers' own professional practice and on change-making in the present.

Chapter 3 has offered a lengthy philosophical exegesis closely aligned with a baseline of particular values. I conclude with a passage from Hughes (1971), which resonates with my working practices and sets the tone for the next Chapter. Reprising Wright Mill's (1959) encapsulation of social science's main instrument—the 'sociological imagination'—Hughes describes it as inhabiting a kind of transitional hinterland:

> [of] free association, guided but not hampered by a frame of reference internalized not quite into the unconscious ... When people say of my work ... that it shows insight, I cannot think what they could mean other than whatever quality may have been produced by intensity of observation and a turning of the wheels to find a new combination of the old concepts, or even a new concept.
> (Hughes 1971, p. vi, cited in Grady 2004, p. 26)

As a creative media educator-practitioner since the turn of the century, the wheels have been turning implicitly for some time. And so it is with an explicit and "alert consciousness poised for insight" (Grady 2004, p. 26) that I begin the story of what happened.

Bibliography

Alasuutari, P. (1995). *Researching Culture: Qualitative Method and Cultural Studies*. California: Sage Publications.

Alexander, R. (Ed.). (2010). *Children, their World, their Education: Final Report and Recommendations of the Cambridge Primary Review*. Abingdon: Routledge.

Anderson, C. (2012). *Makers: The New Industrial Revolution*. London: Random House Business Books.

Anyon, J. (2009). *Theory and Educational Research: Toward Critical Social Explanation*. New York: Routledge.

Appadurai, A. (1986). *The Social Life of Things: Commodities in Cultural Perspective*. Cambridge: Cambridge University Press.

Arendt, H. (1981/1971). *The Life of the Mind*. San Diego: Houghton Mifflin Harcourt.

Bakhtin, M. (1981). *The Dialogic Imagination: Four Essays*. Austin: University of Texas Press.

Ball, S. J. (2013). *The Education Debate* (2nd ed.). Bristol: Policy Press.

Barone, T. (2001). Pragmatizing the imaginary: A response to a fictionalized case study of teaching [online]. *Harvard Educational Review, 71*(4), 734–741. Retrieved February 7, 2018, from http://hepg.org/her-home/issues/harvard-educational-review-volume-71-issue-4/herarticle/a-response-to-a-fictionalized-case-study-of-teachi.

Barone, T. (2007). A return to the gold standard? Questioning the future of narrative construction as educational research. *Qualitative Inquiry, 13*(4), 454–470.

Bassey, M. (1998). Fuzzy generalisation: An approach to building educational theory [online]. In *BERA: British Educational Research Association Annual Conference*. The Queen's University of Belfast, Northern Ireland. Retrieved February 7, 2018, from http://www.leeds.ac.uk/educol/documents/000000801.htm.

Benedict, R. (1934). *Patterns of Culture*. New York: Houghton Mifflin Harcourt.

Bold, C. (2012). *Using Narrative in Research*. London: Sage.

Bradford City of Film (2010–2015). *Bradford Film Literacy Programme* [online]. Retrieved February 7, 2018, from http://bradfordfilmliteracy.com/about/.

Bruner, J. S. (1996). *The Culture of Education*. Cambridge, MA: Harvard University Press.

Bruner, J. S. (2009/1960). *The Process of Education*. Cambridge, MA: Harvard University Press.

Bryman, A. (2008). *Social Research Methods* (3rd ed.). Oxford: Oxford University Press.

Buckingham, D. (2003). *Media Education: Literacy, Learning and Contemporary Culture*. Cambridge: Polity Press.

Buckingham, D. (2009). 'Creative' visual methods in media research: Possibilities, problems and proposals. *Media Culture and Society, 31*(4), 633–652.

Burke, C. (2008). 'Play in focus': Children's visual voice in participative research. In P. Thomson (Ed.), *Doing Visual Research with Children and Young People* (pp. 23–36). Abingdon: Routledge.

Burn, A., & Durran, J. (2007). *Media Literacy in Schools: Practice, Production and Progression*. London: Paul Chapman.

Burnett, C. (2011). The (im)materiality of educational space: Interactions between material, connected and textual dimensions of networked technology use in schools. *E-Learning and Digital Media, 8*(3), 214.

Burnett, C., Merchant, G., Pahl, K., & Rowsell, J. (2012). The (im)materiality of literacy: The significance of subjectivity to new literacies research. *Discourse: Studies in the Cultural Politics of Education, 35*(1), 90–103.

Cannon, M., Bryer, T., & Lindsey, M. (2014). Media production and disruptive innovation: Exploring the interrelations between children, tablets, teachers and texts in subject English settings. *Media Education Research Journal, 5*(1), 16–31.

Cannon, M., Potter, J., & Burn, A. (2018). Dynamic, playful and productive literacies. *Changing English, 25*(2).

Clandinin, D. J., & Murphy, S. (2009). Relational ontological commitments in narrative research. *Educational Researcher, 38*(8), 598–602.

Clough, P. (2002). *Narratives and Fictions in Educational Research*. Maidenhead: Open University Press.

Conteh, J., Gregory, E., Kearney, C., & Mor-Sommerfeld, A. (2005). *On Writing Educational Ethnographies: The Art of Collusion*. Stoke on Trent: Trentham Books.

Csikszentmihalyi, M. (1990). *Flow: The Psychology of Optimal Experience*. New York: Harper & Row.

Dall'Alba, G., & Barnacle, R. (2007). An ontological turn for higher education. *Studies in Higher Education, 32*(6), 679–691.

Denzin, N. K. (2001). *Interpretive Interactionism* (2nd ed.). London: Sage.

Dewey, J. (1997/1938). *Experience and Education*. New York: Touchstone.

Dezuanni, M. (2014). The building blocks of digital media literacy, socio-material participation and the production of media knowledge. *Journal of Curriculum Studies*, 1–24.

Dezuanni, M., & Woods, A. (2014). Developing media production skills for literacy in a primary school classroom: Digital materials, embodied knowledge and material contexts. In G. Barton (Ed.), *Literacy in the Arts: Retheorising Learning and Teaching* (pp. 143–160). Heidelberg: Springer.

EEF. (2015). *About the Education Endowment Foundation* [online]. Retrieved February 7, 2018, from https://educationendowmentfoundation.org.uk/about/.

Eisner, E. (1997). The promise and perils of alternative forms of data representation. *Educational Researcher, 26*(6), 4–10.

Eisner, E. (2005/2002). What can education learn from the arts about the practice of education? [online]. In E. Eisner (Ed.), *Reimagining Schools* (pp. 205–214). Abingdon: Routledge. Retrieved February 7, 2018, from http://www.infed.org/biblio/eisner_arts_and_the_practice_of_education. htm.

Freire, P. (1993/1970). *Pedagogy of the Oppressed.* London: Penguin.

Furedi, F. (2013). Keep the scourge of scientism out of schools. Retrieved February 7, 2018, from http://www.frankfuredi.com/site/article/keep_the_ scourge_of_scientism_out_of_schools.

Furstenau, M., & Mackenzie, A. (2009). The promise of 'makeability': Digital editing software and the structuring of everyday cinematic life. *Visual Communication, 8*(1), 5–22.

Le Gallais, T. (2008). Wherever I go there I am: Reflections on reflexivity and the research stance. *Reflective Practice: International and Multidisciplinary Perspectives, 9*(2), 145–155.

Geertz, C. (1973). *The Interpretation of Cultures* [online]. London: Hutchinson. Retrieved February 7, 2018, from http://www.csub.edu/~mault/pdffiles/ch1. pdf.

Gell, A. (1998). *Art and Agency: An Anthropological Theory.* Oxford: Oxford University Press.

Goodman, N. (1978). *Ways of Worldmaking.* Indianapolis: Hackett Publishing.

Grady, J. (2004). Working with visible evidence: An invitation and some practical advice. In C. Knowles & P. Sweetman (Eds.), *Picturing the Social Landscape: Visual Methods and the Sociological Imagination* (pp. 18–31). Abingdon: Routledge.

Hall, S. (1992). Cultural studies and its theoretical legacies [online]. In L. Grossberg, C. Nelson, & P. Treichler (Eds.), *Cultural Studies* (pp. 277–294). London and New York: Routledge. Retrieved February 7, 2018, from http:// msuweb.montclair.edu/~furrg/pursuits/hallcultstuds.html.

Hattie, J. (2012). *Visible Learning for Teachers: Maximizing Impact on Learning.* Abingdon: Routledge.

Hattie, J., & Yates, G. (2014). *Visible Learning and the Science of How We Learn.* Abingdon: Routledge.

Heath, S. B. (1983). *Ways with Words: Language, Life and Work in Communities and Classrooms.* Cambridge: Cambridge University Press.

Heikkinen, H. L., Huttunen, R., & Syrjälä, L. (2007). Action research as narrative: Five principles for validation. *Educational Action Research, 15*(1), 5–19.

Heikkinen, H. L., Jong, F. P. C. M. d., & Vanderlinde, R. (2016). What is (good) practitioner research? *Vocations and Learning, 9*(1), 1–19.

Heron, J., & Reason, P. (1997). A participatory inquiry paradigm [online]. *Qualitative Inquiry, 3*(3), 274–294. Retrieved February 7, 2018, from http://www.peterreason.eu/Papers/Participatoryinquiryparadigm.pdf.

Hill Bulman, J. (2014). *Developing a Progression Framework for Children's Reading of Film.* PhD Thesis, School of Education, University of Sheffield, Sheffield.

Hollway, W., & Jefferson, T. (2000). *Doing Qualitative Research Differently: Free Association, Narrative and the Interview Method.* London: Sage Publications.

Hughes, E. C. (1971). *The Sociological Eye: Selected Papers.* Chicago: Aldine-Atherton.

Hymes, D. H. (1981). Ethnographic monitoring. In H. T. Trueba, G. P. Guthrie, & K. H. Au (Eds.), *Culture and the Bilingual Classroom: Studies in Classroom Ethnography* (pp. 56–68). Newbury House: Rowley, MA.

Ito, M., Livingstone, S., Penuel, B., Rhodes, J., Salen, K., Schor, J., et al. (2013). *Connected Learning: An Agenda for Research and Design* [online]. Digital Media and Learning Research Hub. Retrieved February 7, 2018, from http://dmlhub.net/wp-content/uploads/files/Connected_Learning_report.pdf.

Jenkins, H., Purushota, R., Clinton, K., & Robinson, A. J. (2006). *Confronting the Challenges of Participatory Culture: Media Education for the 21st Century* [online]. Chicago: The John D. & Catherine T. MacArthur Foundation. Retrieved February 7, 2018, from https://www.macfound.org/media/article_pdfs/JENKINS_WHITE_PAPER.PDF.

Jones, K. (2006). A Biographic researcher in pursuit of an aesthetic: The use of arts-based (re)presentations in 'performative' dissemination of life stories [online]. *Qualitative Sociology Review, 2*(1), 66–85. Retrieved February 7, 2018, from http://www.qualitativesociologyreview.org/ENG/Volume3/QSR_2_1_Jones.pdf.

Jones, K., & Fenge, L.-A. (2017). Gifted stories: How well do we retell the stories that research participants give us? *Creative Approaches to Research, 10*(1), 35–35. Retrieved February 7, 2018, from http://creativeapproachestoresearch.net/wp-content/uploads/CAR10_1_Jones_Fenge.pdf.

Kaplan, I. (2008). Being 'seen', being 'heard': Engaging with students on the margins of education through participatory photography. In P. Thomson (Ed.), *Doing Visual Research with Children and Young People* (pp. 175–191). Abingdon: Routledge.

Knobel, M., & Lankshear, C. (2008). Remix: The art and craft of endless hybridization. *Journal of Adolescent & Adult Literacy, 52*(1), 22–33.

Lather, P. (1991). Research as Praxis. In *Getting Smart: Feminist Research and Pedagogy With/In the Postmodern* (pp. 50–69). New York: Routledge.

Lather, P. (2006). Paradigm proliferation as a good thing to think with: Teaching research in education as a wild profusion. *International Journal of Qualitative Studies in Education, 19*(1), 35–57.

Law, J., & Urry, J. (2003). *Enacting the Social* [online]. Department of Sociology and the Centre for Science Studies, Lancaster University. Retrieved February 7, 2018, from http://www.lancaster.ac.uk/fass/resources/sociology-online-papers/papers/law-urry-enacting-the-social.pdf.

Lincoln, Y. S., & Guba, E. G. (2000). Paradigmatic controversies, contradictions, and emerging confluences. In Y. S. Lincoln & E. G. Guba (Eds.), *Handbook of Qualitative Research* (pp. 163–188). Thousand Oaks, CA: Sage Publications, Inc.

Loveless, A. (2008). Moving from the margins creating space with digital technology: Wonder, theory and action [online]. In C. Palmer & D. Torevell (Eds.), *The Turn to Aesthetics: An Interdisciplinary Exchange of Ideas in Applied and Philosophical Aesthetics* (pp. 189–198). Liverpool: Liverpool Hope University Press. Retrieved February 7, 2018, from http://works.bepress.com/cgi/viewcontent.cgi?article=1001&context=clive_palmer.

Lyotard, J. F. (1984). *The Postmodern Condition: A Report on Knowledge.* Minneapolis: University of Minneapolis Press.

Mäkelä, M. (2007). Knowing through making: The role of the artefact in practice-led research. *Knowledge, Technology & Policy, 20*(3), 157–163.

Manovich, L. (2001). *The Language of New Media.* Cambridge, MA: MIT Press.

Merleau-Ponty, M. (1964). *The Primacy of Perception.* Evanston, IL: Northwestern University Press.

Miller, D. (2008). *The Comfort of Things.* Cambridge, UK: Polity.

O'Reilly, T. (2017). *WTF?: What's the Future and Why It's Up to Us.* Louth: R H Business Books.

Orr, S. (2013). *Making Teaching Work in Media* [online]. Media Education Summit, Sheffield Hallam University. Retrieved February 7, 2018, from https://www.youtube.com/watch?v=SI0jep9bNBs.

Pink, D. (2009). *Drive: The Surprising Truth About What Motivates Us.* London: Penguin.

Pink, S. (2013). *Doing Visual Ethnography* (3rd ed.). London: Sage.

Potter, J. (2012). *Digital Media and Learner Identity: The New Curatorship.* New York: Palgrave Macmillan.

Potter, J., & Gilje, Ø. (2015). Curation as a new literacy practice. *E-Learning and Digital Media, 12*(2), 123–127.

Potter, J., & McDougall, J. (2017). *Digital Media, Culture and Education: Theorising Third Space Literacies.* London: Palgrave Macmillan.

Prensky, M. (2001). Digital natives, digital immigrants part 1. *On the Horizon, 9*(5), 1–6.

Prensky, M. (2012). *From Digital Natives to Digital Wisdom: Hopeful Essays for 21st Century Learning*. Thousand Oaks, CA: Sage Publications.

Pring, R. (2004). *Philosophy of Educational Research* (2nd ed.). London: Continuum.

Prosser, J., & Loxley, A. (2008). *Introducing Visual Methods* [online]. ESRC National Centre for Research Methods, NCRM Review Papers 010. Retrieved February 7, 2018, from http://eprints.ncrm.ac.uk/420/1/MethodsReview PaperNCRM-010.pdf.

Reid, A. (2007). *The Two Virtuals: New Media and Composition*. West Lafayette, IN: Parlor Press.

Roberts, B. (2008). Performative social science: A consideration of skills, purpose and context [online]. *Forum: Qualitative Social Research, 9*(2), Art.58 [99]. Retrieved February 7, 2018, from http://www.qualitative-research.net/index.php/fqs/article/view/377/822.

Scott, D., & Usher, R. (2011). *Researching Education: Data, Methods and Theory in Educational Inquiry* (2nd ed.). London: Continuum.

Sefton-Green, J. (2013). *Learning at Not-School: A Review of Study, Theory, and Advocacy for Education in Non-formal Settings*. The John D. and Catherine T. MacArthur Foundation Reports on Digital Media and Learning. Cambridge, MA: MIT & MITE.

Selwyn, N. (2012). Ten suggestions for improving academic research in education and technology. *Learning, Media and Technology, 37*(3), 213–219.

Shirky, C. (2009). *Here Comes Everybody: How Change Happens When People Come Together*. London: Penguin.

Thomson, P. (2008). Children and young people: Voices in visual research. In P. Thomson (Ed.), *Doing Visual Research with Children and Young People* (pp. 1–19). Abingdon: Routledge.

Thomson, P., & Gunter, H. (2007). The methodology of students-as-researchers: Valuing and using experience and expertise to develop methods. *Discourse: Studies in the Cultural Politics of Education, 28*(3), 327–342.

Thomson, P., & Gunter, H. (2011). Inside, outside, upside down: The fluidity of academic researcher 'identity' in working with/in school [online]. *International Journal of Research & Method in Education, 34*(1), 17–30. Retrieved February 7, 2018, from http://www.researchgate.net/publication/233282142_Inside_outside_upside_down_the_fluidity_of_academic_researcher_identity_in_working_within_school.

Thomson, P., Hall, C., Jones, K., & Sefton-Green, J. (2012). *The Signature Pedagogies Project: Final Report* [online]. London and Newcastle-upon-Tyne: Creativity, Culture and Education. Retrieved February 7, 2018, from http://www.creativitycultureeducation.org/wp-content/uploads/Signature_Pedagogies_Final_Report_April_2012.pdf.

Van Manen, M. (1977). Linking ways of knowing with ways of being practical. *Curriculum Inquiry, 6*(3), 205–228.

Vygotsky, L. (2012/1934). *Thought and Language.* Cambridge, MA: MIT Press.

What Works Network. (2015). Guidance from the Cabinet Office on Public Services. Retrieved February 7, 2018, from https://www.gov.uk/guidance/what-works-network.

Williams, F. (2004). What matters is who works: Why every child matters to new labour. Commentary on the DfES Green Paper *Every Child Matters. Critical Social Policy, 24*(3), 406–427.

Wright Mills, C. (1959). *The Sociological Imagination.* New York: Oxford University Press.

4

The Clip Club: Primary Film-Making & Editing

In this Chapter I explain the context of my first study and how it came about, I then probe the ways in which production practices with the audiovisual are framed, catalysed or inhibited. The narrative for this and the remaining three settings will draw on the themes and values identified in Fig. 3.1. I start with a 'bricolage' (Lévi-Strauss 1966; Turkle and Papert 1992) of moments from an after-school club presented through a range of texts and then interpreted through a practitioner's pedagogic lens. Descriptive passages are supplemented with a contextual reflection on the social conditions from which the data is drawn so that discursive influences are kept close to the material. The concrete data, the practical insight and the contextual reflection provide a foil for the interpretation of my three remaining studies in Chap. 5.

Setting 1: East London Primary School—Clip Club Context

In Chap. 1, I explained my motivation for working with young children and media and my belief, along with others (Burn and Durran 2007; Burn et al. 2012; Cannon et al. 2014, 2018; Lord et al. 2007; Mumford

© The Author(s) 2018
M. Cannon, *Digital Media in Education*,
https://doi.org/10.1007/978-3-319-78304-8_4

et al. 2013; Parry 2013; Potter 2012; Scottish Screen 2006; Selwyn et al. 2010), that film and media-making offers an engaging and levelling route to authorship, especially for those struggling with literacy in the conventional sense. With this in mind, I started an after-school film-making club in the school where I worked called Clip Club.[1] The Club aimed to create a space where some of the more vulnerable children could explore moving image and film-making as an alternative expressive means. This was based on the understanding that film is a familiar medium to primary children, and on the proposition that their implicit knowledge could become a rich fund of explicit and productive learning in the film-making process.

The school was a co-educational Catholic primary school in East London located in a multi-ethnic community in an economically deprived area,[2] I had worked part-time at the school for several years and in that time it had experienced significant challenges including changes of leadership. There had been a number of Heads over several years and each brought a different vision. The Head Teacher at the time of the research was supportive: Clip Club took place outside formal hours, the children came voluntarily and there was no financial outlay. With the exception of a Year 6 girl who left for secondary school after two terms, the same members who had been invited to attend continued to come to the Club over eighteen months. There were two Year 5 girls, five Year 5 boys (aged nine to ten years at the start) and one girl from Year 6 (aged eleven). The year prior to my research I had worked extensively with four of the mentored boys: G-man, Wizard 23 (henceforth Wizard in this account), Dual 2, and Leonardo.[3] Some of the children were considered to have either low levels of literacy, a certain lack of confidence or they displayed levels of anti-social behaviour.

At this point I digress slightly from the particulars of Clip Club, to recount a foundational event in 2011 pertinent to the four boys men-

---

[1] The Clip Club's blog is available here: http://www.theclipclub.co.uk [Accessed 7 February 2018] and documents its activities over an 18 month period. The Club was set up for research purposes and as such operated as a separate entity, distinct from the formal arrangements of the school.

[2] In the Index of Multiple Deprivation—see http://dclgapps.communities.gov.uk/imd/idmap.html [Accessed 7 February 2018]—the school falls within the 20% most deprived areas in the country.

[3] Members all chose pseudonyms for the purposes of online anonymity. The children are familiar with creating user names and this was deemed a continuation of this practice.

tioned above. The (former) national charity Film Education ran an annual film review competition for schools alongside their National Schools Film Week, whose award ceremony took place at headquarters of The British Academy of Film and Television Arts (BAFTA). Having seen some small print inviting filmed rather than written reviews, the then Year 4 boys (aged eight to nine) submitted a two-minute DV edited review of the animation Ponyo (Miyazaki 2008). There had been very few filmed entries (about six out of several hundred) and theirs was the only group effort.[4] The film was officially recognised and the boys were given an award in a newly invented category.[5]

The event inspired me to pursue moving image as an access point to meaning-making with these boys—one that included multi-sensory and intertextual elements. I include this event here as, although on one level the event may be construed as an elite industry-related public relations exercise—inaccessible to the majority, and attended by celebrities and BFI board members—it did give the boys public feelings of success in literacy. Literacy is understood here as a participative social practice in the service of making and exchanging meanings. What is more, these under-standings were made public in a rhetorical sense, rather than battened down in isolated reading and writing tasks, often with limited personal investment.

The girls, Cara and Clara, were new to me: the one quiet and introvert with a strong capacity for reflection and organisation, but lacking asser-tiveness in class, the other ebullient and extrovert but with little interest in literacy lessons. The girls in their different ways, acted as gelling agents for the group, such was their dedication and determination to make the most of the project. Another boy, Nimbus, was something of an anomaly within the group in that he was the Learning Mentor (Mr. P)'s son, and he was regarded by the school as academically gifted. At home he identi-fied as a DIY computer programmer, independent blogger and self-con-

---

[4] The boys' Ponyo (filmed) review is available here: https://fashioningandflow.wordpress.com/2012/03/25/film-educations-young-film-critic-competition-2011/ [Accessed 7 February 2018].
[5] Wizard had sketched the film's Director, Miyazaki, as part of the DV entry—a drawing which ended up on the big screen at the BAFTA in central London. Wizard's interest in drawing becomes significant later in this account.

fessed geek, thus his auto-didactic qualities meant that he did not fit readily into the initial social groupings of the Club.

Given his relationship with the more vulnerable boys, Mr. P had agreed to help me run the Club, and logistically this meant Nimbus joining too. I felt that Nimbus—assertive, articulate and socially confident—would add an interesting dimension to the group on various levels. Computer skills notwithstanding, he eschewed creative activity in the formal curriculum, and on a social level, from interviews, we learn that these children would not ordinarily have had anything to do with each other. The group worked well together, and as their preferences and dispositions aligned with the different roles that film and media production offers, it was clear that their initial mutual suspicion slowly morphed into a solid camaraderie.

The Club lasted approximately eighteen months and took place weekly after school during term time, each session lasting for about an hour. We watched and analysed movie clips, practiced elements of film grammar with Flip DV cameras and subsequently iPads, and made two short films. The first film Run School Run! achieved success at the National Youth Film Festival 2013, and the sequel Run School Run 2! won Into Film's[6] 'Film of the Month' in October 2015.

This was a lengthy project and the material gathered was rich and voluminous. Indeed, in terms of Eisner's hermeneutic heat generated in the reporting of findings, this was the warmest of my studies. By this I mean that the level of empathy and trust that accumulated between participants, amid the sometimes messy friction of our encounters, led to significant insights and personal disclosures. This approach maps a field of detailed exploration as opposed to one that defines a narrow gauge of measurement. I begin with a series of 'pen portraits' based on interview material with: (1) Nimbus, (2) Nimbus, Leonardo and Mr. P (Learning Mentor) and (3) Leonardo.

---

[6] Into Film is a grant issuing charity formed in 2013 from the ashes of the disbanded UK Film Council and the legacy of two film education charities, FILMCLUB and First Light. Its aim is to put film at the centre of children and young people's learning and cultural experience.

Nimbus

Nimbus was a self-assured ten-year-old, proud of his self-styled geek status and keen to be able to apply it. He was articulate for his age and therefore not entirely representative of the group, but he gave us a view of what a young media author could look like, as well as some pointers as to how he might develop. I asked him what he was enjoying about the Club a few weeks into the process.

[To be clear on issues of formatting and referencing, all DV material is supplied online as private links on Vimeo (the password is **wizard**). Links to full audio interviews are available on SoundCloud links]

Audio available at: https://soundcloud.com/shelleuk/phd-thesis-interview-1-nimbus-march-2013/s-BakNN [Accessed 7 February 2018]

Nimbus: What I really like about Clip Club is the fact that you're with all these other people and instead of being limited to being enclosed in this one … well … medium sized room, you can just wander round and film with your team mates or peers, and then share it with the rest of the group without being like ashamed that you had to take two shots of something or anything like that. It's quite good.

Michelle: Mm, nice, yeah, erm, and … what do you think, erm, what do you think you're learning in the editing process?

Nimbus: Well I think I'm learning how to … how like … like before I did this, I thought they did all the sounds and everything on location like. And they just did it while they were filming. But now I found out that basically lots of the times, they get rid of the sound in the clip and they put new sound over it to make it sound like it's real, when actually it's just a sound effect.

Michelle: Cool yeah OK, and what about all those camera shots and things, are you interested in those?

Nimbus: Um, yes I like them, I found a really good website that tells you about all the different shots and all … different types of media and everything like that, it's really interesting. And like who … before this, someone mentioned to me er … or something … they just mentioned something like "oh that's a really good establishing shot" and I was thinking "What?" and it's like … it's like … "Oh yeah, that was a quite good establishing shot actually, it really brought the tension into the moment".

[Michelle sniggers]

Michelle: OK, excellent. And do you think you might look at TV programmes or adverts or films in a different kind of … way?

Nimbus: Yes.

Michelle: In what way?

Nimbus: Like, I would … instead of just sitting back, relaxing, watch … watching it and let it all sink in and have the information going out your ear … erm … I would like…. endure [laughs] it you could say … and might think "OK, that's an establishing shot" or for fun I could like count the pans or the close-ups or something like that. And in adverts, I like, sometimes I count how many times it changes between views.

Michelle: Mm, how many cuts … Yeah Yeah…

Nimbus: Yeah.

Michelle: Cos there's a lot.

Nimbus: Yeah.

Michelle: Quite a lot in adverts, isn't there?

Nimbus: Because adverts are usually fast, cos you know, … yeah … yeah … buy this, buy this!

(Interview with Nimbus, 2013)[7]

A Media Literate Practitioner

Nimbus began by affirming the social significance of Clip Club for him, albeit that at this point his peers were referred to distantly as 'these people', rather than the friends they would become. As someone who spent hours at home on the computer, the fact of physical collaborative team-

---

[7] For conference presentation purposes, I experimented with a videoed version of this interview with Nimbus standing silently, looking directly at the camera, 'addressing' the audience with a voiceover: http://theclipclub.co.uk/2013/03/20/points-of-view-1-nimbus/ [Accessed 7 February 2018]. I also videoed Leonardo using the same technique: https://vimeo.com/127138677 [Accessed 7 February 2018].

work and the sharing of texts were appealing features of the Club. Nimbus did not view himself as a creative collaborator; his forte was solo computer programming and looking under the bonnet of digital technology, a set of skills he regarded as separate from those related to creativity. Indeed, the ironic inflection in his voice when describing 'the tension of the moment' signalled that it felt odd for him to be alluding to the evocative, but somehow he recognised the importance.

Cinematic techniques for building tension and suspense had been the overarching theme for the previous few weeks and Nimbus had assimilated much of this new visual film grammar[8]—for example how certain sounds, camera shots, movements, angles and distances achieve the effects they do—with particular reference to a scene in Wall-E (Stanton 2008). As if to test out his imaginative capacity he whimsically projected himself into an imagined dialogue, in which he was called upon to make explicit his newfound knowledge on the merits of a particular establishing shot. Possessing knowledge was a marker of Nimbus' identity; indeed not knowing was a potential cause for shame in his reality.

Not having an immediate offline community with whom to share his knowledge of computer programming, and finding a receptive one within Clip Club, revealed to Nimbus sides of himself that had previously been in shadow. This discursive schism between informally acquired skills perceived as high value beyond school, and the dearth of outlets in which school children can formally practice them in school, all embroiled in illusory divisions between creative, academic and technical subjects, are apparent in one guise or another in this short exchange with Nimbus.

Practitioner Insight: Tools, Iterative Technique, Dual Contexts

Nimbus's use of the word 'ashamed' indicates that either he himself had felt ashamed and/or that he had been sensitive to others' on account of some public failure—such as getting something wrong in class, or rather, for him, not having got something right first time. The ways in which

---

[8] http://theclipclub.co.uk/2013/02/05/7-tell-me-a-few-things-about-this-shot-in-a-comment/#comments [Accessed 7 February 2018].

digital filming and editing (a) lessens the likelihood for 'mistakes' to be felt as such, and (b) recasts repeated attempts at 'correction' as pleasurable and sometimes irresistible processes of refinement, are a revelation for young learners. The benefits of informed and iterative redrafting as a key element of media composition is an important theme uncovered in my Masters dissertation (Cannon 2011).[9] Furthermore, school systems condemn failure at all costs on account of academic achievement targets and prevailing competitive cultures. My data suggests that these priorities are parsed to the students with negative consequences. Nimbus in particular experienced the sweet dissonance of 'failing well' as he picks up on the intrinsic benefits of review and redraft processes so characteristic of creative media production.

As someone who was unusually alert to the possible continuities between the home-life-world context and that of school, Nimbus revelled in his insider knowledge about the artificiality of media constructs. This is seen in his allusion to texts overlaid with recorded sound beyond the diegetic. In other words, you can cheat when film-making by removing the original recorded sound, and importing additional more evocative soundtracks and effects that artfully mesh with the content. This is useful information, the inference being that he would be able to implement this new knowledge quickly, not only in the Clip Club but also at home and with his friends. Activities at the Club inspired him to expand his visual toolkit by independently researching camera shots, which links with a newly acquired critical perspective on audiovisual texts in his non-school life.

Nimbus and Leonardo

I conducted an interview[10] with Leonardo, Nimbus and Mr. P one lunchtime in the third term of the Clip Club. Leonardo, who was relatively new to the school, expressed himself well but lacked confidence, and finding it difficult to integrate socially, he would gravitate towards

---

[9] Hear young research participant Daniel's words at 03:20′ on the second movie: https://fashioningandflow.wordpress.com/category/case-study-data-analysis/case-study-c-st-elizabeth-primary-school/the-critical-creators/ [Accessed 7 February 2018].

[10] As my research progressed I refrained from asking the 'What?' and 'Why?' questions evidenced here, which were too pointed and overly related to my research. I began asking open-ended ques-

Nimbus in group work. Notably, over time his estrangement changed for the better and he was gradually accepted into the group. I asked them about issues of control when film-making:

Audio available at https://soundcloud.com/shelleuk/phd-thesis-interview-2-mrp-leonardo-nimbus-march-2013/s-uhdHC#t=03:29   [Accessed   7 February 2018]

Part 1:

Nimbus: Control?

Michelle: If I were to throw that one at you? Does it give you control?

Nimbus: Yeah. Yeah, it does, because like, if you were doing a lesson; how to make a film, then what they're going to do is they're going to give you some software, they're going to give you a subject and they're going to say, "Make a film on this", although in Clip Club we had more control over what we did, so like we didn't have to do some sort of particular subject. Well, during the movie-making process we did, because it was making a movie, but we got to choose what the movie was about, instead of someone saying, "Here's your movie. Make a film", and then you've got to work out how to do all this stuff with this just particular subject you might not even be particularly interested in said subject.

Michelle: Right. Okay, well they're great points, thank you. Mr P learning mentor, what would you say, what have you got to say about maybe the social aspects of this process; this experience?

Mr.P: I would say one of the key elements of the group as a whole has been how they've learned to work with each other, and support each other, not just through the process of making the movie and the process of learning how to make films and all that encompasses, it's also elements that I've seen in and around the school with the group. So yes, when they're all in a room, working together, they have a goal; they have an aim; it's very obvious that they want to make this movie, they want to make it well, and to do that they have to cooperate with each other, they have to support each other, they

tions of a 'Tell me about…' nature, allowing for more fluid, less directed responses, about feelings and experiences.

have to find who is strong in certain areas, experiment a little bit and try different things. So all of that is I would say contained but it's there; you're there for an hour on a Tuesday night and you have a common goal. What I've seen around the school outside, which is… I think comes from the strength of Clip Club and the group is their … how they behave to each other outside, in their lessons and in the playground and how they've been very supportive. They're a much stronger group than they ever would have been, and they're all very different individuals that potentially would not have had anything to do with each other before Clip Club. So I've seen a real camaraderie that's stretched out into other areas of the school, and that for me as learning mentor obviously is a huge plus because, you know, it's enough to make you redundant really.

Part 2:
Audio available at https://soundcloud.com/shelleuk/phd-thesis-interview-2-mrp-leonardo-nimbus-march-2013/s-uhdHC#t=09:37 [Accessed 7 February 2018]

Michelle: Right. Okay. Just one more question I think. What do you think … has anything changed about you from the beginning until now?

Leonardo: Well, obvious… well, for me, independence. Independence…

Michelle: Confidence?

Leonardo: Confidence, and at the beginning like Nimbus said, he said that it's not like … the teacher don't tell you, do this, and then make a film about it. It gives us free explanation, so it's not a fixed project.

Michelle: Right. Yeah, it gives you freedom?

Leonardo: Yeah.

(Interview with Nimbus, Leonardo and Mr. P, 2013)

Autonomy, Control and Social Interaction

Nimbus enjoyed learning autonomy and opportunities to indulge this predisposition in school was refreshing for him. Perhaps as a result of this, however, he is dismissive of the obligation to work with content of no interest to him. Even if the specified task were to include film-making, he speculated that the subject matter would be some approved learning topic with a specific objective. A point reinforced by Leonardo, who, referencing Nimbus' remark, offered the loaded observation that the nature of Clip Club gave him "free explanation, so it's not a fixed project". Both Leonardo and Nimbus appeared to be equipped with a meta-cognitive sense and could make objective judgements on the predictable mainstream practices of compliance. This may have been because their family lives were such that they had been exposed to certain experiences that developed independent creativity and/or critique. Whatever the case, it is implied that the open-ended and democratic 'possibility thinking' (Craft 2013) that Clip Club invited was an allure for these children.

Unsurprising Mr. P.'s comments on the social benefits of the project echoed those of his son, Nimbus. Both recounted how the group supported each other in ways that moved beyond the boundaries of the Club to affect relations in the normal school day. As a learning mentor, Mr. P had a broad perspective on the children and as such he occupied an in-between interstitial space. It is from this vantage point that he advocated for the Clip Club's socially beneficial influence which he put down to a sustained collective purpose.

Practitioner Insight: The Role of Review and Redraft

In this and future participants' contributions, we hear Nimbus invoke the rubric of audiovisual language in ways that indicate possible routes to literacy work in which authorial choice, form, structure and artistry are the foci. Not only this but DV editing practices render iterative approaches to creative work a transparent standard procedure, as disclosed by Nimbus in his comment on feeling no shame at taking several shots of the same thing. School-based literacy often exacts grammatically precise "paper-based outcomes" (Burnett and Bailey 2014), with mono-logic as opposed to dialogic appeal. The monomodal has its place in literacy practices, but this account argues for provisional, non-linear, open-ended meaning-making and contingent decisions made 'on the fly'—activities that characterise media production. In the process of editing, media entities (DV clips and sounds in time) become malleable, quasi-tactile raw materials, workable familiar symbols which, ordered in certain sequences, for certain lengths of time, to a certain pace and rhythm, wield an aesthetic power. Giving young people repeated opportunities for recursive digital redrafting gives them powerful control over their own creative learning, a luxury that few schools, in current regimes of practice, feel they can offer in any sustained way.

Clip Club members were free to explain their story and allow it to unfold, in a language that was at once new and familiar to them—the language of the moving image—familiar in that most have consumed it from infancy, and new in terms of the acquisition of intellectual resources to interpret and produce it. Arguably one of the reasons why the children kept returning to the Club, beyond the social appeal, was precisely this fascination with facets of artistry inherent to film-making and the audio-visual medium. Given the tools and sensitive pedagogic intervention, it is a process of inscription that builds on implicit accumulated knowledge, over which young people can exert autonomous and nuanced creative control. These are educational experiences that deliver a balanced sense of relevant learning in the service of self-determined ends.

Leonardo

I interviewed Leonardo separately at the end of the project because he had missed the final session in which I had made some recordings of the children responding to prompt cards about their Clip Club experience.

Audio available at: https://soundcloud.com/shelleuk/leonardo-july-2014/ s-ZeYgI#t=2:30 [Accessed 7 February 2018]

Leonardo: Well, the most surprising thing was when we… when we got to use the… when we… what … it's actually the film because you get to use all of each other's talents kind of, really, and make them interfused; connect them together to make one movie, or film, yeah.

Michelle: Really good, yeah. So what do you think your talent is; your particular talent?

Leonardo: Making people laugh because in the... when the school saw, it everyone was laughing—

Michelle: Mm.

Leonardo: yeah and especially in the blooper … "bald head" [laughs at private joke]—

Michelle: [Laughs] yeah. Yeah, how do you think the screening … was that a good thing for you?

Leonardo: Yeah.

Michelle: Yeah. Yeah. It's quite nice to hear everybody laugh. Okay. Any more?

Leonardo: Yeah, I like it when people laugh because like… like when they laugh—

Michelle: Mm.

Leonardo: —the people who make it will appreciate it, because they've done something or changed … made change.

Michelle: Mm, what do you mean by that? That's quite an interesting thought.

Leonardo: By change, I mean like change their … say you watch a scary movie like they … change, you know, when… after you finish, it might have been too scary that you change how you think and you become paranoid about it.

https://soundcloud.com/shelleuk/leonardo-july-2014/s-ZeYgI#t=5:22 [Accessed 7 February 2018]

Leonardo: Well, I kept coming back to Clip Club because it's fun and you get to like take burdens off you from the day, like especially in the … at the end of Year 6, there's SATS and tests and more tests and even more tests, and (sighs) it was… it made us stressed out and after we could just relax and make films and stuff, yeah…

https://soundcloud.com/shelleuk/leonardo-july-2014/s-ZeYgI#t=7:42 [Accessed 7 February 2018]

Leonardo: What does that say?

Michelle: [reading from card]'Things that I have found out about myself whilst doing Clip Club'.

Leonardo: What I found out about myself is that I achieved something and no one has said, "Do it". I've taken out one hour every Tuesday, once a week, to do something which is what I can use in later life, if I become a film-maker or anything in that department.

(Interview with Leonardo, 2014)

Co-composition and Display

Leonardo had a developed sense of social awareness and seemed to appreciate the range of ability on offer in the group. This was odd considering he was on occasion socially awkward and disconnected from the rest of the children, apart from Nimbus. Nevertheless, his idea of blending their talents—of "interfusing" them—was a sensitive observation, reminiscent of the ecotonal metaphor discussed in Chap. 2, and of the ways in which an environment that welcomes difference can give rise to potent heterogeneous expression. One of the drivers of imaginative project work, along with the artistry of the teacher, is precisely the blending of disparate elements to create new and unexpected forms. As has been mentioned, the children learned to respect personality differences by experimenting with different roles, allowing talents and interests to surface and be channelled into a collective endeavour.

Beyond the obvious indicator of social well-being, Leonardo made an insightful comment on the ways in which laughter created change. Hearing his schoolmates laughing and enjoying something he had created, made a deep impression on him, he felt proud of himself in a way that was intrinsic, rather than generated by some extrinsic reward. His sense of accomplishment was further suggested at the end of the extract where he mentioned his independent decision to "take an hour" of his time for his own purposes. Customarily, the valuing of time is perceived as an adult preoccupation and not the concern of an eleven-year-old, whose time is irrevocably pre-carved in school systems. Furthermore, his qualification of the ways in which he brought about 'change' signifies a metacognitive capacity. In that moment of laughter, he realised that the Club's independent efforts had generated a new and emotional communion with his peers, and to have made his mark in this way was a lasting triumph.

Practitioner Insight: Ownership and Public Celebration

As discussed above, from a practitioner's point of view, the public staging of media and film events is often overlooked in the school context—like some extraneous add-on. Media display is a time-bound spectacle, unlike the largely paper-bound products of analogue art and literacy confined to walls, notice boards or static exhibitions. Conversely, as was demonstrated in the Question and Answer sessions after each screening of the Clip Club films, this public exhibition is a negotiated arena where media authorship and craftsmanship are celebrated, where ownership is claimed and exposed, and where genuine dialogue between peers about learning is oxygenated.

Clara and G-man

Clara and G-man are coupled in this section as they had a tacit and unlikely relationship: she the outgoing and passionate actress; he the quiet, introverted and self-conscious stills photographer. Both were reportedly disengaged and distracted in formal literacy lessons, whereas in Clip Club they appeared to find roles that suited their discrete skills and personalities. Clara's effervescence occasionally caused friction with some of the boys, however at no stage did anyone undermine her acting ability. For much of the time the crew wielded the film-making tools and processes around her, as she funnelled her talent down the lens. Her focus and performance in front of the camera represented the spirit of embodied artistry in time and space. Conversely G-man's meanings were conveyed through engagements with the still image, and were embedded in a modality of phronetic[11] and social interaction. Both children illustrate the ways in which meaning-making with still and moving images provides certain children with the means to excel in ways which would otherwise be denied them.

---

[11] As introduced in Chap. 2, phronesis describes the kinds of practical intelligence that informs improvised solutions.

Iterative and Critical Approaches to Understanding Film Language

After the group watched a short horror pastiche on YouTube: He Dies At The End (McCarthy 2010), I took a photo which seems to encapsulate the ways in which moving image media elicits nuanced understandings from the interests and personal approaches of the individual.[12] We discussed how the film's different shots and angles created tension (video footage was taken of this session by Mr.P.[13]). Cara was generally not interested in performing in front of the camera, she was happy in a producer's role with a clipboard in hand, a shot list and people to organise.

The photo depicts her observations on the horror clip, her hand raised with the quiet compliance of classroom norms, her eyes temporarily distracted to the right, but she appears unphased by the audiovisual documentation of the event. On the other hand, Clara is hyper-aware of the recording and performs her definition of an extreme close-up in which even her fingers are acting. She clamps them evenly around her face, exploring her emotions, as if imagining herself secured by some elegant cinematic brace. Indeed, in an early film trailer exercise the previous year, in which we were exploring fear, she enacted this very shot, panting with wild eyes in a dark classroom cupboard (see Clip 1 below). Clara may have felt that she was again on set, her gestured demo of the close-up in the photo, eyes askance, capturing a momentary meditation on her prior performance.

See Clip 1 https://vimeo.com/142087018 [Accessed 7 February 2018, password = wizard]

The photo points towards the possible different access points for critical understandings of moving image media. Clara represents demonstrative ways of knowing related to the affective, the corporeal and outward

---

[12] Unfortunately, publishing restrictions meant that I was unable to reproduce any of the photos taken in this research in this publication, most of which can be found on the Clip Club site.

[13] See third movie: 'IMG_3668' at 03:10′–04:15′ available here: http://theclipclub.co.uk/2014/01/22/he-dies-at-the-end-short-horror-clip/ [Accessed 7 February 2018].

performance, whilst Cara maintains composed inward reflection, as will be discussed in Chap. 6.

Practitioner Insight: Embodying Film Grammar and Power Relations

The few seconds of footage in Clip 1 evince Clara's fearless predisposition to being filmed close-up and in character from the off. This had made an impact at the time as in the main, most children are at least a little self-conscious. Not so Clara, who embraces her role body and soul, taking full stock of her material environment and the face-framing affordances of the camera to enhance her performance. As will be shown in later clips in this Chapter, there is no compromise in her search for a shot's 'rightness of fit' in relation to both the elements within her control and her inten-tion to deliver on 'whole body' emotion with every take.

As noted earlier, the Club's first film Run School Run! was nominated for a prize at the National Youth Film Festival 2013. The Award cere-mony at Vue Cinema in central London, screened a few seconds of each film, and the one chosen for our film was a stairway sequence ending in an extreme close-up of Clara's face. The success of this style of shot for menacing impact, meant that it was once more put to work in their film sequel. The point is that recursive approaches to working with film gram-mar marries tangible meaning-making practices and outcomes with an aesthetic sensibility to genre.[14]

A striking feature of the shot is its low angle: Mr. P and I documented this discussion whilst sitting on the floor looking up at the children, cast-ing them as the protagonists. Conventionally, educators rarely assume a physically submissive position in relation to pupils, but it is an acceptable option for a researcher. This for me represents the 'punctum' (Barthes 1979) of this photo—the diffuse and almost inexplicable appeal of or

---

[14] The final films (featuring a pupil-Clone magically emerging from the iMovie interface trying to get back 'home' inside the software) will not be analysed, as I am interested in the processes through which they materialised. Nevertheless, both films and the 'Making of' are available here, along with a wistful comment from a Club member made long after the project had ended: http://theclipclub.co.uk/2014/07/11/run-school-run-1-2-making-of-on-youtube/#comment-1542   [Accessed   7 February 2018].

detail within a photo that pierces or arrests attention—namely, the unsettling of routine teacher/researcher question and answer power relations.

This is not to suggest that researchers or educators should invariably adopt a supplicant position, merely that it is worth experimenting with space and positioning in pursuit of eliciting understanding of moving image media, particularly if the discussion orbits shot height, angle and distance. Similarly, from a research point of view, having an 'excuse' to interview children from unusual angles could at once enrich the data as well as provide an arresting visual perspective.

Social (non)Participation: Diving In and Out

G-man was rarely to be seen without my camera around his neck: positioned behind the material and functional nature of the still and DV camera, his identity seemed secure. Socially he felt comfortable with those with whom he was familiar, but would retreat in the company of strangers or large groups of people, resorting to gangster-style postures and shows of disinterest. Somewhat paradoxically, he relished the dynamics of the Clip Club, for as an outlier he could dive in and out of proceedings as the mood or impulse took him—the kind of behaviour well suited to an attentive photographer.

There were a few occasions when G-man's outlying status had more to do with transgression. It was SATS (statutory tests) season, and filming had begun on the climax of Run School Run 2. G-man had been in trouble for most of the formal day for insolence, an incident that Mr. P. had been trying to resolve. G-man absented himself from the shoot, choosing instead to look in from the sidelines. He surreptitiously took a series of shots through a window—its reinforced glass a poignant reminder of his self-imposed estrangement and isolation.

A blog post at the time was a conscious effort on my part to integrate these shots into the Clip Club experience in a way that both acknowledged his semi-participative decisions and moved us on positively:

> G-man takes a rest from taking photos [particularly like the ones from behind the window of Clara fainting, shown below] and joins the editing team the following week.

(Available at: http://theclipclub.co.uk/category/shooting-the-film/) [Accessed 7 February 2018]

I tried to take account of the pressures the children were under during the day, in a way that was neither counter to the school's behaviour policy nor complicit with admonition, this was a tricky negotiation given the space of respite that the Clip Club had come to represent for some of its members. Nevertheless, G-man found his own way of maintaining the dialogue with the group through photography, and this was publicly recognised on the blog.

Practitioner Insight: Roleplay, Mess and Collaborative Resolution

Film production and post-production offer different pathways to learning that take into account individuals' distinct inclinations within a community of creative practice. It offers opportunities to take on purposeful roles with defined responsibilities, be they acting, directing, producing, filming, editing, creating graphics or designing sound. Role-play has the advantage of masking or overruling normative behaviours and learners can trial new identities within safe parameters. Regularly swapping roles taps into children's developed sense of turn-taking and fair play, which contributes to the cohesion of group work. Film production roles are highly practical, they yield tangible results with adequate planning, practice and group co-ordination. When these elements mesh and the intended shot is achieved this generates an acute sense of 'rightness of fit'. Equally intense is the frustration of having to take multiple shots of the same scene, which can test all but the most patient of pupils, leaving others surrendering to impulse.

The Clip Club sessions were rarely seamless learning experiences and frequently there was a need to untangle collaborative collapse. One such was registered on the blog on 16 March 2015:

> The last 2 sessions have been unfocussed and not very productive. We had hoped to get a few shots in the bag but it's been very difficult to even get the 3 or 4 useable ones we have. There may have to be some changes…

It could be that the sessions aren't structured enough, but there was a hope the Clip Clubbers would be more focussed and organising themselves without as much adult involvement.

It could be the fact that Michelle's role at the school has changed and so planning and preparation time for the Club is much less than it used to be [e.g. the batteries ran out in the stills camera, which was annoying, and wouldn't ordinarily have happened]

It could be that people are tired from the pressures of the day—it's SATS time with lots of extra tests and drills and sitting still—and people come to the session with lots of stored energy to get rid of…

(Available from: http://theclipclub.co.uk/2014/03/16/shooting-problems/) [Accessed 7 February 2018]

I thought it was important to discuss what was going wrong and try to resolve it collectively. It was a learning moment to be scrutinised, rather than one in which to pull teacherly rank, and it took at least half the session. The point being made here is that it was the sustained nature of the project and the relations that had had time to develop that facilitated such a dialogue—a space for a slow and collaborative resolution to emerge.

The fact that it was a diary-like entry onto the blog may also have had an effect, as the inner workings of the group were publicly and purposefully revealed. This episode was something of a watershed moment which was felicitously followed a couple of weeks later by a positive 'real world' intervention with educational researcher John Potter and local professional film-makers Xube. They were conducting preliminary research on children's film-making with iPads ahead of their Into Film funded project at another school, and had come soliciting Clip Club advice.

The visitors were impressed with the (newly restored) camaraderie, knowledge—and the willingness to share it—that came across during the interview. Potter has been referenced throughout this book and is committed to the value of involving young people in the development of practices with digital media. The timing and nature of this visit precipitated a positive change in attitude in Club members that seemed to rehearse this very principle.

Flow, Mobility and Autonomy

In Clip 2 of the video footage analysed below, we hear and see photos being taken by G-man and witness how he manoeuvres himself in the practice of his craft. He understands that multiple shots express progression and the sound of the release button is heard several times in this take. There is a sense in which he furtively adds a personal stamp to the film's soundtrack, like some visceral, enduring, aural signature. Whereas Clara is central to the action, basking in the full glare of the lens, G-man finds his own idiosyncratic way of involving himself in the movie, occupying the visual documentarist's twilight zone: in amongst the action but operating tangentially, nimbly, attentively, with stealth; in fact, not unlike the modus operandi of the visual ethnographer.

In this particular shoot the children were largely left to their own devices (literally), as I was occupied with the editors elsewhere. Given adequate guidance, trust and time, as most media projects require, a group of young people will often find the necessary resources to independently produce work of quality by negotiating problems between themselves. Risk-taking is as much a part of school media production for teachers as it is for the young participants (Sinker 2000, p. 211), and perhaps a link can be made here with Loveless' "skillful neglect" (2008), where teachers allow discord to run its course. In this view, pedagogies with creative media might benefit from 'carnivalesque' (Bakhtin 1981) approaches, that is, from messy rule-bending, so that young people's ideas are given time to emerge and coalesce, leading to owned work of which they can feel genuinely proud.

Practitioner Insight: Artful Documentation

The shoot in question produced some thoughtful and artful photography[15] from G-man in terms of composition and framing. It features Clone Clara searching for her human counterpart in an attempt to get

---

[15] This post displays G-man's strong photographic skill—image DSCF4686 in particular—and also demonstrates the use of the Evernote app to wirelessly manage the shot list: http://theclipclub.co.uk/2014/04/11/serious-shooting-earnest-editing/ [Accessed 7 February 2018].

home, and moving towards the camera along a corridor. There is a simple beauty to the configuration of the photo: G-man had captured her in a "movie-dream" moment at the end of the take (Furstenau and MacKenzie 2009, p. 8), when the light happened to mimic professional standards. The focal point of the scene was illuminated from multiple sources: from a left hand doorway, from the front, from large ceiling spots and from a large rear window that diffused light along the z-axis of the waxed floor. Successfully framing the subject in the centre of the shot is difficult at the best of times, and here it is gracefully achieved, composed in such a way that we forget the boundaries of the image and stay with Clone Clara, both vulnerable and menacing amid the mundane functionality of school cleaning equipment and a red fire extinguisher.

Just as G-man had positioned Clara in the middle of the frame for his clandestine shoot behind the reinforced glass above, he does the same here, only this time, far from a self-imposed exile, he is 'flowing' with the whole team behind the camera—moments which were captured on film. G-man's output and affinity with the visual demonstrate that photographic documentation of production is a rich and unexplored dimension of film-making with young people, one that testifies to the importance of independence and mobility for its enactment.

Wizard

See Clip 2 https://vimeo.com/142087018 [Accessed 7 February 2018, password = wizard]

Examination of the corridor shoot clip is an appropriate point at which to introduce Wizard. Occasionally sensitive and brittle, he was a confident artist, actor and dancer: he could rarely keep still and loved being in front of the camera. His interest lay in what it was possible to evoke dramatically, physically and pictorially, and he found his expressive space in graphic art and rhetorical performance.

Multimodal Craftsmanship

It was Wizard's turn at directing and the clip shows him immersed in the moment and, acting on impulse surrounded by his crew. He performs an impish dramatic gesture behind the camera at 00:29', mirroring The Clone's menace and the gothic tone of the take. Slipping into the industrial vernacular: 'Cut!', he switches from a playful and evocative mode to executive directorial mode as the needs of the moment dictate. This ability to switch between modes on the fly, is a useful skill in creative practice and one which might start to be conceived as integral to moving image work and the reframing of literacy.

This study argues that in conventional modes of composition, such as writing, we learn to see-saw between two particular modes: the abstract conception of an intended meaning and—with varying levels of skill and competence—its graphic inscription performed largely in isolation. Shooting film is an alternative writing stage that operates with inclusive, social and embodied practices, and with no loss of sophisticated intellectual investment. Wizard is able to act out his intended meaning and then 'transcribe' it immediately in film.

Practitioner Insight: The Affective, Corporeal and Imaginary

In this extract we feel the co-presence of the children and witness them intently attending to a joint imagined vision. Wizard's expressive sensibility illustrates that vision for us through gesture, and then, through visceral teamwork, they bring that meaning to life in ways that may be beyond them in meaning-making with language. Having completed their respective tasks with a unity of aesthetic intention, they clap and congratulate themselves on getting the shot they wanted: the full stop of the 'cinematic sentence' (BFI 2012; Burn and Durran 2007, p. 94; Donaldson 2014)—a metaphor attributable to UK film director Anthony Minghella, to be explained in Chap. 6. The familiar post-successful-take release of tension was a culmination of artistry in which the scene's shooting problems had been overcome and a 'rightness of fit' had squeezed through. By this I mean that the assembly of affective, corporeal and imaginative relations within the design of their shot had finally coalesced into a satisfying reproducible form.

The pedagogic principle at play in this scenario relates not only to my being hands-off, but also absent for a long period, so that textured independent exploration could be done, mistakes made, ownership tested, shots re-taken and 'failure' better unravelled. If I had been present for the entire shoot, the climactic tension may not have been so intense, as I almost certainly would have been keen to move swiftly through the shot list, in a mode of compromise. This was a salutary learning curve, which brought home the function of trust and patience in an ethnographic, pedagogic and mediating role. Here lie some of the tensions in the well-meaning but possibly overbearing offices of the practitioner, the omnipresent teacher or the watchful participant-researcher.

Media Crafting and Embodied Vocabulary

In the weeks prior to the corridor shoot, Wizard had found other ways of recruiting movement into his performative palette. Using the properties of a point of view shot, he was able to conjoin the role of camera operator with an actorly evil presence, as evidenced in Clip 3 below. After watching the short film He Dies At The End (McCarthy 2010), I had asked the group to practice different types of shots to maximise suspense. Wizard's two friends were absent from this session and it was unusual for him to be working with Leonardo who he routinely ignored. Nonetheless, inspired by the short film and emboldened by his friends' absence that day, Wizard stepped up as camera operator in a way that had been eluding him. Forming an alliance with the camera, he assumed the role of the monster, climbed onto the table and filmed Leonardo's victim character with a domineering high angle shot and appropriate sound effects (the film being shot can be seen in the inset video within the clip). With an imaginative leap Wizard was translating his new film vocabulary, the point of view shot, into a short embodied moving image form, or filmic phrase. For Wizard, the corporeal matters, it was as if film-making was story-dwelling as much as story-telling.

See Clip 3 https://vimeo.com/142087018 [Accessed 7 February 2018, password = wizard]

Practitioner Insight: Technique and Iterative Practices

The point of view shot was first introduced to the children in a short dark animation, Alma (2009), which was analysed in some depth. It was then put into practice in Run School Run 1!, where G-man's camera had assumed the guise of the Clone approaching her victims, and it was noticed again in He Dies at the End (McCarthy 2010). Wizard's table-top shoot sees him practising the shot and we witness a sophisticated series of film techniques: he establishes the scene with a wide shot, steadily pans round the space, slowly closes in from a high angle, and finishes with an extreme close up of the victim and a disembodied voice-over familiar to the horror genre.

I chose this clip to demonstrate the relatively sophisticated sequence of filming technique born out of implicit knowledge made explicit through the iterative processes of watching, analysing, discussing, practicing and making short clips. Some may construe that Wizard's everyday artistry might be achievable through regular informal consumption of certain texts, however, one of the fundamental findings of this study was the need for the minutiae of decision-making in the construction of film to surface, be noticed, acknowledged, experimented with, and their impact explicitly discussed. There will always be another way, another angle from which to tell a story, another route to the 'rightness of fit', it is a question of understanding qualitative relations and the clarity and boldness of one's intentions—all of which I believe are demonstrated in Wizard's clip.

Material and Digital Embodiments

As might be recalled in Chap. 3's account of the mini BAFTA experience, media composition work is not exclusively digital in nature, Wizard enjoyed drawing and intertextual practices that melded the analogue with the digital. In the closing scene of Run School Run2! we needed a back-drop to represent Clone Clara's home. An image search resulted in the

Fig. 4.1 Wizard's drawing of Clone Clara's home inside the computer used as green screen backdrop

drawing in Fig. 4.1. It also featured as the cover design of the DVD they all took home as a tangible memento of their Clip Club experience. There was value in offering the children a physical artefact to take home and I noticed how G-man in particular kept hold of his in the playground and in the stairwell outside his classroom, (where he was often sent to reflect on his behaviour). Retro as it might be, the DVD and its case functioned as a portable material embodiment of their co-designed production; the implication being that for some, concrete manifestations of the virtual can enhance positive feelings of pride, ownership and identity.

Practitioner Insight: Roles and Remix

The fluid translations between digital and analogue texts, software, hardware, digital platforms and material artefacts is indicative of literacy practices in a constant state of flux. Indeed, the idea of re-creating a home inside a computer came from watching a short Swiss animation, Animatou (2007), in which an animated cat finds refuge in the three-dimensional innards of a computer—we used this as inspiration to conclude the film.

It is argued here that an enlarged view of literacy is cognisant of strategies that poach from discourse, that adapt and remix roles, narratives and genres, and textual codes and conventions, using different modalities. Wizard was not only a director, an actor and a camera operator, but a graphic artist and set designer too. The more these roles and intertextual processes can be explicitly named and valued, the more moving image literacy can be regarded as a multi-faceted social and participative literacy practice with relevance both inside and beyond the school gates.

Dual 2

See Clip 4 https://vimeo.com/142087018 [Accessed 7 February 2018, password = wizard]

Dialogic Relations and Home-School Cultures

Dual 2 considered himself the head honcho of the group. He often behaved in class and around the school in ways that were considered unacceptable; but this was not my experience with him in Clip Club sessions. At the beginning of the second year we reflected on our film-making experiences and I asked them to record their thoughts. I suggested they frame it around what they would say to a new recruit from their class. This activity was at once an educational and research strategy: by asking them to reflect on their experience it may also have yielded deeper insights.

Dual 2 set up his address to camera in a walk-in cupboard, he propped up the iPad on a shelf and chose an appropriate background to hide the clutter. His physical stance, back straight and hands behind his back, suggested the delivery of a composed, formal address, and perhaps a quiet gathering of thoughts as might be adopted in a school assembly. As the clip progresses, he relaxes into a more conspiratorial tone as if letting his friends in on a secret.

By giving Dual 2 an audience of imagined peers to speak to, he is free to perform and communicate in a way that aligns with his identity, rather than in a way that he perceives might be appropriate to an audience of adults. His demeanour in this activity suggests that he is accustomed to recording himself, and he seems to enjoy imagining an audience of equals. In one session he asked if he could take some iMovie project files away, so he could show friends how our film was being made on his phone. Sadly, logistics and software compatibility issues meant this was not possible but the willingness to cross-pollinate home and school cultures was apparent in this simple request, and it represents a missing component in terms of more permeable relations between the two worlds. Dual 2 perhaps lacks opportunities to make links between home and school that other children with more support at home are able to make in other ways.

Participation and Collaboration

Dual 2 found the optimum studio-like space to record his observations, which seemed to indicate a certain seriousness of intent and sensitivity towards the private nature of what he was about to reveal. He discloses that this Club is actually OK, because you learn things; in fact, he knows no-one who would think otherwise. His neologism—"inspirative"—like Leonardo's "interfuse"—suggests that he is exploring new (learning) territories of intense feeling that standard vocabulary fails to express.

There are two main thrusts to his hypothetical case for joining the Club: firstly, in a departure from the norm, "you don't get told off", and secondly, it is a place of security and support: in his own words, it represents a surrogate and provisional "family". Dual 2's mode of address at these two junctures re-affirms the intensity of what appear to be deeply felt emotions. There is a point at which he pauses and scratches his head, as if his usual school identity had been short-circuited by some pleasing turn of events. Further, where he likens the Club to being in a team, a family, I am persuaded by his integrity and interpret this exclamation as Dual 2 enjoying the security and stimulation of an alternative habitus—a new and regular community of learning.[16]

---

[16] In another enthusiastic piece to camera, Dual 2 reveals the importance of his local community. He was more thrilled with Clip Club's film festival success locally—'out of the whole of Tower

Practitioner Insight: Agency and the Creative Community

The commonly accepted features of a community of practice (Lave and Wenger 1991) became part of the fabric of the Club on the basis that we were a group of people with a shared interest in film-making, who met regularly and who improved with practice (Wenger-Trayner 2015). Dual 2's commitment to the Clip Club community derived from a sense of agency that was missing in formal education; much of his energy in the school day was spent maintaining a certain social identity and negotiating frustrations.

Film-making is a challenging creative practice that treads a fine line between structured agency and disciplined autonomy, between the planned and the improvised. When facilitated with attention to these dichotomous elements, pupils like Dual 2 are attracted to the freedoms on offer within the safe constraints of a recognisable and familiar art form. The self-direction and intrinsic motivation that many teachers seek to develop in their students is witnessed in Dual 2's clip and the one to follow that sees him co-editing with Nimbus.

> *See Clip 5 https://vimeo.com/142087018* [Accessed 7 February 2018, password = wizard]

Co-composition and Editing as an Iterative Craft

Anyone watching the clip with insider knowledge would recognise the anomaly of Nimbus and Dual 2 working together; there were few circumstances in which this would have happened in the normal course of the school day. They are editing footage in which Clone Clara emerges from her sleeping status to explore her environment. They make a series of collaborative decisions, fine-tuning what is going to make it into the

---

Hamlets' (his home London borough)—than with the fact that it was a national competition. See: http://theclipclub.co.uk/2013/11/12/stoney/#comment-173 [Accessed 7 February 2018] and his accompanying comment: "Please have to look this video [sic] I could not write it so I did it in a video".

cut and what needs to go. Theirs is the language of trial and error, review and redraft as they negotiate their way through footage to obtain the required effects and move the story along. There is a point at which they look to me as if for advice, but then realise that they are the editors and I am in researcher mode. What is interesting is Dual 2's deference to Nimbus, which seems difficult for him as he fidgets his way through certain moments and his patience appears to be tested. Dual 2 is keen to make changes there and then, while Nimbus, perhaps more familiar with delayed gratification or perhaps simply enjoying 'calling the shots', suggests making a mental note of possible changes, seeing the whole clip first, and then making the changes at the end.

Digital editing is an iterative inscriptive process, and going backwards and forwards between abstract thinking and practical adjustment is, in essence, a phronetic activity. To demonstrate this, there are points where the boys appear to be experiencing mutual feelings of flow, control and absorption in their efforts to make precision cuts, so that the integrity of the story is maintained. It is often the case in professional editing that more than one person is involved in the editing—for example, the Director might decide the cut and the Editor executes it. Here the boys are performing both tasks in collaboration, and conflating these roles makes for a rich dialogic exchange.

Practitioner Insight: Phronesis and Rhetorical Performance

I describe the artistry of DV editing as rhetorical performance in that the boys are engaged in a task that actively combines aesthetic sensibilities with pragmatic intention, and which expresses the sophisticated and often contradictory thinking that editing can bring about. There is no right or wrong way to proceed but the boys' distinct approaches signal a difference in character and mode of operation: the one cautious and systematic with an eye on future action, the other impulsive and focussed on results in the now. Despite these differences, they manage to share the keyboard and listen to each other's ideas, sometimes the one instructing the other, negotiating the software as they go. Audiovisual curation at the interface—selecting, re-ordering, and re-assembling digital assets—is thus rendered a dialogic and tangible craft that caters to both the mercurial and the constant. These are the kinds of skills and dispositions that literate multimodal composers might develop alongside writing, for creative, narrative or explanatory expression across the curriculum.

Media Composition Practices in Action

See Clip 6 https://vimeo.com/142087018 [Accessed 7 February 2018, password = wizard]

Clip 6 involves a brief montage of the children's engagement in green screen manipulation, that is, in that perceived professional dimension of film-making related to video effects. The split screen where Clara is face to face with her Clone, had been Dual 2's idea a few weeks before, and they had researched how to achieve the effect on YouTube. Filming it, however, had not been altogether successful, as it required more precise alignment than was possible to achieve without a tripod. The green screen was a workaround suggested by Nimbus: his suggestion was to cut out a misaligned background and superimpose the figure of the Clone onto the original footage. This was phronetic intelligence in practice. After several attempts the resultant effect was not perfect, in that the Clone is perceived on screen as smaller than her mirror image. However, with a pragmatic leap of the imagination, it was deemed that this could in fact fit the plot, as her otherworldly powers were on the wane.

In a similar fashion the last green screen sequence (from 08:31′ in Clip 6) involving the Clone arriving home inside the computer, sees the team working together intuitively to achieve the visual objective. At first Clara resorted to lurching rigidly across the screen, suggesting she was at a loss as to how her character should behave—her improvisation skills, so evident in other scenes, seemed to have forsaken her. Nimbus suggested that she interact with the imagined scenery on the bare screen "so that it would look as if she's in her house." The rest of the sentence was barely audible because I started talking over him. Nimbus meekly reclaimed the idea as his own under his breath: "That was my idea" all of which went unnoticed until watching the footage back—so concentrated was I on Clara's performance and on getting a decent shot. What was heard was G-man's response after my: "Oh yeah, a bit of interaction with the ... Nice.", whereupon he affirmed: "It's her home!" G-man and the others were jointly engaged in imagining the clone's home. Indeed, as Clara fiddled with the backdrop, tweaking fanciful domestic apparatus, his tone implied the sentiment 'why would she be doing anything else?'

Time constraints and the visceral in-the-moment quality of film-making increase the likelihood of this type of metacognitive refinement, or "possibility thinking" (Craft 2013). In this instance, they were not only having to imagine how the shot would eventually turn out, but they were also de-centering themselves sensitively enough to be able to imagine how a rationalising audience might be thinking when it was eventually screened.

Leaps of imagination are a feature of putative higher order thinking in the literary world of written composition, but for some they can remain distant and unarticulated if the verbal is the preferred mode of encoding it. Moving image production manifests conceptual thinking in more concrete ways, hence the literacy value for those who struggle to articulate themselves in the spoken or written word. What is clear from these clips is the children's determined and purposeful agency their mobile and material improvisation and their social agility. There were no lesser roles in the production of these shots, the children were pulling together to make them work—rhetorically, dialogically, reflexively and phronetically.

Practitioner Insight: Technological Constraints

In the last section of green screen montage I found myself being more teacherly for the sake of expediency; but this, and the fact of directing Clara to walk across the screen felt odd. I had gradually been relinquishing control of the Clip Club sessions, and throughout the project Clara has displayed a consistently reliable and creative autonomy in her acting, as well as an uninhibited desire to explore her 'found' mise-en-scène. Her movements in this green screen shot were restricted. In prior scenes she successfully exploited the z-axis (that is, the long depth of field in a shot) with a sense of freedom and expansiveness. In this scene, reminiscent of a theatrical set with flat scenery, she was limited to walking several steps along a blunted horizontal axis within the narrow confines of a static letter box format.

In pointing this out I draw attention to the fanfare that often appends amateur special effects software. The thrill of mimicking professional practice can also be accompanied by a constrained dramatic performance and a dampening of actor agency. This is as relevant an observation in the microcosm of school practices as it is in a macro sense in the wider social world. As will be discussed later, algorithmic software design necessarily determines the creative agency and autonomy of users, which suggests the importance of encouraging users' own creative strategies where possible, and making them aware of the non-inevitability of having to select from a database.

Contextual Interpretation: Clip Club

Social and Participative Forms of Literacy

My research with the Clip Club children suggests that many young people have unexplored and undervalued knowledge and skills related to media, film and popular culture, along with a ready disposition to make, communicate and be part of a productive team. The boys involved in the 'filmed' film review award ceremony at the BAFTA headquarters, testified to an enthusiasm to participate in ways that were familiar to them and over which they felt they had some mastery. Furthermore, Nimbus and Leonardo were able to reflect on the merits of learning that involved social interaction and the sharing of complex film-making processes. Indeed, the Clip Club's longevity and two resultant short films were a testament to the children's collective and hitherto unrecognised interests and capacity to commit to sustained literacy practices.

It is in these respects that my work is redolent of the thoughts and opinions of popular 'creativity guru' Ken Robinson (2011, 2013) whose entertaining and influential promotion of universal and hidden artistic talent appears to have accrued public and cross-sector endorsement. Though sceptical of his essentialising tone I concur with some Robinsonian rhetoric in as much as many young people's talents remain undervalued and redundant in formal school contexts, rather than uniformly undiscovered. And as Robinson's popularity is likely the result of a backlash against reductive curricula and a lack of opportunity for young people to express their interests and preferences, my findings become laden with political significance.

Both thoughtful individuals, Nimbus and Leonardo articulate two elements lacking in their school experience—relevancy and autonomy. Clip Club created a space in which participants exhibited dispositions for social reciprocal relations, for productive action, and for rhetorical communicative performance—arguably the required attributes of the new literacy practitioner—to offer anything less in a modern literacy programme curtails the rights of the learner in today's digital economy.

Conditions of Possibility: School and Industry Constraints

My material draws attention to the constraints under which primary children operate in the formal curriculum. Leonardo articulates the stress related to national testing and heaves an audible sigh in the process.[17] He sees Clip Club as a release from the strictures of the formal system, rather like some form of compensation for what he calls "the burdens of the day", whereas a holistic grasp of this relevant expressive art form should function as a core entitlement. However, such are the constrained conditions of possibility in much formal schooling, that collaborative interaction with digital media as routine is unlikely to be a popular choice

---

[17] Listen @ https://soundcloud.com/shelleuk/leonardo-july-2014/s-ZeYgl#t=05:43 [Accessed 7 February 2018].

amongst overburdened teachers—many of whom lack confidence with moving image manipulation. Nor in the eyes of the inspectorate is digital media production valued as a legitimate learning practice. Most formal assessment is analogue and individualistic, set up to audit the quality of book-marking, individual teachers and pupils' progress—assessing collaborative digital work is antithetical to these procedures. With this in mind, there is a boldness of spirit in schools interested in pursuing moving image production as a standard meaning-making practice, as will be seen in the following Chapters.

Somewhat paradoxically, despite being a place of fun and refuge, Leonardo has absorbed from public discourse the perceived instrumental benefits of gaining media skills as they relate to the work place. Throughout my research and in other professional evaluation work, young people consistently profess the usefulness of film and media production experience to their future careers, seeing it as an adult work-oriented activity. This binary between practical media as work and/or play, and why in the former case the benefits should be deferred until adulthood, is a recurring tension in media education, and a theme that will be further explored in Chap. 6.

A further potentially problematic dimension relates to the re-production of film industry protocols and their constraining influence on youth practices. It seems there is a lack of imagination on the part of some practitioners and software impresarios to re-construe professional standards and practices for younger users. We tend to fall into them unquestioningly, we reproduce linear pre/post-production models, the festivals and awards, all of which arguably preserve "cinematic life" (Furstenau and MacKenzie 2009) as mythic and out of reach. The enthusiastic embrace of industry tropes does little to move the medium on as an expressive art form in the everyday lives of teachers and pupils.

A Gestalt of Hybrid Transactional Pedagogy

At the beginning of the book I made a distinction between formal, informal and non-formal education, and Clip Club fell in the latter category in that it was run under the aegis of the school but was not accountable to it. There is no doubt that the non-formal nature of the Club had an impact on Dual 2 who struggled in the formal school structures. As indicated above, the opportunity to engage in sustained after school media production may be an appropriate outlet for some less privileged pupils to express themselves and to prepare them for a sense of belonging that is neither school nor home. The Clip Club provided a transitional staging post—or 'third space' (Potter and McDougall 2017) between these two domains through engagements with popular culture and moving image production.

Moreover, formal pedagogic approaches might embrace the latitude for local community building offered by non-formal, hybrid education models, whose ethos is often less individualistic and more collaborative, where 'failure' is given time to be reinterpreted as a process of iterative review and regroup. The moments of friction in the Clip Club alluded to earlier, were resolved sensitively and democratically with attention to the wider context. The children were offered time and space for critical reflection on proceedings in which they were emotionally invested. It is also possible that this experience and the Club's positive encounter with professional adults seeking their advice, spurred the children on to higher levels of achievement, the implications of which will be examined later.

An appropriately facilitated creative media session accommodates different talents and interests through iterative production practices and the negotiation of different roles. In a space free from assessment and prescriptive standards, Nimbus for one, in a prolonged series of Clip Club literacy events, was able to experiment with his less confident creative side, explore social collaboration, and indulge his interest in computer science. These practices are the hallmarks of the kinds of dynamic literacies elicited by this research, and what was being generated was a gestalt of greater significance than the films themselves.

This is an idea corroborated by Dual 2's address to camera. He sensed that the success of the Club was built on participation in a co-dependent flattened hierarchy of social and material relations, leveraging new technologies for a collective purpose. Pedagogies related to creative digital media underscore efforts to create a supportive and inclusive teaching habitus which is both conducive to learning and dismissive of ranking and categorising systems. Just as Clip Club learners, in the run up to shooting their short films, engaged in editing a series of "temporal gestalt(s) of sound (and) image" (Furstenau and MacKenzie 2009, p. 14, drawing on Merleau-Ponty 1964, p. 54), so a temporary historical gestalt was created amongst its participants.

From a research perspective, through this partial anatomy of experience in a particular local community, it has been possible to lay out the dimensions of creative digital media composition, which may prove fruitful in other contexts. It is to this task that this volume now turns as focus shifts to the development of international film and moving image education and the ways in which this is applied in the UK.

Bibliography

Alma. (2009) [online]. Short Film, Directed by R. Blaas. Spain. Retrieved February 7, 2018, from https://vimeo.com/4749536.

Animatou. (2007). Short Film. Directed by C. Luyet. Switzerland.

Bakhtin, M. (1981). *The Dialogic Imagination: Four Essays*. Austin: University of Texas Press.

Barthes, R. (1979). *Camera Lucida: Reflections on Photography*. London: Vintage.

BFI Education and Film Education. (2012). *Film: 21st Century Literacy—Integrating Film into Education* [online]. London: British Film Institute, Creative Skillset, Filmclub, Film Education, First Light. Retrieved February 7, 2018, from http://www.independentcinemaoffice.org.uk/media/Misc/film-21st-century-literacy-advocacy-report.pdf.

Burn, A., & Durran, J. (2007). *Media Literacy in Schools: Practice, Production and Progression*. London: Paul Chapman.

Burn, A., Potter, J., & Parry, B. (2012). *Montage, Mash-up, Machinima* [online]. DARE: Digital, Arts, Research, Education. Institute of Education, University College London. Retrieved February 7, 2018, from http://darecollaborative.net/2012/06/20/montage-mash-up-and-machinima/.

Burnett, C., & Bailey, C. (2014). Conceptualising collaboration hybrid sites: Playing *Minecraft* together and apart in a primary classroom. In J. Davies, G. Merchant, & J. Rowsell (Eds.), *New Literacies around the Globe: Policy and Pedagogy (Routledge Research in Literacy)* (pp. 50–71). Abingdon: Routledge.

Cannon, M. (2011). *Fashioning and Flow* [online]. MA Dissertation, Institute of Education, London. Retrieved February 7, 2018, from https://fashioningandflow.wordpress.com/.

Cannon, M., Bryer, T., & Lindsey, M. (2014). Media production and disruptive innovation: Exploring the interrelations between children, tablets, teachers and texts in subject English settings. *Media Education Research Journal, 5*(1), 16–31.

Cannon, M., Potter, J., & Burn, A. (2018). Dynamic, playful and productive literacies. *Changing English, 25*(2).

Craft, A. (2013). Childhood, possibility thinking and wise, humanising educational futures. *International Journal of Educational Research, 61*, 126–134.

Donaldson, S. (2014). *Maximums and Minimums* [online]. Film Literacy Advisory Group (FLAG) Blog. Retrieved February 7, 2018, from https://filmliteracyadvisorygroup.wordpress.com/2014/11/20/maximums-and-minimums/.

Furstenau, M., & Mackenzie, A. (2009). The promise of 'makeability': Digital editing software and the structuring of everyday cinematic life. *Visual Communication, 8*(1), 5–22.

He Dies At The End. (2010) [online]. Short Film. Directed by D. McCarthy. Ireland. Retrieved February 7, 2018, from https://www.youtube.com/watch?v=YRlvnDUtBbI.

Lave, J., & Wenger, E. (1991). *Situated Learning: Legitimate Peripheral Participation.* Cambridge, UK: Cambridge University Press.

Lévi-Strauss, C. (1966). *The Savage Mind.* Chicago: University of Chicago Press.

Lord, P., Jones, M., Harland, J., Bazalgette, C., Reid, M., Potter, J., et al. (2007). *Special Effects: The Distinctiveness of Learning Outcomes in Relation to Moving Image Education Projects: Final Report* [online]. London: Creative Partnerships. Retrieved February 7, 2018, from http://www.nfer.ac.uk/publications/SPF01/SPF01.pdf.

Loveless, A. (2008). Creative learning and new technology? A provocation paper [online]. In J. Sefton-Green (Ed.), *Creative Learning* (pp. 61–71). London: Creative Partnerships, The Arts Council. Retrieved February 7, 2018, from http://www.creativitycultureeducation.org/wp-content/uploads/creative-learning-booklet-26-233.pdf.

Merleau-Ponty, M. (1964). The film and the new psychology. In H. L. Dreyfus & P. A. Dreyfus (Eds.), *Sense and Non-sense* (pp. 48–59). Chicago: Northwestern University Press.

Mumford, S., Parry, B., & Walker, G. (2013). *Pockets of Excellence: Film Education in Yorkshire and the Humber* [online]. Leeds: IVE Creative (formerly CAPEUK). Retrieved February 7, 2018, from https://weareive.org/impact/pockets-excellence-film-education-yorkshire-humber/.

Parry, B. (2013). *Children, Film and Literacy*. Basingstoke: Palgrave Macmillan.

Ponyo. (2008). Film, Directed by H. Miyazaki. Japan: Toho Company.

Potter, J. (2012). *Digital Media and Learner Identity: The New Curatorship*. New York: Palgrave Macmillan.

Potter, J., & McDougall, J. (2017). *Digital Media, Culture and Education: Theorising Third Space Literacies*. London: Palgrave Macmillan.

Robinson, K. (2011). *Out of our Minds: Learning to be Creative* (2nd ed.). Chichester: Capstone.

Robinson, K. (2013). *Finding Your Element: How to Discover Your Talents and Passions and Transform Your Life*. London: Allen Lane.

Scottish Screen. (2006). *Moving Image Education & a Curriculum for Excellence* [online]. Glasgow. Retrieved February 7, 2018, from http://www.movingimageeducation.org/files/pdfs/mie-and-a-curriculum-for-excellence-2006-booklet.pdf.

Selwyn, N., Cranmer, S., & Potter, J. (2010). *Primary Schools and ICT. Learning from Pupil Perspectives*. London: Continuum.

Sinker, R. (2000). Making multimedia—Evaluating young people's creative multimedia production. In *Evaluating Creativity* (pp. 187–215). London: Routledge.

Turkle, S., & Papert, S. (1992). Epistemological pluralism and the revaluation of the concrete [online]. *Journal of Mathematical Behavior, 11*(1), 3–33. Retrieved February 7, 2018, from http://www.papert.org/articles/EpistemologicalPluralism.html.

Wall-E. (2008). Film. Directed by A. Stanton. USA: Disney-Pixar.

Wenger-Trayner, E. (2015). *Introduction to Communities of Practice* [online]. Retrieved February 7, 2018, from http://wenger-trayner.com/introduction-to-communities-of-practice/.

5

Film and Digital Media Production in Schools

In the next three case studies I continue to present audiovisual materials, interpreting the implications for literacy and learning of media composition processes from a pedagogic and practitioner's point of view. As in the last Chapter, each setting's account will conclude with a reflection on the socio-cultural context in which material was gathered and the constraints and potentialities related to the conditions of production. Setting 2 is located in an after-school context in a North London Primary School which was following an international educational film-making programme over two terms. Setting 3, referred to here as Film in a Morning, records Year 7 media composition practices in the formal English curriculum of Riverside School, a secondary school in south London, in partnership with Institute of Education (IoE) tutors and their student teachers. This setting is pivotal as it offers an unusual bridge for non-formal practices to cross over into formal institutions. Finally, Setting 4, Riverside School English and Drama Department, follows specific pedagogic practices in a series of Year 7 English lessons, working on the development of critical awareness through still and moving image work.

© The Author(s) 2018
M. Cannon, *Digital Media in Education*,
https://doi.org/10.1007/978-3-319-78304-8_5

Setting 2: North London Primary School—Le Cinéma: Cent ans de Jeunesse

The second setting was a Church of England primary school in North London located in an environment not unlike Clip Club, in that it shared a similar demographic only smaller, with a one-class yearly intake. There was a diverse ethnic mix of pupils typical in this part of London, and of its 168 pupils, approximately two thirds qualified for the Pupil Premium.[1] I tracked a weekly non-formal after school film-making project for ten Year 6 pupils over two terms, led by a Year 4 teacher. This was the fifth year that Ms. J had been running the club with different groups.

There was a significant extra dimension to this club in that the resultant short film was to be conceived, filmed, produced and edited by the children and then screened at the British Film Institute (BFI) months later, as part of a national film education programme. The programme itself originates in France and had been running for over twenty years as Le Cinéma: Cent Ans de Jeunesse (Cinema: a hundred years 'young', henceforth CCADJ) at the Cinémathèque française in Paris.[2] The BFI had been one of the CCADJ's cultural partners since 2009, developing its own national version of the programme, now with over twenty workshops in the UK. The north London school where my study was based was one of these workshops.

Over two decades CCADJ had grown from a home-spun national celebration of one hundred years of French cinematic culture, into a yearly programme involving hundreds of teachers and young people across Europe (and beyond—with Guadeloupe, Brazil, Cuba and India now on board). The overall purpose continues to be that young people and educators watch, interpret, discuss and practise making films as an art form with intrinsic worth, as opposed to a medium with strictly entertainment

---

[1] The Pupil Premium (or PP) is government money made available to schools 'with disadvantaged pupils' that need extra resources to close 'the attainment gap'. With 98 pupils on the 'PP register' out of the 168 total, the school received £99,000 in the school year 2013–2014 which was spent on booster classes for 'low achievers' in English and Maths.

[2] Every year the project develops a blog to which all pan-European participants are encouraged to contribute: http://blog.cinematheque.fr/ and the UK equivalent: https://markreid1895.wordpress.com/2013/07/23/plan-sequence-the-long-take/ [Both accessed: 7 February 2018].

or instrumental value. Over the course of fifty hours of contact time, participants are given a series of small, low-risk and highly structured production exercises guided by their teacher and a professional film-maker. These culminate in a 'film essai'—an eight-minute short film, or moving image experiment, to a given brief.

Apart from its international reach and longevity, the programme has other distinguishing features: film theory, professional development and pedagogy are taken as seriously as the children's learning; its content is different every year; there is no formal element of competition, nor any appeal to Hollywood glitz; the age range of participants is from seven to eighteen years old; and many of the young film-makers unite in Paris for summer screenings of their work. A key component of the programme is the invitation to film-makers of all ages to discuss their authorial choices after the screening in a public multilingual Q & A. But perhaps the most important characteristic is the focus on the aesthetic affordances of film as a medium and as an art form. Certain familiar dimensions of film-making, such as acting, narrative, script-writing and dialogue are de-emphasised, as is the exploration of social issues which often drives projects with young people, in favour of visual story-telling, and the sequencing and quality of shots.

Every year the CCADJ Creative Director and French cinéaste Bergala (2002; Bergala et al. 2016), creates a typology, focussing participants' attention on one aspect of cinematic grammar or filmic sensibility. Past themes have included: camera movement, colour, light, depth of field, mise-en-scène, the weather, games and playing, or the more conceptual hiding/revealing in film. For 2013–2014, and hence the one relevant to my study, the theme was le plan-séquence, or the long take.[3] This is defined as one sustained shot—moving or static—which mainly includes a sequence of events. The theme will be described in further detail in Chap. 5, suffice to say that it was inspired by the century old practices of French film pioneers, the Lumière brothers. CCADJ was found to be a site of rich international experimentation with teaching and learning

---

[3] A 'long take' is distinct from a 'long shot'. The former describes duration while latter describes the distance between the camera and the subject, which is more commonly known as a 'wide shot'.

approaches, all the while embedded in the long established traditions of European film culture.

There is a heady mix of discourses at large in this programme that appear to contradict some of the preceding prose championing progressive inclusive educational practices, indeed, some may even construe a programme founded on a certain cultural didacticism. This might be seen in the ways the CCADJ programme embraces a classic sage-on-stage input strategy, and the manner in which canonical art house production values seem to be cultivated at the expense of Hollywood and more popular film tropes. These tensions will be explored later, but first I wish to examine a more positive and enriching view, one which is supported by Mark Reid, Head of UK Educational Programmes at The British Film Institute. Reid first enrolled a UK secondary school in the French programme in 2009, seeing the model as an innovative approach to teaching and learning about film with specific learning outcomes. Rather than privileging narrative content or social issues, its aesthetic is rooted in film as an art form that attends to aspects of theory, language, form and iterative making practices.

Relations Between Theory and Practice Through Artistry

Building on decades of abstract thought on film, CCADJ actively works at maintaining the balance between theory and practice, and between reflection and material experimentation. This key principle resonates with my research in that explicit attention is given to film literacy or the reading and writing of film. That is, time and parity is given to group processes of watching, practicing and critical reflection in repeated cycles over the weeks of the programme. Continuities with cultural histories are maintained by watching specific clips from a wide range of nations and times past, with viewer-learners' sensibilities attuned to one particular film aesthetic. This annually determined theme could be abstract in nature, or it could relate to practical camera work, whichever the case, developing the authorship and artistry of students is fundamental to the way the programme works. Chez CCADJ, the affordances of tools, the local and social environment and elements within the cinematic frame are in constant dialogue with each other—an orientation to learning which, it is argued here, illustrates the kinds of situated cultural practices that progress relevant and dynamic literacies.

My study of material from a London based primary school following the CCADJ programme offers a glimpse of such a model, but first I briefly relay its key principles in the words of Nathalie Bourgeois, Director of the Programme and Co-ordinator of European educational projects at the Cinémathèque française:

> This extract (my translation below), is available in French from 0:35′ to 3:11′ @ https://soundcloud.com/shelleuk/ccadj-nathalie/s-PH5ty#t=0:35 [Accessed: 7 February 2018]:
> The most distinguishing feature of this programme is the connection between reflection and experimentation. That is, we gather a group of adults—teachers, practitioners and cultural partners or coordinators—around a specific subject every year. We could just get together and discuss the theme and how we would develop it in the workshops. However, how this project differs is that we develop an actual experiment with real pupils in the classroom, and at the same time share an object of study. And at the end of the year, we reflect on how the shared experiment went, and also discover something of ourselves in the process. I think we could call it experience at the human level: because there are over forty workshops, and we can actually meet and see each other's work. I think that's unique. https://soundcloud.com/shelleuk/ccadj-nathalie/s-PH5ty#t=2:10 [Accessed: 7 February 2018]:
> Another thing which is important and quite rare is the partnership between the teachers and film-makers. It's not that we have a session for teachers and a session for the professionals. At the beginning of the year we all meet and we unite over some aspect of cinema. We don't just talk about pedagogy, we talk about film. It's an educational experience for teachers and the cultural partners, who don't often have the opportunity to follow film education programmes; and for the film-makers too, who are faced with a theoretical question before any consideration is given to pedagogy. I think that's really important, that film is a central aspect of the pro-gramme—an 'object' that we question.
> (Interview with Nathalie Bourgeois, 2015)

Bourgeois' account highlights the importance of maintaining a dynamic relationship between theory, its robust implementation, and follow-up processes of open and critical evaluation. The adults' practices and interactions—what she terms le va et le vient (or coming and going) between theory and practice—mirror in many respects those amongst the young participants. They too engage in multi-operational practices related to: the phronetic (the negotiation of tools and techniques in workshop style environments); the critical (the particular film grammar theme); and the dialogic (recursive display and discussion at every stage)—which in turn are replicated in linked communities of practice in other schools. The model is self-perpetuating, most years propagating additional national or international practitioner-pedagogue alliances in different learning spaces. Its successful global reach may well be attributable to accessible meta-linguistic foci, and the iterative movement between robust structures of delivery and the creative agency this begets—from the London borough of Lambeth to Guadeloupe[4] and Cuba.

Bourgeois alludes to a central theme, which for 2013–2014 was the long take. Groups worked around a theoretical typology devised by Bergala (2002) to execute short film exercises, or indeed, that anatomise visual structures of meaning related to the long take. Examining such an exercise will indicate how literacy incorporating the moving image can be re-conceived as an array of cultural practices that move us beyond the narrow definitions to which centrally mandated UK curricula subscribe, towards vibrant, social and global interactions.

The below exercises were translated by Alastair Satchel, coordinator of Understanding Cinema[5]—a project inspired by CCADJ, and run by Scotland's Centre for the Moving Image in Edinburgh.

---

[4] The French CCADJ blog contains the full array of rules and protocols and presents clips from workshops in their respective locales around the world: http://www.cinematheque.fr/cinema100ansdejeunesse/en/experiences-de-cinema/all-questions-of-cinema.html   [Accessed: 7 February 2018].

[5] Alastair made a short explanatory movie of Understanding Cinema's activities in 2013–2014: https://vimeo.com/102957237 [Accessed: 7 February 2018] including comments from teachers and pupils. Some of their young participants' films were shown at the Edinburgh Film Festival 2014.

Exercise 1

Watching: Lumière Minutes—recording the world around you

Each participant will film a minute of material in the manner of the Lumière Brothers. The shot will be from a fixed position, lasting one minute and include the sounds recorded on location at the time of filming. The minutes can be filmed either inside or outside.

Choose a place, a subject, a moment and record it, without influencing anything in the shot. Once each student has recorded their minute, show all of the clips they have made together in one go.

You can ask your groups to choose locations for their minutes together in small numbers. Within those groups each participant must film a different moment, in the location chosen, or about the chosen subject, making sure to set up their own framing and choose the right moment for themselves.

The exercise could not be simpler in practical terms. From their knowledge of the clips and the long take typology, they were to frame and film a sixty second unscripted local moment.

Lumière Minutes on a North London Dual Carriageway

One late November afternoon I set out with Ms. J., the class teacher, Ben, our tutor-film-maker, and the Year 6 children, to capture some Lumière Minutes along a busy north London dual carriageway. The shop fronts, businesses and buildings that the children would habitually pass were now potential film sets. Each location scout was obliged to think about the strengths and weaknesses of their location, to interact with the people in it, and to ask for permission. They also had to deal with knock-backs from certain fast food chains—sites that may routinely have welcomed their custom.

Johnny, who was very clear about where his film was to take place, chose the ordinarily forbidden zone of a rundown tattoo parlour, into which the unusual combination of chaperoned child with a professional camera was granted entry. Pushing further, Johnny asked if he could shoot his Minute during a client's procedure. Other children had variously chosen a nail salon, a grocer's, a garage, a bus stop, but the parlour seemed the most audacious location, screened off from public view and laden, for some, with cultural taboo. Johnny may have been curious about its workings and he was now authorised to venture in, engage with the adults, capture its culture, and shape and share a representation of it.[6]

Johnny appears to be calling the shots in a realm not readily associated with childhood and in which normative power relations seem to have been suspended. As witnessed in the link below, the event is recorded very close to the action: a cling film covered side table, a plastic cup, some kitchen roll, a household spray bottle, vinyl wall hangings, a poster of Jack Nicholson's Joker, a bright spotlight, a drum and base soundtrack and the buzzing needle, all set within a cramped space of questionable hygiene—it resembles some Gothic surgical tableau, layered with cultural and ritualistic resonance.

Included in Bergala's typology for the long take was the representation of mutation. That is to say, choosing to film a long take is an effective way of conveying process which involves some kind of modification or variation of intensity over time. This, he proposes, could be wrought through bodily transformations, the development of a mood, a dawning realisation, or simply a change in the weather. Johnny's choice of filming a tattoo artist at work fits the brief well: we see him administering—and performing—a change. Not only this, the parlour is conveniently lit, audiovisually evocative, and with little in the way of distracting dialogue from the focused audience. Moreover, it fulfils what Bergala would describe as the aesthetic function of the long take rather than a narrative function. Part of this aesthetic function is to be sensitive to viewers' experience through the artistry of framing and mise-en-scène, if narrative serendipitously emerges, then that is as a bonus.

Filming their individual Minutes, the children were intently following the action through the viewfinder: everyday details were transformed in some way or became cinematic in scope. As previously seen in Clip Club's film language analysis sessions and Clara's filmed improvisations, it is argued here that literacy events in response to the visual, begin with the

---

[6] All the 'Minutes', (including the tattoo parlour from 02:05′), are recorded here: http://makingislearning.com/2014/01/25/north-london-obs-january-2014/ [Accessed: 21 September 2014].

simple act of noticing the peculiarity and profundity of one's material surroundings.

Aesthetic/Film Sensibility

I wrote a blog post at the time reflecting on the quality of attentiveness that the children bestowed on what they were watching.

> Striking how they've taken to this exercise without any kind of complaint—just filming an apparent 'nothing', no fiction, no fighting, no acting, no dialogue, no action, no genre-imitating, no plot, no story … except of course we captured most of those things in a filmed slice of real life. Or is it a 'slab' of real life? in the way of Geertz's 'thick description'? There was a real feeling of thinking on your feet and scouting for locations, keeping quiet and behind the camera. One time the camera operator couldn't help commenting on the drama of his Minute: "Perfect!" … as he catches the bus driver not allowing a woman on the bus and her reaction.
> (Available from: http://makingislearning.com/2014/01/25/north-london-obs-january-2014/) [Accessed: 7 February 2018]

Imbuing quotidian experience with meaning is for Bourgeois one of film's unique attributes. She speaks of "film sensibility" and the ways in which working with film sensitises the maker to visual nuance and the sensorial. She claims it activates a kind of knowing that is metacognitive, a consciousness that has to do with perception, thus provoking in the film-maker a "sincere attention" to the environment and the visual. The sincerity of which Bourgeois speaks is less to do with genuineness and more to do with a response that is personal. A link might be made here with G-man's ethnographic sensitivity and his close photographic attentiveness to filming and its procedures. The proposition is that drawing attention to filmic theoretical typologies (in this instance, the long take) helps to deliver the viewer-maker of his/her preconceptions; in other words, they can short-circuit conditioned feedback loops that may arise otherwise.

Available in French at https://soundcloud.com/shelleuk/ccadj-nathalie/s-PH5ty#t=13:08 [Accessed: 7 February 2018]

... having this perceptive acuity already creates the conditions through which this sensibility can be felt. And when I spoke of sincerity I think this word is appropriate because it's the opposite of 'a priori' givens—hence the reasons for showing the film clips, which are often a kind of immediate confrontation. Having to think about sound or about the context, breaks the contact with the film, either because of the milieu or the question posed. Attention is kept in a sincere way without being muddled with a priori knowledge and prejudices.

(Interview with Nathalie Bourgeois 2015)

Johnny, whose autonomous choices had been bold and original, was exhilarated on leaving the parlour; he had captured his moment born out of an intense and sincere engagement with a real setting of his own choosing. In so doing, a cluster of normally distinct worlds came together for a brief improvised collaboration—ecotonal[7] in nature—in ways that possibly rehearse a nascent moment of social participative empowerment. If literacy is conceived less as a stable threshold and more as a moveable, contingent condition (Belshaw 2012, p. 205, drawing on Martin 2006), that is sensitive to social engagement and siting (Burnett et al. 2012), then this may have been one such experience.

Moments of Translation and 'Practise, Practise, Practise!'

Each participating CCADJ workshop produces a final 8–10 minute short known as a film essai. Bourgeois distinguishes this from a short film which, despite its brevity, is nevertheless considered a finished entity. The essai, which comes from the French essayer—to try, describes the nature of the exercise: it is less the pursuit of a festival-ready oeuvre that reflects well on all parties, and more about creating a partial structured response to a film aesthetic, containing a simple narrative but not driven by it.

The final essai brief was this:

---

[7] It will be remembered that ecotonal refers to the biodiverse territory that constitutes edge conditions between two distinct eco-systems, such as estuaries or mangrove swamps. The two worlds collide productively, creating rich sites of resistance, adaptation and habitats for new forms of life.

A troubling encounter: at a certain moment a character or characters have an encounter which troubles them.

Create a film around the provocation above which includes several long takes. The film can be edited together, including elements of montage if you so wish. The film will last a maximum of 8–10 minutes. *In one of the long takes the camera must forget the character or characters and become autonomous, follow another path and then find the character or characters again.* This section should create an emotional or sensational response in the viewer watching the clip.

The material I present relates to the production of the above brief and comprises four clips of audiovisual material edited into one file:

Clip 1: participant generated footage from a film shoot in the street outside school

Clip 2: participant generated footage taken in the editing suite and edited (by me) into a sequence of 7 short sub-clips (2a–2g)

Clip 3: a scene from the final film to illustrate content

Clip 4: the BFI screening of the film and the public Q & A

Clip 1 is taken by a Year 6 child participant, Callum. He liked to be the centre of attention, he was a good actor, a good dancer and a good beat-boxer; he seemed to need more managing than most. He reminded me of Clip Clubbers, Wizard and Dual 2: he was a confident showman amongst his peers with occasional issues of concentration. I asked him if he would take some DV and photos of the shoot with my iPad. The reasons for this request were threefold (a) to yield participant generated material (b) to make a 'Making of' movie if there was time and (c) to give him something to do that would make him less of a distraction to others.

The premise of the children's film was the bullying of a new girl who was falsely accused of stealing the school's gold cup award. Clip 1 features a girl catching up with the new girl outside school in order to strike up a false friendship. Watching Callum's 'filming of the filming' in Clip 1, you will see a small inset screen depicting what was actually being shot for the final film.[8]

---

[8] The in-picture camera view in Clip 1 (as used in Wizard's table-top filming) simultaneously screens the junior producers' work. This is a potent dual perspective—now common editing functionality—that researchers would do well to explore in terms of presenting material in non-linear and multi-layered ways.

Watch Clip 1 at https://vimeo.com/132088709 from 00:00' to 00:56' [Accessed: 7 February 2018, password = wizard]

In his capacity as iPad documenter of the film-making process, Callum sets up his shot behind the camera and begins recording the third take of this particular scene—hence, he is familiar with the design of the shot. There then ensues a series of silent signals: the sound operator, Becky, gestures to Johnny, positioned over the road, to instruct the first actress to begin walking. The two actresses are not within earshot of the crew but wear radio microphones so the sound can be picked up in the editing phase. Callum first frames the action on the signal to Johnny and then moves over to the main action, composing it so that both girls and the DV camera's viewfinder are within shot. Finding he can move in with the camera, he steadily gets a closer look. He then leaves the action and pans round to his left filming myself and Ms. J., and finally the camera alights on the two actresses who have just finished their scene. I am gesturing for him to get out of the way of the actresses and Ms. J. gives the thumbs up to them all for a successful take.

In the same way it suited G-man's sense of self to dart in and out of Clip Club film shoots with his stills camera, Callum was able to break away from the main area of concentration in a gesture of independence that provided him with an alternative route to express himself. In other words, by acting on impulse in a structured way rather than in a way that might be perceived as disruptive, he found another path on which to practise his craft that was separate but pertinent, and still within the integrity of the group.

Possibly as a response to the overall CCADJ film essai brief which dictated the bifurcation of the camera at a certain point (that is, a cinematic technique in which the camera independently diverges away from the main subject/s, only to rejoin it/them moments later), Callum chose to leave the approaching girls and pan a near 360 degrees, to rejoin the girls behind him—even eliciting an empathetic response from the bystanders, in accordance with the brief. In ways that recall Wizard's first autonomous point of view 'sentence' with the camera (where he was crawling on the table with a DV Flip camera in the last Chapter) we see Callum's first experiments in framing, close-up, pan and bifurcation with an iPad. This book calls for the examination of such seemingly meaningless acts of moving image cognition and theoretical assimilation, casting them as moments of translation. This describes those particular learning moments in which prior knowledge or implicit experience is re-framed, transformed and embodied in alternative modalities, in ways that anchor our subjectivities.

Reid likens our first moving image efforts, regardless of age, to our first attempts at any creative production, no matter the art form or media, commenting as follows:

> Available at https://soundcloud.com/shelleuk/mark-reid#t=23:10 [Accessed: 7 February 2018]
> it's time-consuming and difficult, and every time somebody shows me a film they've made, invariably I ask myself, or imagine asking them, "Do you remember writing your first paragraph, or writing your first poem?" because it's probably a bit like that, you make and you've never made one before, and you're 30, and you're like a 6-year-old who's written a poem about a flower for the first time. It takes a long time to learn how to manipulate a language, to express yourself in a language … You just do it, you just practise, practise, practise.
> (Interview with Mark Reid, 2015)

The fact of having repeated opportunities to make and refine DV communicative efforts based on structured short form exercises, rather than a one-off, high stakes film-making approach, is enshrined in CCADJ methodology. This resonates with the ways in which a more fluid and fragmented approach to literacy is envisaged that lifts meaning off the page, and creates a disposition amenable to le va et le vient—or iterative interactions—between forms of praxis, aesthetic improvisation and communicative modalities.

There are echoes here of Lanham's 'AT/THROUGH bi-stable oscillation' (1994), explained in Chap. 2, as the means through which a sense of stable meaning emerges through texts. Lanham's insight concerning the ways in which we recursively fool ourselves by looking AT symbols (or INTERACTING WITH digital symbols in the modern era), and then THROUGH to illusory constructed meanings, will be picked up again in Chap. 6. For now it is enough to note that trends in transmedia take-up, suggest that "multi-stable oscillation" (McKee 2005, p. 124) with tools, symbols, modes, and meanings, may more accurately describe multimodal sense-making practices.

Practitioner's Insight: Tacit Communication, Tools and Anatomy

In keeping with my anthropological approach to interpretation, I notice how Callum's clip demonstrates the richness of non-verbal communication in film-making processes. The silent signalling evident in Clip 1 brings to mind Wizard's dramatic gesturing and the spontaneous clapping in the Clip Club corridor shoot. In evidence is a range of facial expressions, gestured instructions and signs of approval indicative of a complicity within the group. This is the stuff of organised teamwork, communicative strategies with which many children will be familiar, not least from competitive sports. Educators might reflect on opportunities for intuitive and interpretive skills development in contexts such as film-making, and how they might be applied in more formal sites of learning.

These moments of social and cohesive artistry, where much is achieved in tacit communication, accumulate to create the conditions for a group of young media authors to become attentive to processes of refinement, as opposed to gaining kudos for being first to finish some individual task. Along with the complicity of a joint vision, and as part of the phronesis of pedagogic practice, it is possible for a shoot to accommodate action in the wings. For understandable reasons, most schools prevent playfulness around the objects of technology, invoking something of an essentialist aura around them. However, this account suggests that relaxing this reverence towards technology can sometimes bear fruit—even tools can be imaginatively repurposed, with the same tactile value as props, in playful integration with the network of human and non-human actors on a shoot.

In this view the equipment in use folds into the social arrangements; from iPad to boom, material technologies can become haptic ports of security for children involved in media-making. In a manner reminiscent of G-man on the sidelines, Callum took a series of photos of the sound operator, Maria, wielding the boom like an air guitar. Judging from the many photos that Callum took, there was a sense in which he was silently colluding with and indulging Maria's air guitar performance, like some videographer on a music video shoot. In formal structures this side-show may have been viewed as off task, but in the informal world of creative media where material is rarely trashed, the air guitar fantasy moment would be fertile footage for the 'Making of' movie.

When committed to from the start by junior journalists, the supplementary 'Making of' movie encapsulates the heart and soul of the production process, its secret stash of jokes. As such these texts have a value, in as much as the unveiling of films' anatomy piques viewers' curiosity and draws them in to the artifice, so that taken for granted consumption is interrupted (ESRO 2015, p. 28). For the makers themselves, processes of unpicking and stitching the illusion start much earlier in the editing suite.

Watch: https://vimeo.com/132088709 from 00:57 to 04:19
[Accessed: 7 February 2018, password = wizard]

DV Editing and Literacy: Making the Cut

This section views literacy as socially contingent and embodied, and elsewhere as a set of entwined cultural practices that develop a certain disposition for creation with media. For example, the data shows the children's collaborative reviewing and redrafting of digital material based on reasoned critical response and aesthetic sensibility. Their words and body language evince the negotiation of doubt and ambiguity, consultation and modification, trial and error; and finally, decisive action. This analysis reveals a series of learning moments related to the participants' level of autonomous engagement, their use of implicit moving image knowledge and their interactions with the screen, the editing software, the teacher and their peers.

Clip 2 is filmed in the editing suite of a local secondary school.[9] Unable to attend this session I asked Ms. J if one of the children could film it for

---

[9] As editing is the realm of the practitioner, there is no separate Practitioner's insights in Clips 2a–2g, they are subsumed within the initial interpretation.

me with an iPad as I was keen to capture editing in progress. This practical solution proved advantageous in terms of acquiring footage of editing through the eyes of a child participant—right down to the preferred portrait orientation associated with movies taken on mobile phones. The camera operator on this occasion, Tara, appeared to film with all the selfless composure of a fly-on-the-wall documentary film-maker, making no intervention and dividing her time equally between the editing couples. This impressed me a great deal on seeing the footage, probably because 'invisible' camera work of this nature mobilises skills of unbiased restraint.

Pairs of children occupied three editing stations, each responsible for cutting an allocated number of scenes, with Ms. J. and Ben in the background as tutor-mentors. From Tara's thirty minutes of continuous footage, I put together a montage of the children editing in which I tried to capture the spirit of the process in terms of language, action and intent.[10]

Clip 2a @ 00:57'–01:19' features Sally and Eva, editing the final moments of the film 'essai' including the requisite bifurcating long take. Eva is seen fully engaged in authorial choice: headphones on, she gestures at the screen and speculates on the effect of cropping the long shot in question, articulating herself verbally and physically as she goes. Her hand gestures replicate the movement of the camera as it turns a 90-degree corner and then frame a hypothetical zoom. Just as Clara in the Clip Club had found hand gestures useful in the description of her close-ups, we can start to see how the verbal articulation of moving image editing and analysis is an inclusive and expressive practice, no less sophisticated in terms of conceptual grasp than the written act.

In Clip 2b, 01:19'–02:32', Johnny is asking for permission to delete a "giant part" of the clip. This comment is easily overlooked—he has assimilated that a mere few seconds of film on a timeline is valuable storytelling space, which could be put to better use: too long a clip means lagging action and potentially losing viewers' attention, too short a clip makes for a disjointed or incoherent viewing experience. Ben, the mentor, turns the decision back to the editors who have in fact already risked

---

[10] I had communicated in advance that quick bursts of contiguous filming were preferable to continuous, but even at this stage in their film-making, the urge to reproduce one long take, as default film-making practice, is difficult to shift. Although given the context, there is an inherent irony in her decision to opt for one long take—this year's CCADJ theme.

making the cut and found the decisive moment for themselves. These particular editors have learned that through patiently watching clips, you hit upon the 'rightness of fit' required of continuity editing. This means, the right clip, in the right sequence, cut to the right length, at the right place and pace, in order to advance the story smoothly. All of these decisions coalesce allowing a certain mood to emerge within in an even tonal range, assuming that is what is required of the narrative. In this instance, Johnny and his partner achieved a complex editing outcome as a result of the various viewing, making and theoretical strands of learning over the months of the programme, and arguably as a function of audiovisual engagement accumulated over years of everyday media consumption. This concrete accomplishment does not fail to go unnoticed and is applauded by Ms. J., in Clip 2e.

In Clip 2c and 2d, @ 02:35′–03:14′, Ms. J. entreats Maria and Stephanie to act on their own decisions, and to make them in the spirit of strong visual storytelling; that is, artfully and efficiently composed clips, whose juxtaposition adds value in some way. This is at least the aspiration, a less strong outcome might become the subject of a critical and constructive debate. Maria on the left is concerned about the inauthentic look of the classroom with "too many empty seats" ; to cut that part of the scene she needs reassurance from Ms. J:

Clip 2c @ 02:35′

Ms. J: Do what you think. I mean, is this part really important? Is it necessary in the film? What do you think? So, do what you think. If you think that bit is…

Maria: Shall we just cut it off?

Ms. J: Yeah. Do what you think.

Clip 2d @ 02:52′
[stopping the film and pointing at the screen]

Maria: If you look there, do you think that this bit is actually important? Do we need it?

Stephanie: [quietly] No, if she's showing that she's doing well, then we don't really need it.

Maria: Erm, [pointing] there's too much space there, like too many empty seats. So let's take this one.

This brief exchange between Ms. J. and the editors reveals the dynamic between the teacher and the pupils, between the pupils themselves and the pupils and the interface. They are at first hesitant to delete material in order to improve the scene, perhaps because it is not inherently wrong.

One of the important skills in editing is that editors must make decisions based on their own judgement. As Nimbus found, in the absence of definitive notions of right and wrong, they must build on their 'negative capability'.[11] DV editing entails managing ambiguity, namely the negotiation of endless possibility within the conventions of moving image storytelling. Rather like the art of a sculptor, minute additions and subtractions of material on the timeline are creative acts emitting specific meaning effects. The challenge is to trust in and feel the 'rightness' of aesthetic choice from the raw variables, and manipulate them under the constraints of time and technology. Digital making conditions of this nature inculcate feelings of autonomy and control that may lead to a sense of self as a confident agent of change, especially in the screening and Q & A phase. This was indeed the case for Clip Club's Leonardo who "made change" having shown his film to over a hundred of his peers. These conditions are at once socially contingent and choreographed by the mentors.

In Clip 2e @ 03:16', Ms. J. is congratulating Johnny and his partner on a job well done. Using her hands to reinforce her comment: "I really like the way you edited that together, you're doing a good job there". She could equally have been applauding a group of adults on their first experience of DV editing, who, from my own personal experience, may well have felt a similar sense of achievement. Regular feedback is an important part of the process as media texts are most often meant for audiences' consumption. Johnny and his partner take the praise, and immediately put the headphones back on to get back to work, this time with an increased sense of purpose: "Right!"

---

[11] 'Negative capability' was a term fleetingly used in a letter by Keats, critiquing Coleridge, whom he thought wrong to be privileging knowledge over beauty. The phrase describes: "when man is capable of being in uncertainties, Mysteries (sic), doubts, without any irritable reaching after fact & reason" (Mee and Gittings 2002, p. 40). Keats' cherished 'half-knowledge' which connects with Eisnerian 'knowledge in the absence of rule', seems to have gained a particular resonance in modern times.

In Clips 2f and 2g @ 03:27′–04:15′, Sally and Eva at the central editing station have to negotiate their strong individual sense of what is "right" or "nice" in terms of successful edits. In an interview, Ms. J. advised me that these girls' acute visual sense was apparent throughout the project, and that they were able to abstract the look and sequencing of shots at the filming stage. Making competent and quick work of their choices, taking turns and collaborating well, the girls' overall demeanour manifests the fun of editing, demonstrating an exuberance of ludic (playful), haptic (touch-oriented), imaginative and cognitive interplay.

Other pairs' working relationships were slightly different in that there seemed to be a more dominant personality taking the lead, Johnny and Maria respectively, yet it seemed clear that the quieter children were indeed 'present' and their ideas were heard and acted on. This is a significant finding as pair work can often lead to disparately matched couples, but media composition practices have the propensity to generate contemplative dialogue at the interface, in accessible and unthreatening ways. At the end of Clip 2g, Sally and Eva are so engrossed that they fail to hear Ms. J.'s question, they need to be physically nudged to jolt them out of their editing flow.

Editing decisions made on the fly constitute the phronetic dimension of media composition practices that necessarily link with the corporeal, the imaginative, the cognitive and the affective elements of digital storytelling. Ms. J. and Ben repeatedly gave the children the authorisation, the encouragement and perhaps most importantly the trust and responsibility, to make the cut, and draw on shared intuitive understandings of moving image tropes. The editing excerpts presented bring into relief the ways in which successful pedagogies related to media production assume a more hands off approach, and can bring about a succession of critical and autonomous learning moments.

Watch Clips 3 and 4: https://vimeo.com/132088709 from 04:18′ to 09:45′ [Accessed: 7 February 2018, password = wizard]

BFI Screening Public Display and Process Exegesis

Earlier it was acknowledged that media texts are most often made with an audience in mind and that CCADJ learning protocols build in both a public screening, and a question and answer session. Clip 4 shows the group answering questions about their production from an authentic audience of peers and adults in one of the smaller BFI cinemas. The primary film-makers in the audience have all answered the same CCADJ brief and are thus primed to be asking questions of each other's productions. I include Clip 3—a scene from the end of the film—so as to provide context for the disquisition between young film-makers.

Before examining Clip 4, I invoke Bourgeois' comment on the significance of this stage of the programme. She refers to the moment of screening as a kind of alchemy:

> Available in French at: https://soundcloud.com/shelleuk/ccadj-nathalie#t=23:00 [Accessed: 7 February 2018]
>
> It's a significant moment because that's when their film becomes detached. People from your workshop are all there, and you show it to everyone else and suddenly, a little alchemy occurs on that day because the film becomes a separate object, and that's powerful. It's the thing that counts over and above the comparing of films [in a film festival context], it's the event that has taken place that's important.
>
> (Interview with Nathalie Bourgeois, 2015, transcript in Appendix G2)

The metaphor is aptly chosen as it recalls the moment in the Cycle of Digital Making (Fig. 2.2) when texts are detached from their makers and released into the public sphere. Alchemy involves the transmutation of one material to another, and if we embrace this metaphor, then it is the screening event that enables a change in the relationship between the children and their film—an '(im)material translation' perhaps—from a set of localised meanings conceived in a private space, to diffuse meanings in a communal space. In addition, film screenings, conceived as literacy event sites, de-centre the individual maker and effect a change in wider society (see Burnett et al. 2012 for more on this and "(im)material relations"). The Clip Club's Leonardo expresses it thus in Chap. 4 regarding making his audience laugh:

> Available at https://soundcloud.com/shelleuk/leonardo-july-2014/s -ZeYgl#t=3:23 [Accessed: 7 February 2018]

the people who make it will appreciate it, because they've done something or changed ... made change.
(Interview with Leonardo, 2014)

What further facilitates the children's sense of agency and ownership is the non-hierarchical, non-competitive nature of the event. Formal literacy is entrenched in scales of individual aptitude in culturally specific competencies that seem to build in success for some and failure for others, from an early age. Open non-judgemental fora such as the post-screening discussion hints at a more dynamic, inclusive version of literacy, as celebration. The idea is that the Q & A is of benefit to all, through the stimulation of a critical sense via the communication of participants' production challenges and decision-making processes.

The public dissemination phase is a moment that requires sensitive pedagogic orchestration for the alchemy to be fully realised. Rather than asking about the meaning of the text, so often a trait of formal literacy understanding, the facilitator, Mark Reid, asks the children to explain how they achieved the final winding long shot, and commends them on their resourcefulness. This is an approach which ascribes value to the often unarticulated but accessible nuances of the film-making process.

Practitioner's Insight: Improvisation, Historical Continuity and Critique

Earlier, in the Clip Club corridor footage, we heard that the junior film crew re-shot the scene nine times. Choosing to do that repeatedly, unsupervised, is testament to their commitment to crafting their product until it was "right", until it "worked". From Eva's first comments on the BFI stage we witness a similar disposition. The group is accepting of "lots of trials and errors" because by that stage in the programme they anticipate the various logistical ("people coming in the way") and technical ("too much bumping") challenges. The long take brief immediately presented practical problems related to moving camera work, problems that had to be solved through iterative experimental strategies. The more sophisticated the operation the more phronetic wisdom, or ingenuity on the fly, is called upon to achieve the required effect. Maria reveals the use of a trolley—with the camera placed on top—as a substitute for a professional tracking system, dolly or Steadycam. Indeed, the film-making process affords frequent opportunities for improvised problem-solving, independent productive agency, and insights into the creative process.

The Cycle of Digital Making (Fig. 2.2) speculates that ideas for creative output often arise from reflection on observations and feelings remembered from past experiences (following Dewey 1997/1938, p. 64), suggesting that by widening the cultural repertoires of young learners their pool of imaginative and filmic resources will be enriched. Mirroring this, Reid's line of questioning accentuates the often overlooked importance of historical continuity in the act of media composition. In recognition that ideas for moving image narratives are often rooted in personal or viewing experiences, he is interested in knowing about the group's creative influences. At 06:50′ Johnny refers to the Lumière Minutes of a few months prior, stating that a stealing incident had inspired their choice of plot. Evaluation practices such as tracing the threads of thought and cultural derivation related to film and moving image work, (and other creative arts disciplines) are the kinds of metacognitive skills that can be developed orally and possibly publicly, especially with respect to work that evolves over a sustained period.

The screening is a celebration as well as an evaluation. In my interview with John Potter, a parallel was drawn between creative media evaluation techniques and established assessment methods in Higher Education's Creative and Visual Arts programmes, where the emphasis is on discussion:

Available at https://soundcloud.com/shelleuk/john-potter#t=09:27 [Accessed: 7 February 2018]

there is a strong correlation between artistic practice, the studio practice, and the practice of discussion and critique which still persists in … our fine art degree system now. I think there's something to be said about the ways in which people will look at a screen together, and work out whether something is working or not, and what more they have to do, which is similar to the way somebody would talk about a collage that has been created.

(Interview with John Potter 2015)

Potter's choice of "collage" as an analogy is apposite in terms of the ways in which editing is a crafted process of assembly. Furthermore, the public BFI screening aligns with older students' art and design shows—inviting provocation and inquisitiveness as much as admiration. In a move that strategically does away with the trappings of industry and festivals, the annual CCADJ screening is an event, where primary children come together and exchange their knowledge and experience of filmmaking with peers and adults—almost in the mode of a research presentation: the brief/problem is aired, methods are designed, a representative outcome is achieved, followed by a public reception.

The children however are not uniformly receptive to the screening event. We witness the relatively mature observations of novice filmmakers, such as Eva's explanation of the benefits of a simple plot, alongside others' discomfort at being so exposed on the stage line-up. For Callum, to the right in yellow (and Gman before him), the occasion is overwhelming and he withdraws when beckoned to contribute. This said, he has been fully immersed in practical film production for a sustained period, the '(im)material' experience of which will be stored in what might be called his visual archive. As discussed in Chap. 2, and as Reid himself contends (2014, following Gee 2011/1990), to be literate is to fully participate in the culture, the language, the values and the meaning-making practices of a community—the screenings are one way of reaching towards this.

Contextual Interpretation: CCADJ Programme

Socio-cultural Conditions of Possibility

One of my research questions relates to the constraints and discursive conditions of possibility (Scott and Usher 2011) that encircle film and media production projects. To throw more light on this, I asked key commentators linked with CCADJ to reflect on what distinguishes the programme from other film and moving image education initiatives the UK. Reid picked out several features relating to its culture and infrastructure that led him to initiate the first UK workshop:

Audio   available   at   https://soundcloud.com/shelleuk/mark-reid/s-
wVzWW#t=12:50 [Accessed: 7 February 2018]

It's been going for 20 years, every year it's new, it has a common set of
constraints that aren't new every year, but there's a new instantiation every
year. It's a programme that has a 'va et vient' between teachers and film-
makers, which is important … It's about film language, it's not about social
issues, it's a gateway into cinema from all over the world, you don't get a
gateway like that in UK film culture, the UK always looks towards America,
and the French look everywhere else.

(Interview with Mark Reid, 2015)

From this snippet and in other parts of the interview references to
iterative practices come to the fore which are prerequisites for the types of
cultural diversity and historical continuity alluded to in my theoretical
and interpretive frameworks respectively. Both in Bourgeois' and Reid's
accounts recursivity is seen in: the ricochet between CCADJ's longevity
and yet its fresh annual appeal; its recurring methodological structure
and its renewed content; its practices of exchange and interaction between
teachers and practitioners (the va et vient or coming and going to which
they both refer); its continual revisiting of visual form over content or
social foci (although social issues do feature as a means of exploring visual
thematics); and finally, its holistic and eclectic embrace of old and new
classics from world cinema.

For Reid, these are the cultural principles and structuring characteristics, that differentiate CCADJ from other European models of film education. The inference being that, while there are recurring projects of
quality in existence, for example here in the UK,[12] many others are
expert-led, short-term, industry/career-facing, one-off funded projects,
driven by age-specific content, inspired in the main by US/English language cinematic outputs. It does seem that the UK approach to film education, and hence to the development of moving image sensibilities, is
frequently functional or instrumental in comparison with European cultural and educational practices. It may be that the film education field

---

[12] One such programme is the annual UK networked BFI Film Academy: http://www.bfi.org.uk/
education-research/5-19-film-education-scheme-2013-2017/bfi-film-academy-scheme/bfi-film-
academy-uk-network-programme, although this too is industry-facing and specifically aimed at
older students.

could benefit from programmes conceived with a wider view, including film as a discrete historically situated complex art form (see FLAG, Film Literacy Advisory Group, 2015, with these principles in mind).

My research supports the re-imagining of schools' engagement with film and the moving image as both a cross-disciplinary medium of expression, and as a particular dimension of the Visual Arts. As such, it is worth reflecting on the contextual challenges with which progressive pedagogies would have to contend if such a vision were to be contemplated.

Negotiating Constraints and Permeable Pedagogies

From what has been said about the prescriptive nature of the programme and its exclusive siting, some with a more pragmatic outlook might be sceptical about the French approach and its celebration of the European film canon. Indeed, there is a dissonance between the transactional model of pedagogy that has been hitherto championed in this book, and what appears to be more of a transmission model implemented by CCADJ. Potter, who conducted research on the project in 2012, had initial misgivings about the model and its perceived overly structured design. At first he thought it would:

Available at https://soundcloud.com/shelleuk/john-potter/s-3P9LY#t= 13:05 [Accessed: 7 February 2018]
inhibit rather than allow [pupils] to develop their own mastery. The idea that there is a mastery is going to inhibit their creativity in some way, and actually that isn't what happened, but I think it could have worked liked that without the pedagogy ... the role of the pedagogue was so important in ensuring that that did not happen. It pushed the students out of their comfort zone, but allowed them to remain inside the zone of their own agency,
[I interject with 'their habitus?']
... habitus, yes, because it enabled them to think that they could reflect that back through the lens of some of the techniques that they were learning, and make a better film than if they'd run around with the camera pointing it in any direction, without any consideration for some of the structures of film-making.
(Interview with John Potter 2015)

Potter reasons that CCADJ's prescriptive constraints and the practice of specific techniques help to extend all participants' horizons of possibility, at the same time as shaping practice and output. He stresses that this is only possible with the application of a pedagogy permeable to the needs, interests and insights of the students; in short, one that respects their habitus (Bourdieu 1984). Interview material gathered from participating tutor-mentors concurs with this hypothesis, and lends weight to the notion that tutoring in film-making requires artistry sensitive to the synchronous negotiation of structure, agency and production.

We see this tension played out in observations made by Ms. J. after her fourth year of participation in the programme:

Audio available at https://soundcloud.com/shelleuk/phd-interview-8-ms-j-june-2014/s-TF3fj#t=17:02 [Accessed: 7 February 2018]

Mark [Reid] said to me last year, he was like, "Your film really stood out, it was like a cut above," and he said, blah, blah, blah, and the shots and this and that. And I, sort of, cracked a joke and I went, "Yeah, but you know me, Mark, I just blag it every year." And he went to me, "Never say that, [Ms. J], you should never say that, you should always retain composure and say, 'Well, of course', you know." [Laughing] but yeah, and I did think it was partly because I had the group, but it's also because I know what I'm doing more now, you know what I mean? And I know what I need to do to get them ... and when I first started the project I was like, "I don't want to drive this, I don't want to influence you," so I took too much of a step back where I didn't want to tarnish it in any way, I didn't want to touch it, I wanted it all to come from them. But now I understand more that actually they need some of the techniques, they need some of the knowledge and they need—I don't know what the word is—I guess they need the training, and that's my job to train them. And that's not me taking over and controlling it and making it my film. Because from every idea they have I can see it. The minute they tell me the film I can see the whole thing and I know exactly how I'd shoot it. I know everything about it. So I always have to go, "No, no, so how would you do that, kids?" Because I know how I'd do it.

(Interview with Ms. J., 2014)

Her opening comments seem to downplay or even to deny her talents, at the same time as displaying a nuanced and reflexive practice. It is arguable that this negativity is seeded by formal school structures that simply do not value her skills. There is a tension between the pedagogic freedoms associated with running an after school project, and its low status in terms of support. In contrast, both Reid and Potter are strong advocates of the need to invest in robust career professional development for teachers in the field of creative media production, hence Reid's recognition of an enhanced expertise. Despite the local vacuum in which she had been working, the recurring nature of CCADJ meant that Ms. J. had a rare opportunity to hone her film production pedagogy, enabling a more sophisticated practice to develop, porous to the interests and responses of her pupils.

From what she discloses in the interview and from my own experience, it seems that many budding moving image educators fall between two camps: there are those who take an auteur approach by taking creative control, and then those who operate in a hands free way. This more invisible mode, as was Ms. J.'s initial strategy, may emerge from discourses that over-determine the so-called untarnished freedom that film production is questionably seen to afford. Alternatively, teacher detachment may simply be down to a lack of confidence that training might address. Ms. J. learnt from experience that the way forward with film-making with young people is to adopt a measured and facilitative approach, akin to workshop/studio practice, with relations based on trust, empathy and respect.

Considering the entrenched structures and rigid divisions of the school day, it is debatable the extent to which existing pedagogies can be more accommodating of pupils' and teachers' life worlds, and more reflective of their digital interactions outside school. In many ways, after school ateliers (or creative workshops) make it easier to conceive of pupils as apprentices, engaging in flexible, transactional environments with access to experienced mentors. The media production zone, both for CCADJ and Clip Club participants, was a haven in which it was safe to experiment, pose questions, build relationships and learn from each other, all the while developing everyday artistry in slow and often messy iterative exchanges.

Informal Contexts and the Case for Twilight Pedagogies

In the nomenclature of the Inspectorate there is an expectation for schools to provide evidence of pupils' rapid and sustained progress (OFSTED 2012), which is something of an oxymoron. It is questionable how this progress might be reliably manifested in a drive-by approach to lesson observation, and debatable how useful such a strategy can be for the students themselves to get a sense of their own advancement. This study suggests that progress is rather a commitment to a process whose outcomes are long term, thus presenting a challenge to existing pedagogies and inspection routines. I interviewed primary teachers from Lincolnshire who follow the CCADJ programme, asking them about the ways in which their twilight media-related pedagogy may be affecting their daytime practices. One primary teacher responded thus:

> Audio available at https://soundcloud.com/shelleuk/phd-thesis-interview-10-primary-teachers-ccadj-mid-project/s-RuoWT#t=02:50 [Accessed: 7 February 2018]
>
> Well, normal lessons—you do your starter and say "we're doing this for this hour … now apply it yourself for 20, 25 minutes and then let's come back and have a look at it". Whereas, this is so much more "let's experiment and have a play around", and over the course of one hour-long film club you might have nothing at the end of it, like an actual product, but all that experimentation you've done over the course of that hour is really, really useful. I think that gradual build-up is very different to in lessons, for me anyway … you're not prescribing to them: "You are doing this today!" They're experimenting and trying it out for themselves and working as a group to find it themselves which I think is much more different and very exciting as well.
>
> (Interview with primary CCADJ teachers, 2014)

In wistful tones, this teacher draws a distinction between the sanctioned pedagogies of prescriptive input based on efficiency, and what appear to be experimental, undetermined practices with 'nothing' to show for it, apart from tacit wisdom of experience. The implication is that while orthodox practices produce legitimate product in the form of tangible progress and testable knowledge, the CCADJ context for learning, espouses informal practices that nurture certain dispositions for social and reciprocal relations. Mature purposeful practice of this nature is known as praxis, that is, often improvised productive action based on theoretical discussion and, in this context, percipient film sensibility.

Perhaps mentor-style pedagogies are more easily facilitated in the primary context, where there is one teacher per class, and a degree of curricular flexibility. As the stakes rise in secondary, the appetite for transactional creative pedagogy is less identifiable and limited by a more oppressive regime of individual test preparation in distinct subject areas. These are conditions unconducive to group media composition practices, though not impossible, as the ensuing case studies attest.

I conclude by summarising the ways in which the non-formally located CCADJ programme shows us ways forward for the design and evaluation not only of film-related but digital media projects in general. The emphasis is on a critical egalitarian process driven by agentive social learning, within a framework of structured production and evaluation, sensitive to present and past influences. I will proceed with presenting media composition practices in the formal secondary school environment, where such activities are even less frequent and constraints more institutionally prescribed. If contemporary ideation on literacy is aiming for action-oriented participation, ways of conceptualising modern illiteracy are thrown into question. The studies that follow engage with issues of digital equality head on, with pedagogic ideology rooted in democratic ideals, and leveraged with digital tools.

Setting 3: Film in a Morning—Riverside School and UCL Institute of Education

Setting 3 combined representatives from three institutions that joined forces and created a brief film-making experience for Year 7 boys as well as a group of PGCE student teachers. Over one morning, the project comprised:

* a class of Year 7 boys from a state secondary school located in central London just south of the river Thames

• two PGCE course tutors, an MA student, a technician and a dozen student teachers of English and Drama at UCL, Institute of Education, (University College, University of London, henceforth UCL IoE)
• learning spaces provided by the nearby BFI Education Department

Riverside school is a specialist sports college and has a well-thumbed, spartan old-school air about it, with its many floors, irregular nooks and crannies, vertiginous Victorian stone stairs and peeling paint. The school is non-denominational and so the ethnicity of the pupils is more diverse than the previous two faith schools, and in terms of social grouping by income, the students come from families in the low to middle range, erring on the former.

The two UCL IoE teacher educators who coordinated the project, Theo Bryer and Morlette Lindsey, had been enthusiastic supporters of media production in English and Drama teaching for a number of years.[13] Since 2010 they had been developing an extra workshop for student teachers interested in filming and editing short DV texts, in response to literature. So, as an alternative to, or supplemental to, a written response to a poem or a novel, student teachers were encouraged to manage a critical and creative learning experience for their future pupils by harnessing the audiovisual and the performative. What was, in 2010, an initiative entitled Film in a Day, involving a suite of BFI iMacs, has transformed into Film in a Morning involving iPads, the iMovie app and a roving sense of mobility.

I took an interest in this project a year after its inception, and began following its progress on an informal basis, filming and blogging about it, because I felt it marked two important trajectories. One related to the development of DV production and subject English in critical and creative ways, and the other related to the professional development of teachers and their creative confidence with the digital. It was felt that this setting was to offer an unusually multi-perspectival view of new literacy practices, enacted in a formal setting with an important extension into

---

[13] This project was written up by myself, Theo and Morlette in the journals: Media Education Research Journal and Changing English (see Cannon et al. 2014 and Bryer et al. 2014 respectively).

the realm of ITT (Initial Teacher Training). Unique to this project was the fact that groups of student teachers and pupils were learning to be audiovisually co-productive, working together in small collaborative huddles.

I took up more formal research with this project because of its links with the formal English curriculum; the dialogic and interactive dimension; the flattened socio-pedagogic hierarchies and the proximity of thought and creative output as afforded by the iPad—all of which are consistent with explorations of new media technologies, production processes, new pedagogies and the ways these can be folded into formal school practices.[14] Through the examination of photos and extracts of interviews with teachers and the boys, I examined the types of hybrid pedagogy that embrace partnership and collaboration with pupils. With pedagogies in place that support co-composition and short-form digital outputs fired by implicit media awareness, a more democratic view of knowledge exploration and cultural production is formed that could start to influence mainstream practices at local level.

Colleagues Theo Bryer, Morlette Lindsey and myself collaborated on writing up the practices of this project in detail: Media Production and Disruptive Innovation: exploring the interrelations between children, tablets, teachers and texts in subject English settings (Cannon et al. 2014). The article attends to many of the constituent elements of this book as a whole; particularly to the ways in which digital disruptive innovation (Pendleton-Jullian 2009) can unsettle orthodox classroom practices with an ecology of "randomness and riskiness" (Burnett 2011a, 2011b). Perhaps this setting, more than any other in this book demonstrates the fecundity of the third space (Bhabha 1994; Gutiérrez 2008; Potter 2011)—a rich and permeable space of learning somewhere between the life-world, the school-world and the virtual-world that accommodates multiple productive modalities (Potter and McDougall 2017). Similarly, and as referred to in Chap. 2, Pendleton-Jullian (2009) usefully applies her ecotone metaphor (a fertile zone in the natural world, where

---

[14] The edited footage from the 2012 Film in a Day project is on my Masters blog, viewable at the bottom of this post: https://fashioningandflow.wordpress.com/2012/02/20/film-student-teachers-the-london-nauticals/ [Accessed: 7 February 2018] Watching this 5 minute edit contextualises the project in ways that are difficult to match in writing.

distinct biodiverse regions meet) to hypothetical environments where pedagogic innovations meet institutional practices. Film in a Morning is the site of one such rich territory, and it rehearses the dynamics of porosity that both inhabit and bracket the Production/Composition quadrant of the Cycle of Digital Making (Fig. 2.3).

Improvised Co-production and Playful Agency

The project was conceived as a way of stimulating pupils' personal critical responses to a magic realist print text, the novel Haroun and the Sea of Stories (Rushdie 1990). Set in a sad fictional earthly city, the text spirals out into a fantasy world reminiscent of Alice in Wonderland, The Hobbit and The Wizard of Oz. The teachers assembled for training in a function room at the BFI and, prompted by an array of everyday objects as props, they had one hour to familiarise themselves with the iMovie app and create and edit an audiovisual text. Their brief was to 'transform something ordinary into something magical' by composing four photos and a few seconds of moving image. The student teachers then replicated the exercise with groups of Year 7 boys the same morning.

It was a cold sunny January morning and most students avoided the brighter external conditions, opting to make do with the potentialities and possible constraints of the inside space. The room was notable for the one pane of glass where natural light could enter, which possibly explains the BFI's choice of hanging a panoramic photo of an outside view as a fake window onto the Thames. In contemplation of the enclosed area underneath the arches of Waterloo Bridge, there is a sense of being hemmed in, as if the student teachers had been let loose with a brief in a bounded playground. They had been given the challenge to exceed the confines of the ordinary and capture that excess as an act of literacy. At play with their pedagogy, they were offered the chance to improvise with audiovisual material and cultural production. In summary, these activities represent aspects of rhetorical performance and reflexivity emerging from intuition and dialogue between the students and their environment.

The activity recalls the CCADJ exercises in terms of the time-limited, stripped down brief, the imposed rules and the permission to feel a sense of imaginative agency under the prevailing conditions. I observed a mood of playful spontaneity and possibility thinking as iPads were handed out and props opportunistically grabbed; the task was on to choose a mise-en-scène ripe with visual potential amongst found semiotic resources. As Bryer notes (Cannon et al. 2014) co-opting and freighting the everyday with meaning in opportunistic ways, is an exercise in envisaging alternative realities. In addition, the anticipation of a peer screening fed a sense of deadline and impending performance.

One group experimented with stop-motion animation, using the wall as a backdrop and bringing plastic bricks to life.[15] Another resolved to transform a black leather glove into a sinister presence in a sink with a tap. One teacher awkwardly contorted himself so the other could get an appropriately angled and framed shot; the pair then immediately reviewed their work. The iPad's large screen enabled them to experience their roles as actors in, producers of, and audience for their own work in rapid succession. As such, by using the language of creative collaboration as was seen in the CCADJ editing suite, they were in a position to make judgement calls, do retakes and negotiate provisional adjustments as necessary. They were manipulating in social and empirical ways the building blocks of film and media composition, which once experienced, even in microcosm, seemed for most to instill a peculiar curiosity and/or confidence with the medium and the desire to do and learn more.

Practitioner's Insight: Media Crafting and Artistry

Without any previous experience, the above film-makers had chosen a kitchen sink as a setting which happened to offer a series of cinematic affordances: it was well lit with the overhead lights of the bar area; the shiny metallic chrome would render a pleasing clean contrast with the dark gloved hand; there was potential in the textures and reflective surfaces for a rewarding close-up; and there was a natural source of noise and contained movement with the running water. With the addition of menacing music from the iMovie app database, this was traditional film trailer

---

[15] More information on the richness of learning with animation in the primary years, particularly in poetry, can be found in Bazalgette (2012).

fodder, and eventually made for an amusing clip as a result of the students' attention to perspective, suspense and the sensorial.

This brief sequenced clip has remained in my memory for reasons of artistry, shortly after the clip was deleted. The emphasis was on the process over any precious attachment to the text, serving as a reminder that short-form digital texts are dispensable, and can be redone and reworked. Indeed, there being no one chance to get it right, as can be the case with other visual art forms, proves liberating for those less confident with oral or inscribed storytelling.

What the iMovie app interface loses in functionality (as compared with the full desktop version), it gains in tactility, mobility and intuitive design. In terms of creative process, the resultant work is close to the hand-wrought in the mode of craft—a different mode from the offices of the hand-written. Pinching, reverse-pinching, dragging, splitting, splicing, cutting, trimming, pressing, moving and (double) tapping in sequences of iterative actions, signal a new dynamic lexicon in relation to literacy, where linear typographic codes cede ground to craft modes. The properties of the hand and eye are more directly connected to the symbolic material than they might be through the mediation of a mouse. Not only this but the accessibility and wireless mobility of the tablet could start to displace assumed power relations in the classroom, as widely accepted pedagogic modelling and positioning is disrupted in favour of clustered creative practice.

Critical and Hybrid Pedagogy

These student teachers appeared to be practising a form of rigourless play with no clear assessable success criteria; but by overlaying Reid's analogy comparing first film efforts to young learners' first poems, seemingly trivial media exercises become politically potent. Learners act in self-directed ways, assume responsibility for cultural production and then evaluate their achievements based on their own cultural repertoires. This book argues that the earlier these processes are modelled in Initial Teacher Training (ITT) programmes, the more familiar learners become with the critical, creative and personally-involving (co-)construction of texts, and the less reliant they feel on gaining mastery over always-already scripted content.

I interviewed a group of student teachers at the end of the morning after working with Year 7 students, and they found the experience beneficial in a variety of ways. For example, one student overcame feelings of inadequacy related to digital editing—not being "a huge technology person". Another was surprised that the pupils had not used the app before but they "cottoned on quick". Both these views are arguably derivative of the binary digital immigrant/native discourse (Prensky 2001), where the myth goes that young people are perceived as adept producers and knowing masters of the mystical digital, while adults remain bemused bystanders. Happily these misplaced technological and generational determinist views (Selwyn 2009) were unsettled through the Film in a Morning process.

A more confident student teacher found the morning useful at the level of her practice. She questioned whether it was acceptable for teachers to encourage reflexivity in her pupils with regard to improving their media outputs. I found myself puzzled, re-phrasing her question thinking she must be asking how rather than if it was possible:

Available at: https://soundcloud.com/shelleuk/phd-thesis-interview-ioe-student-teachers-film-in-a-morning1/s-6R82a#t=06:25 *[Accessed: 7 February 2018]*

Sarah:	Would you push the kids to improve upon what they'd done? What do you think?
Michelle:	[Do you mean:] How do you do that?
Sarah:	Well I mean, have you seen it done? Should it…? Is…? Cos more the point of this session was very exploratory…. But should it be, maybe at a later point more critical? You know kind of like critical and reflective. Was that strong? Why wasn't it that strong?

Available at: https://soundcloud.com/shelleuk/phd-thesis-interview-ioe-student-teachers-film-in-a-morning1/s-6R82a#t=07:03 *[Accessed: 7 February 2018]*]

Sarah:	It can be hard for kids though to know why something works and something doesn't and like, you kind of have to ask the right questions. Erm … but I don't… It's not some-

thing I've done a lot. It's something that I need to work on in Drama.

Liz: It's like leading without leading

(Interview with student teachers after the Film in a Morning activity, 2014)

The issue of if and how to encourage the revision of media texts echoes Eisner's invocation (2005/2002) to practise the art of "aesthetic judgement made in the absence of rule". According to Eisner, exercising the kinds of wisdom that go beyond the ratiocinative is crucial to the educational experience. Youth media production can occupy this ambiguous territory, as a function of the popular cultural stock from which material is often drawn, and the generous rule-resistant nature of audiovisual assembly. At the end of the exercise it seems Sarah was searching for the criteria for success herself, on behalf of her pupils, and perhaps needed more support on how to invite and convey media-making critique in mentor-like ways. There is a sense in which meanings inhere in the moments before learning, hence the value of post-production reflection.

It is laudable that Sarah be raising meta-thinking as an important part of media education, but lamentable that she should have to question its validity, suggesting that Film in a Morning apart, compliance with the teaching of content and how to deliver it, is still the dominant pedagogic model in ITT. This said, it did seem that even after this short DV editing exercise, the teachers were edging towards a more nuanced pedagogy that might incite learners to collaborate and take ownership of their own improvement—an engagement more likely to happen in a climate of trust and open-ended experimentation.

It could be that in addition to the inherent benefits of film and media-making for which I have been arguing, these activities have a utility as tools to ignite independent critical thinking, across the subject ranks of ITT, even at this early stage of their career (McIntyre and Jones 2014). If self-reflexive questioning is recognised as an important attribute of the modern pedagogue, then modelling this skill so that students are encouraged to critique their own and others' work constructively and publicly emerges as a salient facet of literacy. This approach advances evaluation beyond what can often be tokenistic peer-to-peer reviewing of texts.

Over the course of my research with children I have found that asking them tangentially about their learning rather than the more pointed what they think they are learning, is more fruitful. To round off this setting, I present an interview that demonstrates this technique, whilst reinforcing the value of children's oral and reflective commentary in acts of literacy.

Contextual Interpretation: Film in a Morning

Formal Frustration

As a wide ranging question that can invite eclectic and intimate responses, I often ask my research participants about aspects of their practical media work that may have surprised them in some way, either in relation to themselves or in relation to external phenomena. In conversation with two Year 7 boys some two weeks after completion of their magic realist text, Isaac replied with: "I was surprised that we thought about it so quickly",[16] suggesting that he may not have been used to acting impulsively in a creative setting. Turning fantastical ideas into embodied action and inscribing them digitally, all in the space of an hour, was an empowering and refreshing change that interrupted their more procedural daily routines.

On further questioning about the editing process, Isaac revealed metacognitive insights about his media composition work:

Available at: https://soundcloud.com/shelleuk/phd-thesis-interview-year7s-film-in-a-morning/s-AszEh#t=02:45 [Accessed: 7 February 2018]

Michelle:	Yeah. It does take ages, doesn't it? editing… And you've got… (pause) What do you think you've got to be, if you're … if you're editing?
Isaac:	You have to be focussed and … um … permitted to do it
Michelle:	Permitted to do it
Daniel:	And relaxed
Michelle:	And relaxed. And what was that first thing you said?

---

[16] This interview extract and some of the observations appear in a joint article written about the project by myself, Bryer et al. (2014), for the Media Education Research Journal).

Isaac:	Focussed
Michelle:	Focussed, right yeah. I like this word … I like the idea of you thinking you need permission, that's interesting. Can you talk a bit more about that?
Isaac:	That you can't just do anything, without …well… you can't just do anything that you … (pause)
Michelle:	… that you feel like
Isaac:	Yeah, that you feel like. It has to be appropriate and (that…)
Michelle:	Yeah. OK. Alright. So you're talking about following certain rules? Maybe? Are you? I'm not quite sure … when you say permitted do you mean, you're given the permission to do it by a teacher or do you mean something else?
Isaac:	Like, not permission but…
Michelle:	Erm, I think I know what you mean. Erm, (pause)
Isaac:	Like, we want to do it.
Michelle:	Yeah. Yeah. You're allowed to just use your imagination, maybe? Is that what you mean? Just given a bit of freedom? Could you talk a bit more about that? Just kind of … doing
Isaac:	Like imagination … you can think about anything you like, and dream about anything you like and no-one can stop you from doing that, so … it's a bit like that … the freedom to think about whatever er … you like … and then (pause) and then it's just, it's the same like that because we use our imagination to think about the story, so … we like freedom to, erm to think about what we like.

(Interview with Year 7 students, 2014)

Isaac chose two adjectives to describe the states conducive to good DV editing, being—"focused" and "permitted"; the former relates to his cognitive engagement (commonly associated with editing), the latter to an impersonal warrant from some external authority. A permitted state springs to his consciousness rather than any unfettered state. Arguably, needing permission is indicative of the disruptive unconventionality of the project, and the extent to which institutionalised young learners have internalised school rules. Daniel's contribution with respect to being "relaxed", may indicate how the social nature of media composition practices worked for him, especially as they involved collaborating with stranger-adults who willingly reciprocated ideas and shared a certain parity of skills, knowledge and enthusiasm.

The extract hinges on Isaac's quietly emphatic "we want to do it", the implication being that they are routinely denied opportunities for free reign creative production; even more so in today's climate of academic credentialising and the de-privileging of the arts. There is a certain melancholy in Isaac's claim, in so far as he and his peers do in fact buy into this kind of work. Although grateful for the experience, they lament the mere glimpse of a social practice of direct relevance to their world beyond the confines of the school. I phrased it thus in a related article:

> If indeed Isaac did use the word 'permission' in relation to being authorised to 'dream' (as, in the interests of transparency, I am aware that he may have been influenced by my enthusiasm to interpret it as such), then schools might question the wisdom of current instrumental curricular regimes. Isaac experienced a liberating, if wistful, shift in orientation, an ontological adjustment in a supported environment where the boys' own cultural capital was shaped, shared and collectively valued.
>
> (Cannon et al. 2014, p. 29)

It has to be recognised that replicating this activity and its impact in mainstream classrooms in the format just recounted—that is, densely populated with facilitators, hardware and enthusiastic adults asking secondary questions—is unrealistic. Be that as it may, the rich outcomes are indicative of a pupil-teacher relationship that blurs traditional roles, and exposes dispositions open to both creative collusion and improvisation that pivot around questions prefaced by "What if" imaginings (Liu and Noppe-Brandon 2009).

The final case study is set in the same school and engages with the tensions inherent in one department's valorising and implementing of formal moving image literacy, whilst complying with largely analogue statutory demands and centralised accountability procedures. It demonstrates how multimodal communicative infrastructures and a pedagogy committed to both the digital and the analogue, combine to form a rare productive tension in the ecotonal margins of mainstream education.

Setting 4: Riverside School—English and Drama Department

I had originally thought that this fourth study would follow a formal Year 7 English class as it progressed through a project incorporating media production. However, after observing the English and Drama teacher and his innovative teaching methods, I moved the focus away from the students and their engagements with media, to the progressive practices of Mr. C., Head of English and Drama. I believe the formal pedagogy that he enacted indicates ways forward not only for English teaching, but for practices across the curriculum. Mr. C. incorporated: digital, visual and moving image literacy; DV production with mobile technologies; blogging; and the use of an open-source social media platform—as routine interacting elements within the ecology of the classroom and department.

At the heart of the department was an open source online digital platform, functioning as a teaching, learning and communication hub. The Wordpress platform, created and maintained by Mr. C., was accessed by all department staff, students of English and their families. Programmes of work, lesson plans, resources, homework, reflections, feedback, blog posts and other digital outputs were moderated and published on a daily basis. The pupils no longer exclusively wrote in books and could choose to make their online work private or open to the public.[17] It was thus as paperless an environment as could be manufactured in a school setting, with few resources beyond a set of iPads. At the same time as developing a pioneering approach to teaching, learning and formative assessment (Black and Wiliam 1998), the department ran parallel 'OFSTED-friendly' analogue classroom practices and achieved above average results within the regular structures. For context, at the time of writing, despite the English department's successes, the school as a whole was having fre-

---

[17] Despite being publicly accessible, divulging the website address would identify the school, and issues of ethics prevent me from doing this. It does seem at odds with the department's generous ethos of transparency, as Mr. C. was happy to be identified. However, I opt to retain the school's, the pupils' and the teachers' anonymity, especially as the previous study is implicated. Issues of privacy and consent in openly networked school environments point to a possible future schism in orthodox educational research, possibly provoking a shift towards more flexible practices.

quent OFSTED inspections as a result of its Requires Improvement status.

An ethos of transparency permeated the running of the department, in which agentive digital making was a quotidian, un-simulated social practice. My research relates to Mr. C.'s enterprise in terms of how it was able to generate a pedagogic climate of collective buy-in, through strategies of openness, trust and dialogue with its constituents; that is, it aspired to creating a community of practice (Lave and Wenger 1991) amongst staff, pupils and parents.

This relates to my research questions with respect to the enactment of open pedagogic practices that incorporate dialogic ways of being, varied and inclusive modes of communication, mobile and social media technologies, and a commitment to the development of a critical consciousness. By way of illustration teachers organised the content of their pupils' termly work thematically so that the boys engaged in a holistic project incorporating a range of textual production. More importantly, parents and pupils were offered the opportunity to collaborate on the design of these learning units, with the boys ultimately choosing (and committing to) which approach (and therefore which teacher) appealed to them. All the units were published on the online platform and the boys' written and audiovisual work, was viewable and open for peer review. These were some of the more democratic pedagogies that characterised Riverside, constituting an appropriate environment in which to study teaching and learning practices that embrace the affordances of digital media production and that were cognisant of influences external to the school. In an interview Mr. C. acknowledged the somewhat subversive 'under the radar' edge to his practice which will be explored later in the Chapter.

Andrew Burn and colleagues are familiar with Riverside's practices and their summary below lays out the implications for pedagogies with digital making in the formal school sector and beyond:

> [This] head of English is fully aware of the ways in which the lines between director and enabler become blurred. In this context it seems that pedagogy is founded on a belief in agency and activity as well as an understanding of the wider lives of learners and of the media and cultural landscape. In a busy urban school this individual engages in flexible working practices

which engage and involve learners and makes a point of building personal networks on social media and through TeachMeets which move across the boundaries between home and school and which sustain innovation in the context of a wider performative culture.

(Burn et al. 2014, p. 10)

Mr. C. brings to the department an alternative pedagogic vision imported from his native New Zealand (NZ). In 2007 and after a lengthy and inclusive governmental review over several years, a new NZ curriculum[18] was formulated, a set of reforms on which Mr. C. had collaborated. This future-facing curriculum embraced the digital, and was cognisant of the well-being of the individual and their productive and participative stake in society. From my observations, this seemed to be the ethos that drove Riverside School's English and Drama department. Their practices presaged the ways in which formal arrangements could both harness the existing informally acquired digital skills and interests of many young people, and identify those in need of more support.

After some initial rudimentary classroom observations in prior months, I observed three Year 7 classes over one week, taking note of interactions between Mr. C. and his pupils. I had recognised by that stage in my research that in terms of examining the literacy implications of practices involving media composition, new pedagogies were integral to the success of these practices. Without a critical investigation of a potential model of confident modern pedagogy, there would have been something missing from my research efforts with respect to the necessary climate in which these alternative practices are given a chance to flourish.

Being more distanced in my approach within this setting, and staying with insights without distraction, allowed me to witness activities that constituted a playful merging of school-not-school life-worlds (Sefton-Green 2013). In the actual practice of fieldwork, I occupied the role of Denzin's "intimate public journalist" (2001) and Jones' "collage-maker" (2006), such was the intertextual richness of these particular research encounters. I examine a pupil's drawing, photos taken during a moving

---

[18] Available at: http://nzcurriculum.tki.org.nz/The-New-Zealand-Curriculum [Accessed: 7 February 2018].

image exercise with iPads, extracts from an interview with Mr. C., and a video interview with Year 7s. This is with a view to exploring how digital media production was integrated into a programme of English study that focussed on the development of *critical textual response*. I do not intend to outline the programme nor the resultant texts, I focus on processes related to literacy conceived as producing meanings in a variety of modes, which are in active, material and digital dialogue with the environment.

Preparation for Praxis and Critical Thinking

The week prior to my visit the boys were introduced to various shot types that constitute basic film grammar. For example, they were challenged to draw storyboard frames that represented the scenario illustrated in Fig. 5.1 from different angles, positions and perspectives. These included: the establishing shot, the (extreme) close-up, the mid shot, the wide shot, the bird's eye view, the over-the-shoulder shot, shots taken at high, low or skewed angles, or from different people's point of view.

According to Mr. C., simple drawing exercises based on film language usefully set up hands-on audiovisual production activities related to theories on the construction of film narrative. In a few lessons time, having watched and analysed a specific short film[19] and had practice at enacting their own directorial choices, the boys were to create a more considered filmed response, using a range of techniques aimed at developing their overall critical and creative textual understanding. Mr. C. proposes that the stage of making, translates abstract concepts in concrete ways which relate to thought processes that can be re-applied in other media such as writing. Their drawings arguably illustrate a latent knowledge of filmic techniques used for specific dramatic and narrative effects, as the example in Fig. 5.2 demonstrates. The child has chosen to illustrate the extreme close-up, and in doing so demonstrates a dramatic cinematic technique, that draws audiences into the minutiae and drama of a given moment.

---

[19] The NZ film in question was Two Cars One Night (2004) which was nominated for an Oscar in 2005 for Best Short. It follows an encounter between a young Maori girl and boy waiting in a car park. Available here: https://www.youtube.com/watch?v=R6Pc6cBP-8U [Accessed: 7 February 2018].

Fig. 5.1 Board capture of stimulus for studying camera shots and angles

According to Cousins (2012, p. 31), the invention of the close-up is one of film's unique visual affordances (as distinct from the constant distance that theatrical audiences maintain), whose intimacy and emphasis seize our imagination, as was the case for Clip Club's Clara. The eye in Fig. 5.2, bounded by the frame, radiates narrative rendered by the artist's aesthetic attention to: colour, shape, line, positioning, cropping, mood, perspective, proportion, texture and geometry. Particularly evocative is the clarity and contrast of the black outline and pupil, the dark brown skin, the blue iris encircled with the jagged blood-shot white of the eye, the short lower lashes and the smudged dark circles that complement the eye's weary half-closed state. Notably, unlike the contours of the lid, defined with care, the shading under the eye smudges over the edges of the frame, connoting tired limp movement—an excess or perhaps an absence of emotion.

The image interpellates the viewer with a direct gaze and its detail poses questions about possible fictional narratives. It could be that filmic approaches to literacy offer direct pathways to understanding inference,

Fig. 5.2 Extreme close-up shot of an eye, drawn by a Year 7 pupil

perspective, mood, context and critical interpretation, in ways that are more personally relevant than those spoon-fed by the teacher. A point made by Mr. C. in my interview with him:

Available at https://soundcloud.com/shelleuk/phd-interview-mr-c-river-side-school/s-OSuBH#t=39:38 [Accessed: 7 February 2018]
So instead of me showing them a film and then telling them how to respond to it critically, and what valid critical responses would be, and then asking them to reproduce what I've said in their own writing, as a film criticism, or a film review, they are being asked instead to look at aspects of the film that they find interesting or that they have thought to be successful, and to reproduce those in their own process of film-making. So that they can explore what the director's role is in making a film, so that then when they are ultimately asked to respond to the film, and the director's decisions within the film, they'll do it from a place of knowing as opposed to a place of being told. So they will be able to, I hope, come up with both more sophisticated and also more authentic responses to the original text, and they'll be able to talk with a sort of sophistication that I need them to, but about the things that they see rather than the things that I tell them are there … this is the exploration, learning phase.
(Interview with Mr. C., 2014)

In Mr. C.'s class a drawing is as valued as other forms of response in terms of what it reveals about the pupil's visual literacy and can be built on with collective feedback, more watching and more practical outputs:

Available at: https://soundcloud.com/shelleuk/phd-interview-mr-c-river-side-school/s-OSuBH#t=0:31 [Accessed: 7 February 2018]
... viewing and making is actually a very parallel process to reading and writing, so you teach them in a literature class ... you can teach them in the same ways, and you can use the benefits of one in the domain of the other...

Available at: https://soundcloud.com/shelleuk/phd-interview-mr-c-river-side-school/s-OSuBH#t=2:52 [Accessed: 7 February 2018]
... they're going to ultimately create a film that demonstrates an appreciation for those skills and techniques, and they'll also write about the original film, where they reflect on how the film-maker did this. So it's not radical at all, it's completely within the domain—it's entirely within the domain of English learning in secondary school, the work they're doing. You know, it's not a deviation or a holiday from it.
(Interview with Mr. C., 2014)

Mr. C. is conscious of the status of film and moving image in the UK education system, hence his reference to it as a perceived holiday, and maintains a pragmatic stance on its use. He employs whatever means necessary to help cultivate the capacity to be critical.

In the New Zealand curriculum there is parity between reading and writing, and viewing and making; they are regarded as separate but interacting communicative means. As such, he is a confident negotiator within these domains, relatively free from the dogma of hierarchical cultural value that often stifles claims on the benefits of practical media work in the UK. As revealed in the Film in a Morning study, critical understanding of film and moving image has yet to establish itself in UK ITT programmes, marking out creative and bold forms of critical pedagogic practice as the realm of the outlier.

Practitioner Insight: Pedagogy Porous to the Popular and the Public

Mr. C.'s boys were given an opportunity to respond to the drawing task in a visual and personal way. The young artist who drew the eye (Fig. 5.2) may have imagined himself as the figure standing in front of the truck (Fig. 5.1)—his zombie self—which may explain the macabre detailing. For many boys at the rudimentary stages of film production, action or horror movies are rarely far from their sphere of influence, and scenes of bullying and violence loom invariably large in early autonomous production work.[20] Nevertheless, valuing and building on this knowledge of popular cultural references, and then framing them in critical ways, rather than dismissing them, is a useful and accessible starting point for further development in the English curriculum.

One of the ways that such development can take place is through ongoing, online peer assessment. Once equipped with the basic typologies and formulae of film language and visual critique, the boys were able to display their newfound knowledge on their personal online journals. Their work was thereby available for collective feedback, that is to say, the reviewing of posts was not the exclusive task of the class teacher, but an authentic self-selecting social practice by a range of external interested parties. This helped the boys keep track of their learning and make responsible choices about what they wished to publish and how to present it. Although the virtual dissemination of material on a blog does not guarantee an audience, it bears witness to a personally relevant body of work tied to its author. In other words, it is not separate and distant like last year's discarded exercise books or past exam papers, but forms part of an ongoing digital identity, where progress pertinent to the learner is preserved and 'conversations' are pursued.

---

[20] See Bazalgette and Staples (1995), for further discussion on the Hollywood 'cultural imperialism' that dominates children's and 'family' films on offer, and that my study suggests heavily influences young people's initial efforts at production.

Making Meaning Between a Rock and a Hard Place

After the drawing stage, Mr. C. had students do photographic and/or short moving image exercises with iPads, practising shot types that might, for example, metaphorically express a concept, such as loss or regret. One particular boy, Simeon, caught my attention, as he found it difficult to sit still and concentrate in class. Even as the short film played and most of the class were wrapped in attention, he was fiddling with his bag and making a paper plane. I saw him in the playground and took a shot of him taking a photo. This photo has a similar resonance to that of Clone Clara in the corridor taken by Clip Club's G-man, in the sense that it is freighted with symbolic as well as literal meaning. It appears to acknowledge the pull of creative media practice and the tensions that circulate around its formal implementation. I catch Simeon as he teeters on the stone base of an iron pillar to get his high angle shot. I notice his dishevelled appearance, shirt hanging out, collar awry, shoes laces undone, and then a directorial poise in the way he has chosen to snugly wedge himself between the wall and the supporting pillar, using his feet and elbows to balance and keep the camera steady. There is a marked difference between the distracted boy I noticed shifting around on his seat in class, and the boy fixedly framing a shot from a consciously selected vantage point. Could it be that he is, as Ken Robinson (2013) might describe, in his element?

The precariousness of Simeon's position seems to be noticed by an onlooking member of staff in a neighbouring class. He is the basketball coach on Teaching Assistant duty and is pictured to the left of the image looking out of the window, and wondering what was going on with the apparently unsupervised Year 7s. A scene that some might have regarded as chaotic, constituted playful engagement with the task, the environment, the iPads and each other. The TA had entered a different realm of educational activity that seemed to involve agility, intention, competence and co-operation, in other words, teamwork.

The muted grey and blue colours and the vertical and parallel lines that crisscross the photo connote institutional rigidity, within which Simeon is constrained but self-directing and agentive. His cocked leg and angle-poised body speak back to these constraints in a resistant and subversive act of creation. The off-centre, flat, grey pillar seems to dominate and splice the image in two, until we realise that it is the people who matter in this photo—they occupy the lines that compose the rule of thirds.[21] The 'punctum' (Barthes 1979) for me in this photo is Simeon's hanging shoe-lace, a limp reflection of the iron pillar, and perhaps a 'truthful' representation of his current social power beyond this media exercise.

Simeon and his partner enthusiastically practice a variety of moving and still shots for later more purposeful narrative sequencing.[22] Reminiscent of Wizard filming on the table (in Clip 3, Chap. 4), he is amassing a visual vocabulary with which to build meaning. Indeed, somewhat incongruously in terms of the aesthetic relevance of film-making discussed earlier, Mr. C. likens this process to the collection of raw materials for construction:

> Available at https://soundcloud.com/shelleuk/phd-interview-mr-c-river-side-school/s-OSuBH#t=5:28 [Accessed: 7 February 2018]
> They create an overall plan and they make, they film and record the parts, sometimes out of narrative sequence, and then they form a narrative sequence from those parts, and it's very much a building process. It's almost like engineering, structural engineering as opposed to writing which is as I said, a lot more linear.
> (Interview with Mr. C., 2014)

This book argues that the process of making is one of the key attractions of digital media manipulation for many young people. Conceptual thought, emotion, and social and environmental sensibilities can be translated into palpable chunks and slices of movable material. Clearly the utilitarian functionality of an engineering analogy has its limitations, but it serves to highlight the possible frustrations that some might feel by going in cold with abstract mono-modal writing as the primary technology with

---

[21] The principle of the rule of thirds is thought to improve the balance and composition of a shot. By placing an imaginary 9-square grid on a photo, its key elements should align along the intersecting lines.

[22] Available at https://vimeo.com/111458298 @ 00:08'–00:30' [Accessed: 7 February 2018 password = wizard].

which to express understanding. The structural as well as aesthetic dimensions of literacy activities could be grounded, from the earliest years, in the practical co-creation of audiovisual meanings.

Local Conditions of Possibility

In this section I focus on specific elements within Mr. C.'s pedagogic environment that facilitate practices with digital making, picking out relevant details in videoed interview material.[23] I asked a group of boys to talk to me about Mr. C.'s English lessons. Echoing some of Leonardo's observations, the boys make reference to the use of iPads for learning, the acquired skills that might be useful "in future life" and, notably, in this particular session involving filming, the fact of "not having to write", as if, in other contexts writing were some arduous chore. This account claims that reluctance to write is partly down to its consistent and stringent monitoring, and the prescriptive nature of what counts as good writing (Barrs and Horrocks 2014). As Nimbus acknowledged earlier, the content that they are asked to re-produce routinely fails to connect with their own interests and sensibilities.

Below I list some of the boys' comments in the video that are suggestive of a strong bond between teacher and student, and of a more relaxed and egalitarian pedagogic approach. Mr. C.'s method of building dialogic relations involves mutual respect, listening, trusting, responsibility-taking and agency:

- it's fun
- he likes our ideas
- he gives us many chances
- he's patient
- he tells us off for good reasons
- you respect him and he respects you back
- he gives us encouragement
- [media production tasks] give us ideas

---

[23] Available at https://vimeo.com/111458298 @ 03:17'–07:42' [Accessed: 7 February 2018, password = wizard].

It might be said that this is a generic list of characteristics applicable to many teachers who are popular with students. The difference in this instance is that the boys had been trusted to get on with this particular production task on their own. Mr. C. knew he would be absent that day, and having completed the groundwork, he trusted the Year 7 boys to deliver on their own creative learning—which they did—albeit within the confines of a small boat-yard-cum-playground, weighed down with bags and dressed in naval uniforms. Mr. C.'s decision to leave them to it, although the exception rather than the rule in terms of his practice, took trust, agency and responsibility to a higher level, a realisation which I myself experienced in the latter stages of the Clip Club.

Contextual Interpretation: Riverside School English and Drama Dept

From the time of the study, over the preceding three years, the school's GCSE English results had significantly improved, and my study tentatively suggests that this could correlate with an overall increase in student engagement.[24] My research data proposes that engagement is a social process, and claims on success in the educational domain are as much down to the quality of the relationship between teacher and pupil as they are to content, tools and teaching methodology. Collective doing and the pooling and respecting of ideas, build the kind of shared history on which such relationships can thrive.

Two of the bulleted points raised by the boys above stand out—those of generating and listening to ideas. Potter, an experienced primary teacher as well as academic, claims that listening to pupils' responses is a crucial element in building the necessary dialogic relationship on which effective teaching depends (Back 2013), especially concerning media projects, as most young people are experienced readers of visual texts with implicit knowledge to share, when given the opportunity. Potter notes:

---

[24] For those interested in academic progress measured in statistics, in 2013, the year that Mr. C. became Head of Department, 61% of pupils achieved A*–C in English Language GCSE; in 2014 that percentage rose to 76%, with a further increase in 2015 to 85%. Some might draw conclusions from this data, but my study is more concerned with qualitative interpretation.

Available @ https://soundcloud.com/shelleuk/john-potter/s-3P9LY#t=
21:24 [Accessed: 7 February 2018]
[teachers'] questioning has to be quite skillful and you need to be quite
skilled in your listening to what comes back. There used to be, in the curriculum for teacher education in the late 1990s and early 2000s, there used
to be a standard that teachers had to meet which was something to do with
listening to what children say and building on it. That went in 2002, quite
tellingly, as a standard. But to me that's the heart of teaching. Listen to
what people are telling you about what they know, then you know where
to take them.
(Interview with John Potter 2015)

Time that was once allocated to speaking and listening, and hence to
the potential for building relationships with pupils and for which teachers used to be accountable, is increasingly encroached upon in the name
of bureaucratic demands to cover content and produce spurious data on
school performance. Throughout my experience in schools and as a
researcher, I have come across teachers who have buckled under the pressures of complicity with forms of managerialism that are at odds with a
vocational motivation. Educational environments in which the reaping
of data is the primary objective are doomed to jar with engagement in
creative media projects, as they remain stubbornly resistant to numerical
measurement.

I quote from my interview with Mr. C. at some length to illustrate his
handling of such issues. When I first entered his classroom the pupils
were briefed that I was not an official Inspector, but an observing
researcher, an ally, who could be trusted with real information; in fact,
no-one, including Mr. C., "would get into trouble for saying the wrong
thing". My interview unearthed some trenchant comments on schools'
efforts to erect an acceptable front for the Inspectorate and the potential
deleterious effects on students:

Available at https://soundcloud.com/shelleuk/phd-interview-mr-c-river-
side-school/s-OSuBH#t=20:12 [Accessed: 7 February 2018]
I think the whole system of school assessment leads to the entire school
population erecting a façade in order to be meeting the approval of the
observer. And I think that's an absolute industry in the UK, and that

schools are judged on their capacity to effectively erect that façade as opposed to anything else. And I think that's going to create enormous ripple effects through society over time, because it's duplicity and it's institutional duplicity, and it's enforced and encouraged by the system as it is ... So you know, the kind of requirements that they have of the performance of schools leads to the schools—by absolute necessity—operating a dual system, a system for the Inspector and then the real system. And the kids are part of that, so I was just telling them to know that that stranger in the room wasn't an Inspector, so that they didn't start doing—because that would invalidate your research, because they would give you the answers they felt you wanted to hear.
(Interview with Mr. C., 2014)

Mr. C. raises an interesting point: my reading suggests that there is little in the way of research on the impact of official inspections and the potential systemic dishonesty with which many young people are ipso facto complicit. In the schools where 'institutional duplicity' operates, this might seed at best a critical perspective in pupils,—though it is more likely to generate a cynical disaffection with the system. Either way, it is at some considerable cost to pupils' overall sense of integrity.

Although recently acquired information suggests that OFSTED is warming to Riverside's approach to English, my research in 2014 saw the department resorting to secret measures:

Available at https://soundcloud.com/shelleuk/phd-interview-mr-c-riverside-school/s-OSuBH#t=18:14 [Accessed: 7 February 2018]
The things that I am doing relating to making, I do in secret. Because there's no language or process to acknowledge or value that work. But because I do believe in it being broadly valuable to the students—not just because of the experience being good in and of itself, but because it actually assists them to develop the kind of faculties that will lead to their quite conventional success ... So I don't think I'm working at odds with the system, I just don't think the system gets what it is that I think I'm doing.
(Interview with Mr. C, 2014)

The candidness with which Mr. C. speaks is in stark contrast with the stealth with which the department occasionally finds itself operating, as indeed was the case during one school-sited Film in a Morning activity. It clashed with an OFSTED inspection and the project was diverted to the basement, preferably out of sight (Cannon et al. 2014).

Overall what is revealed here is a department confident in its methods and committed to developing an inclusive, critically-oriented and digitally enabled community of practice, regardless of discursive accountability constraints. Even as it complies with the formal system, students can choose their programme of work and hence their teacher. They are given the kind of democratic responsibilities for their learning that supports engaged participating citizens, enjoying un-simulated control and equality. Mr. C. is, however, the first to recognise that such a vision is under constant review and compromises are ever present between formal procedures and these more fluid practices. In the end, with pupils' incipient critical understanding as a focus, an alternative methodology is presented here that could serve as a functioning proto-pedagogy for the integration of digital media production as a trans-disciplinary school practice.

Young Literate Media Practitioners

To conclude Chap. 5, I briefly re-visit the Clip Club, as I believe one particular movie clip gives us a glimpse of the skills and dispositions that comprise young literate media practitioners working in collaboration. Watching this clip now, in the light of the preceding three studies, offers opportunities for a multi-layered understanding. Clip 7 picks up editing activity once the green screen clips at the end of the film had been transferred to iMovie:

> *See Clip 7 https://vimeo.com/142087018 [Accessed: 7 February 2018, password = wizard]*

One of the casualties of the multitasking participant-observer is the fact of missing key events that should have been filmed. One such occasion was the moment the green screen was replaced with Wizard's blue computer backdrop (Fig. 4.1)—this is invariably a moment of substitution magic. The moment when elements of the human and the hardware merge, and meaning translates into a different realm of visual understanding is most often met with cries and gestures of delight.

The editors set to work, fixing imperfections and making decisions on how and where to cut. They notice that the creased green fabric had been imprecisely positioned and the background was uneven in terms of shading and coverage. As is often the way in an editing or design process, when faced with technical hitches, an improvisatory mode kicks in. This meant using the Cut Away effect—where the green screen clip is cut diagonally to obscure the 'error', by revealing more of the background. Fixing the problem produced yet another effect, the meaning of which is interpreted literally by Nimbus: "Oh my God, you're just going into nowhere!" then, more imaginatively by Clara: "It looks like I'm coming from a different room". At that point the effect is ratified and given narrative integrity by G-man who makes an interpretive claim on the 'mistake' with a sense of knowing disclosure: "No! make it look like diagonal because then it looks like she's going through some portal door". Nimbus, pleasantly surprised, endorses G-man's suggestion: "Oh yeah, that is actually kind of a good idea!" which, with tacit agreement, becomes integral to the ending of the film.

For many, making and agreeing meanings on the fly and taking appropriate remedial action makes digital video editing an engrossing experience. Clara appears to be enjoying a sense of creative collusion, and as was her way throughout the project she vocalises what others might only be thinking. As if cooking up some alchemy herself, she chants: "We're experimenting here people!". This simple exclamation, along with G-man's audibly satisfied: "We made a decision!" alert us to the pleasures of practical media projects: trying things out, making autonomous decisions on meaning and being open to serendipity. Feeling such authorial empowerment has to do with praxis: the translation of abstractions into a palpable modality that in turn transmutes into material action. The joint vision of a story to be told had existed darkly in their imaginations in the weeks prior, but had finally materialised in the viewer.

Presenting Chaps. 4 and 5 has felt like a sinewy odyssey, where temporal interpretations of participants' words, actions and artefacts, have been harbouring in the different dimensions of my interpretive model (Fig. 3.1). As the data churned, changing volume and shape within my imagined elastic Möbius strip, certain key findings emerged. One of these was the way in which media production offers a sense of control over one's learning, if enabled in a supportive and authorising environment. These and many of the other insights that have been garnered over the course of this study will be interrogated further in Chap. 6, once more making use of Fig. 3.1 as a framework for discussion.

Bibliography

Back, L. (2013). *The Art of Listening*. London: Bloomsbury Academic.

Barrs, M., & Horrocks, S. (2014). *Educational Blogs and Their Effects on Pupils' Writing*. CFBT (Centre for British Teachers) & LCLC (London Connected Learning Centre).

Barthes, R. (1979). *Camera Lucida: Reflections on Photography*. London: Vintage.

Bazalgette, C. (2012). *Key Findings of the Persistence of Vision: Animation and Poetry Project* [online]. Retrieved February 7, 2018, from http://www.themea. org.uk/archive/persistence-of-visionanimation-and-poetry-in-primary-schools/.

Bazalgette, C., & Staples, T. (1995). Unshrinking the kids: Children's cinema and the family film. In C. Bazalgette & D. Buckingham (Eds.), *In Front of the Children: Screen Entertainment and Young Audiences* (pp. 92–108). London: British Film Institute.

Belshaw, D. (2012). *What is Digital Literacy? A Pragmatic Investigation* [online]. PhD Thesis, Durham University, Durham. Retrieved February 7, 2018, from http://neverendingthesis.com.

Bergala, A. (2002). *L'hypothèse cinéma. Petit traité de transmission du cinéma à l'école et ailleurs*. Paris: Cahiers du cinéma.

Bergala, A., Whittle, M., & Bachmann, A. (2016). *The Cinema Hypothesis— Teaching Cinema in the Classroom and Beyond*. Vienna: Austrian Film Institute.

Bhabha, H. K. (1994). *The Location of Culture*. London: Routledge.

Black, P., & Wiliam, D. (1998). Inside the black box: Raising standards through classroom assessment [online]. *Phi Delta Kappan, 80*, 139–148. Retrieved February 7, 2018, from http://weaeducation.typepad.co.uk/files/blackbox-1. pdf.

Bourdieu, P. (1984). *Distinction: A Social Critique of the Judgement of Taste*. London: Routledge.

Bryer, T., Lindsay, M., & Wilson, R. (2014). A take on a Gothic poem: Tablet film-making and literary texts. *Changing English: Studies in Culture and Education, 21*(3), 235–251.

Burn, A., Potter, J., & Reid, M. (2014). Media arts, digital culture and education—Guest editorial [online]. *Media Education Research Journal, 5*(1), 5–14. Retrieved February 7, 2018, from http://merj.info/wp-content/uploads/2014/11/MERJ_5.1_Introduction.pdf.

Burnett, C. (2011a). The (im)materiality of educational space: Interactions between material, connected and textual dimensions of networked technology use in schools. *E-Learning and Digital Media, 8*(3), 214.

Burnett, C. (2011b). Shifting multiple spaces in classrooms: An argument for investigating learners' boundary-making around digital networked texts [online]. *Journal of Literacy and Technology, 12*(3). Retrieved February 7, 2018, from http://www.literacyandtechnology.org/uploads/1/3/6/8/136889/jlt_v12_3_burnett.pdf.

Burnett, C., Merchant, G., Pahl, K., & Rowsell, J. (2012). The (im)materiality of literacy: The significance of subjectivity to new literacies research. *Discourse: Studies in the Cultural Politics of Education, 35*(1), 90–103.

Cannon, M., Bryer, T., & Lindsey, M. (2014). Media production and disruptive innovation: Exploring the interrelations between children, tablets, teachers and texts in subject English settings. *Media Education Research Journal, 5*(1), 16–31.

Cousins, M. (2012). *The Story of Film*. London: Pavilion Books.

Denzin, N. K. (2001). *Interpretive Interactionism* (2nd ed.). London: Sage.

Dewey, J. (1997/1938). *Experience and Education*. New York: Touchstone.

Eisner, E. (2005/1993). Forms of understanding and the future of educational research. In E. Eisner (Ed.), *Reimagining Schools* (pp. 150–162). Abingdon: Routledge.

ESRO. (2015). *Children's Media Lives* [online]. London. Retrieved February 7, 2018, from http://stakeholders.ofcom.org.uk/binaries/research/media-literacy/childrens-media-lives-year-1/childrens_media_lives_report_FINAL1.pdf.

FLAG (Film Literacy Advisory Group). (2015). *A Framework for Film Education* [online]. London: British Film Institute. Retrieved February 7, 2018, from http://www.bfi.org.uk/sites/bfi.org.uk/files/downloads/ bfi-a-framework-for-film-education-brochure-2015-06-12.pdf.

Gee, J. P. (2011/1990). *Social Linguistics and Literacies: Ideology in Discourses*. Abingdon: Routledge.

Gutiérrez, K. D. (2008). Developing a sociocritical literacy in the third space. *Reading Research Quarterly, 43*(2), 148–164.

Jones, K. (2006). A Biographic researcher in pursuit of an aesthetic: The use of arts-based (re)presentations in 'performative' dissemination of life stories [online]. *Qualitative Sociology Review, 2*(1), 66–85. Retrieved February 7, 2018, from http://www.qualitativesociologyreview.org/ENG/Volume3/QSR_2_1_Jones.pdf.

Lanham, R. A. (1994). *The Electronic Word: Democracy, Technology, and the Arts.* Chicago: University of Chicago Press.

Lave, J., & Wenger, E. (1991). *Situated Learning: Legitimate Peripheral Participation.* Cambridge, UK: Cambridge University Press.

Liu, E., & Noppe-Brandon, S. (2009). *Imagination First: Unlocking the Power of Possibility.* San Francisco, CA: John Wiley & Sons.

Martin, A. (2006). A European framework for digital literacy [online]. *Nordic Journal of Digital Literacy, 1*(2), 151–161. Retrieved February 7, 2018, from http://www.idunn.no/dk/2006/02/a_european_framework_for_digital_literacy.

McIntyre, J., & Jones, S. (2014). Possibility in impossibility? Working with beginning teachers of english in times of change. *English in Education, 48*(1), 26–40.

McKee, H. (2005). Richard Lanham's the electronic word and AT/THROUGH oscillations [online]. *Pedagogy: Critical Approaches to Teaching Literature, Language, Composition, and Culture, 5*(1), 117–129. Retrieved February 7, 2018, from http://www.users.miamioh.edu/mckeeha/lanham_review.pdf.

Mee, J., & Gittings, R. (2002). *John Keats: Selected Letters (Oxford World's Classics).* Oxford: Oxford University Press.

OFSTED, Office for Standards in Education. (2012). *Changes to Education Inspections Announced* [online]. Retrieved February 7, 2018, from https://www.gov.uk/government/news/changes-to-education-inspections-announced.

Pendleton-Jullian, A. (2009). *Design Education and Innovation Ecotones* [online]. Retrieved February 7, 2018, from https://fourplusone.files.wordpress.com/2010/03/apj_paper_14.pdf.

Potter, J. (2011). New literacies, new practices and learner research: Across the semi-permeable membrane between home and school. *Lifelong Learning in Europe, 16*(3), 174–181.

Potter, J. (2015). *Forward to the New Age of STEAM(M)! Digital Media, Education and Computing* [online]. Media Literacy, Learning and Curating. Retrieved

February 7, 2018, from http://digitalcurationandlearning.com/2015/02/25/ forward-to-the-new-age-of-steamm-digital-media-education-and-computing/.

Potter, J., & McDougall, J. (2017). *Digital Media, Culture and Education: Theorising Third Space Literacies.* London: Palgrave Macmillan.

Prensky, M. (2001). Digital natives, digital immigrants part 1. *On the Horizon, 9*(5), 1–6.

Reid, M. (2014). Film, literacy and cultural participation. In S. Brindley & B. Marshall (Eds.), *Master Class in English Education: Transforming Teaching and Learning* (pp. 84–98). London: Bloomsbury.

Robinson, K. (2013). *Finding Your Element: How to Discover Your Talents and Passions and Transform Your Life.* London: Allen Lane.

Rushdie, S. (1990). *Haroun and the Sea of Stories.* London: Puffin/Penguin.

Scott, D., & Usher, R. (2011). *Researching Education: Data, Methods and Theory in Educational Inquiry* (2nd ed.). London: Continuum.

Sefton-Green, J. (2013). *Learning at Not-School: A Review of Study, Theory, and Advocacy for Education in Non-formal Settings.* The John D. and Catherine T. MacArthur Foundation Reports on Digital Media and Learning. Cambridge, MA: MIT & MITE.

Selwyn, N. (2009). The digital native—Myth and reality. *Aslib Proceedings, 61*(4), 364–379.

Two Cars, One Night. (2004) [online]. Short film. Directed by T. Waititi. New Zealand: Defender Films Ltd. Retrieved February 7, 2018, from https:// www.youtube.com/watch?v=R6Pc6cBP-8U.

6

Five Dimensions of Critical and Creative Media Practice

Over the course of this book I have adhered to five core principles that have functioned as a series of interconnecting vertebrae in the backbone of the work. I adapted a framework related to the evaluation of narrative in action research (Heikkinen et al. 2007), whose components chimed with my practice as a researcher and as a creative media practitioner. I developed these conceptual tools—workability, reflexivity, dialectics, evocativeness (everyday artistry), and historical continuity—into a model of values that guided interpretation of my research material. I now use these tools to ground a discussion on the suggested relationships between moving image literacy pedagogies, creative media composition and the local and wider contexts of practices in this realm. As a reminder, the ensuing sections engage with the following questions:

How does creative media work constitute a wider literacy in formal and non-formal school spaces?
What can established pedagogy learn from moving image production processes?
How do social discursive factors determine practical media work in schools?

© The Author(s) 2018
M. Cannon, *Digital Media in Education*,
https://doi.org/10.1007/978-3-319-78304-8_6

To help organise the discussion of these questions, arguments will be presented under five headings that relate emergent themes from my findings to each core principle. Choosing to structure sections in this way does not preclude the potential for material to overlap and cross-pollinate, indeed, hybridity is woven into the fabric of the discussion. The sections are entitled:

1. Iterative Practical Experiences (workability)
2. Disposition for Praxis (reflexivity)
3. Disposition for Reciprocal Communication (dialectics)
4. Rightness of Fit (everyday artistry)
5. Spaces of Translation (historical continuity)

Firstly, I look at the ways in which media-making practices re-orient the teacher's identity as less the one who knows and more the one who navigates, guides and coaxes participation. I explain how these flattened, agentic relations are made possible through the tangible meaning-making affordances of digital media, and how recursive practice at producing and consuming moving image texts is as vital to non-verbal forms of literacy as reading and writing are to the verbal.

Iterative Practical Experiences

Literacy, Pedagogy and Non-linearity

From workability, I developed the notion of (digital) phronesis—a pragmatic sense linked with intuitive 'wisdom'—which is called upon in moments of experimental engagement with digital tools and with the learning environment. My research explores the benefits of repeated opportunities to engage with digital and material resources in 'more than linear', iterative ways in order to experience the drafting and re-drafting of texts, and the display and open discussion of meanings. The phronetic element in media production, understood here as the dynamic strand of literacy missing from currently restricted conceptualisations, embeds agile and transmedia technical competences (as well as linguistic) into a portfolio of skills, for participation in the human conversation. Equally, limber and versatile responses of the teacher facilitate development of these types of skills and dispositions.[1] As recognised by Potter (2012, p. 21), the pairing of new literacies with new pedagogies was mooted two decades ago:

> If it were possible to define generally the mission of education, one could say that its fundamental purpose is to ensure that all students benefit from learning in ways that allow them to participate fully in public, community, and economic life. Literacy pedagogy is expected to play a particularly importance role in fulfilling this mission.
> (New London Group 1996, p. 60)

The democratising influence of digital classroom practices has made these civic aspirations more feasible, however it appears that it is down to the knowledge and commitment of enthusiasts at school level to make this form of literacy a reality (Waugh 2016).

Figure 6.1, as well as being a timely reminder of the theoretical context of this discussion, traces the winding path of production processes, stewarded by teachers versed in the nature and function of media ecologies. Quadrant 3 is the site where assimilated cultural material is re-composed, and then re-distributed as new workable forms of knowledge, via 'literacy events' (Kendall and McDougall 2013; Potter 2012). The nature of the events might be virtual, such as blogging (Barrs and Horrocks 2014) and posting to YouTube, or physical exhibitions such as the CCADJ/Clip Club public screenings.

Such participatory knowledge-making practices (Rorabaugh 2012) are itinerant but purposeful in nature, and participants are conceived as meandering through virtual and physical production spaces (as evoked

---

[1] Designer and architect Pendleton-Jullian (2009) elaborated the metaphor of the 'sailboat' versus the 'kayak' to explain modern approaches to pedagogy and the need for nimble responses to innovatory practices, the one terrain necessitating: control and foresight—"setting sail and tacking with the wind and currents to keep on course" (2009, p. 7); the other, the navigation of complex 'white water' topologies and "highly developed disciplinary expertise (musculature) and creative dexterity. The imagination is the undercurrent for this creative dexterity, and it fuels movement forward at a steady pace and as bursts of adrenalin." (2009, p. 8)

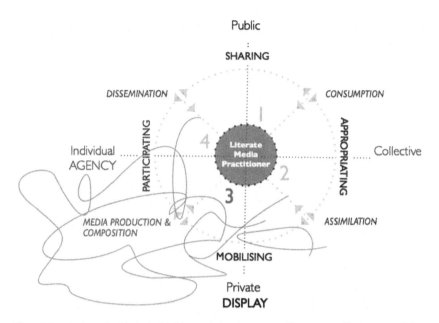

Fig. 6.1 Cycle of Digital Making—iterative, non-linear media composition processes

by the wavy line in Fig. 6.1), alternately experimenting and re-grouping (Dezuanni 2014). In previous Chapters, we witnessed certain young participants' inconsistent focus, where attention was sometimes diverted, re-calibrated and drawn back on course (not unlike a deliberately bifurcating camera movement). This negotiating of blind alleys and re-tracing of steps are commonplace occurrences in media composition, and modern pedagogues might more frequently be called upon to marshal nomadic learners, and to become attuned to their personal creative processes and popular cultural preferences.

Theorising Meaning-Making in Media Composition

Beyond the teacher, a more abstract binding agent that keeps learners motivated and on track could issue from the 'oscillatory processes' (Lanham 1994; McKee 2005) and the anthropologically derived notion of 'symbolic behaviour' mentioned in Chap. 2 (A. Reid 2007, p. 25). In this view, early forms of human representation and the superior wielding of symbolic language, are linked to the development of consciousness and social hierarchies, respectively. A. Reid speculates that the externalisation of early man's abstract thought conferred communicative and competitive advantage. As conceded earlier, this book is by no means a socio-anthropological tract, I merely wish to make an association between this evolutionary theory and Lanham's (1994) ideas on the anatomy of meaning-making.

I am reminded of a moment at the end of Chap. 5, in the video clip featuring four Clip Clubbers at the editing interface, where Nimbus is trying to fix a visual anomaly and G-man suggests leaving it as it is because that way Clone Clara "looks like she is coming through a diagonal portal."[2] This was an entirely appropriate and credible shift in thinking, drawing on a popular sci-fi motif. It is also the kind of imaginative or intuitive leap (Sennett 2008, p. 211) that can be brought about by looking AT (or INTERACTING with) the stylistic surface of a multimodal text and THROUGH to possible meanings. G-man's metaphorical re-working of the visual was collectively accepted, the production 'mistake' was re-interpreted, and a re-imagined version of the narrative put in its place. In other words, his 'decorous trickery'[3] was tacitly approved (Lanham 1994, p. 81).

Chapter 2 spoke of the 'decorous trickery' involved in aesthetic textual assembly for specific rhetorical effects. Lanham's theory unveils the advantage for text-makers of imagining themselves as insiders: iteratively looking AT the stylistic formulation of the text (the decor) from the inside, and then THROUGH to abstract meanings (the trickery), to then retreat back inside, to finesse the rhetorical meaning effect. The proposal is that as we write linear texts, the intended meaning—coded in abstract monomodal print—aims to be clear cut and controllable, whereas the process of composing moving image texts muddies these

---

[2] Clip 7: https://vimeo.com/142087018 [Accessed 7 February 2018, password = wizard].

[3] It should be noted that 'trickery' does not connote mischief; but it is an everyday communicative social practice at which some are more rehearsed and critically dexterous than others. Differences in aptitude are perhaps unavoidable, but this study advances that all learners be given opportunities to become critical wielders of rhetorical performance, in all its 'decorous' digital modality.

waters. Contrary to cultures of print literacy, the often mechanical processes of audiovisual inscription are more concrete and tangible, and the meanings at the point of production and reception, are elusive, emergent and subject to change. As well as cerebral, the iterative AT (INTERACT)/ THROUGH meaning-making dynamic in film and DV composition can be thought of as a sensory, immersive and emotional process of embodied translation.

For many these are rewarding and pleasurable processes that prompt more accessible and equitable literacy practices, or as Lanham phrases it, "the radical enfranchisement of the perceiver" (1994, p. 17)—even at the earliest stages of primary education. If literacy can be re-conceptualised in socially enfranchised, practical and experiential terms, then arguably it could be aligned with cognitive engagement and transformative action— notions often associated with praxis.

Disposition for Praxis

Literacy, and Metacognition

Praxis, understood here in an emancipatory frame, is autonomous action informed by clarity of purpose and a reflexive critical sense (Anyon 2009; Freire 1993/1970; Lather 1991; McDougall 2011). In this section I make suggestions as to how film and moving image education can incite metacognitive[4] reflection through pedagogies that nourish learning conditions for praxis and pupils' dispositions towards the same.

Chapter 4 alluded to a photo of two Clip Club girls taken from a low angle: Clara demonstrating the purpose of the close-up, and Cara waiting to answer, which she did in a succinct and undemonstrative way, indicating a more contemplative approach to learning. I suggested that this could signal the different access points that media composition practices can rally. Pupils, with their range of interests and personalities, seem to locate a metacognitive trigger through film and media-making, as a

---

[4] In this context, I interpret 'metacognitive' as taking active and productive control over one's learning and its contextual significance, rather than brain functionality.

function of the multifarious practical, aesthetic and executive decisions that have to be made. Towards the end of Chap. 5, I connected praxis with the converging pleasures of manipulating, viewing and interacting with media representations, in the process of DV editing. This nexus of pleasure, immediacy, control, purpose and reflexivity are ingredients in the development of a holistic metacognitive engagement, which helps to define a new literate state of being, related to flow in creative acts (Csikszentmihalyi 1990).

Two instantiations of this practical and reflective orientation, were Wizard's improvised table-top sequence, and Callum's autonomous bifurcating shot, where the camera left the main action, turned about him and rejoined the subjects. I suggested that these were examples of deliberative action to produce filmic sentences or cinematic phrases perhaps. The way in which meaning is made from the printed word through the manipulation of grammatical code and stylistic convention bears comparison with meanings made from digital assets through audiovisual protocols. Running these processes and interpreting media representations requires reflexive and critical engagement.

Moving Image Lexis and Pedagogy

The film sentence metaphor was used in a speech by the late Anthony Minghella in 2005 at a BFI convention entitled The Charter for Media Literacy. There have been further film-related analogies to syntax—by the Head of Film Education at Creative Scotland (Donaldson 2014), by Burn and Durran (2007, p. 94) and by the Film: 21st Century Literacy advocacy report (BFI 2012). If such comparisons with the printed word can be made then the case for developing a film-making lexicon in schools becomes ever more pronounced.[5] In his speech, Minghella expressed dismay at the ways in which the rich complexity of moving image is consistently ignored in mainstream education:

---

[5] Merleau-Ponty hints at the correlation in an essay on film and perception, alluding to the "flair or tact of the director, who handles cinematographic language as a man manipulates syntax" (1964, p. 55).

...given the way in which moving image can manipulate us, allow us to inhabit many differing points of view, take us on journeys to other times, places and cultures, indict us, shock us, and delight us, surely it's time for our education system to hold the teaching of the sentence we watch as no less important and crucial than the teaching of the sentence we read.
(BFI 2012, p. 6)

Expressed in these terms, film's marginalisation is indeed perplexing. The advantage of working with moving image production in short manageable exercises that produce clips, is that learners become habituated to particular formulas and techniques which are internalised as a repertoire of visual expression and conceptual thought. Just as one's understanding and production of language in speech and writing improves through regular practice and exposure, a corollary might be drawn with the incremental development of film language.

On the understanding that film and the written word have distinct affordances as productive media, Minghella's cinematic sentence metaphor may be a useful place to start with respect to both forms' use of narration (Donaldson 2014) as a structuring technique to organise and convey conceptual thought. Mr. C.'s embrace of moving image as one of the building blocks to develop critical thinking at Riverside School (including the Film in a Morning project), attests to the academic resonance of audiovisual representation to express critical understanding of literature.[6] Furthermore, a system was in place whereby Riverside English pupils could choose the communicative means through which to explore and express their textual understandings—a strategy which, it is argued here, is a form of pedagogic and egalitarian praxis in practice.

Freire, one of the first proponents of an action-oriented 'humanising' education, was acutely critical of content heavy and paralysing 'banking' models[7] of education taught by 'teacher-bank clerks'. He invested teachers with proactive agency:

---

[6] See also Jones with Hearing (2013) and Hearing (2015) on the use of 'fictive' film and documentary video (respectively) as a creative academic research tool for critical understanding of social phenomena.

[7] 'Banking education' is a Freirian formulation describing styles of pedagogic practice where "instead of communicating, the teacher issues communiqués and makes deposits which the

From the outset, her [sic] efforts must coincide with those of the students to engage in critical thinking and the quest for mutual humanization. His [sic] efforts must be imbued with a profound trust in people and their creative power. To achieve this, they must be partners of the students in their relations with them.
(Freire 1993/1970, p. 56)

With this he lays out many of the precepts of both Riverside English department and the French CCADJ teaching models, where hierarchies are less entrenched and relationships are based on trust, partnership and cooperation. Both are enquiry-led environments, where question-posing is as valued and as safe as problem-solving. Riverside's open digital learning platform and transparent practices are manifestations of honest critical relations. A good illustration of this is Mr. C.'s pragmatic explanation to his pupils of my presence in the classroom—that I had not come to inspect, and they need not adjust their behavior. An aura of candidness appears to rehearse Lather's definition of praxis-orientated terrain:

Emancipatory knowledge increases awareness of the contradictions distorted or hidden by everyday understandings, and in doing so it directs attention to the possibilities for social transformation inherent in the present configuration of social processes.
(Lather 1991, p. 52)

Although conscious of the potential for over-claiming, my research indicates that transparent social arrangements in media production enabled classrooms encourages marginalised voices to be heard, agency to be felt, self-awareness to propagate, and aesthetic sensibilities to be heightened.

Freirian philosophy on pedagogic relationships appears to be enjoying a resurgence (Rogers and Winters 2010; Joaquin 2010) which is unsurprising in the context of prevailing cultures of prescription and accountability. However, a degree of caution should accompany Freirian thinking: there is a an element of patriarchal demystification in his thesis, along

---

students patiently receive, memorise and repeat … the scope of action allowed to the students extends only as far as receiving, filing and storing the deposits." (Freire 1993/1970, p. 53)

with a de-emphasis on social and participative knowledge building (Street 1984; Smith 2002/1997) that could have an unhelpful polarising effect. This orientation runs counter to the social constructionist paradigm that pertains in contemporary scholarship on media education. Inciting educational change and developing spaces for praxis is as much about keeping a dialogue open with policy makers as it is about resistance.

Moving on from media production's relationship with critical thinking and action, I now begin to examine the ways in which practical work with film and moving image nurtures conditions conducive to congenial interactions.

Disposition for Reciprocal Communication

Social Literacies in the Present

In order for conceptions of literacy to diversify, we need to take account of relations between and amongst pupils, teachers, the learning community and their respective responsibilities, which when operating unencumbered by bureaucracy, are commonly stamped with a certain reciprocity. I choose the phrase reciprocal communication because it carries a human inflection—that of sustained giving and taking in kind. This section takes its cue from Potter's recommendation (who in turn draws on and Buckingham 2003; Marsh 2010; Street 2003; Sefton-Green 2000):

> we need a way of understanding children's engagement with digital video as a rapidly changing social literacy practice … we further need to align this with a socialized view of creativity that is much more closely connected with group work, situated peer review, and an awareness of group roles in cultural production than connected with individual auteurs and the realization of a personal expressive goal.
> (Potter 2012, p. 148)

We can assume that for Potter and the other commentators mentioned, that social and dialogic interaction is a key dimension of literacies associated with film and the moving image. Whereas social exchanges are in step with creative iterative practices examined earlier in relation to meaning-making, they grind against those practices that revolve around individual achievement with written outputs and top down assessment procedures.

The different areas of film-making in particular enable the formation of a pool of mutual and interdependent understanding from which others can learn, and the scope of this understanding is not limited to the spaces of production. Along with the widely documented social benefits of film-making (BFI Education and Film Education 2012; Lardoux 2014; Lord et al. 2007), it is in the crucial stage of display that participative literacy competencies further accrue. Quadrant 4 of the Cycle of Digital Making (see Fig. 2.2)—that of participation, dissemination and sharing—is integral to the production of literacy events. Clip Club's Leonardo is a case in point, from the beginning of the project he expressed a desire to peer teach, to spread his newfound knowledge and to show his classmates how to film and edit. It will be remembered that he was also moved by the laughter that his work generated during the school screenings. These are the largely overlooked depths and sensitivities related to audiovisual literacy work when framed as social and participative.

It seems almost fatuous, in academic discourse, to mention the fun element of making media, so widespread are children and young people's references to their enjoyment therein. But should it be so taken for granted, when in the same breath they readily and almost as frequently associate film and media activities with the world of work? In several of my research interviews (as heard and seen with Leonardo and the Riverside boys, respectively) and in my professional experience, young people reveal the extent to which they have absorbed adult preoccupations related to the link between media skills and industry. The narrative often goes that they believe filming with iPads is a good thing because it will help them 'get a job'. Creative production for its own sake does not feature in most young people's life worlds, even though they routinely comment on how much fun they have in the process in other contexts. My account questions why the 'fun' should be deferred until adulthood and even then framed around careers, when there is potentially much to be gained from filmic expression in the present—socially, culturally, and in terms of personal and academic fulfilment.

To disregard structured filming with iPads and the screening of this content, as frivolous play, fatuous screen-time or precocious work experience, is to miss the pedagogic and social potency of the activity. Recalling for a moment the importance that A. Reid (2007) places on the externalisation of thought and its embodiment in symbols, we can start to see a correlation with Potter's ideas on the stage at which play becomes a creative and political act. In this extract, if one substitutes his references to 'internalised speech'[8] and 'thought', with film, the practice of public display becomes more salient:

> the internalized speech [film] cannot take its place in the culture, become widely understood, until it becomes externalized; at this point the inner, context dependent thought [film] gradually unfolds its meaning as "symbol-for-others"; it is creative, rather than playful at the point at which it is assimilated within a culture as a "literacy event".
> (Potter 2012, p. 37)

Inspired by Vygotsky (1978, 2002/1933), for Potter, play with others (and in particular the range of roleplaying that film production offers) is seen as an integral part of the development of communicative skills. Moreover, public screenings of novice moving image texts have a mobilising quality that add heft to layers of meaning that get swept into what I have been referring to as the discursive human conversation.

Theoretical Observations on the 'Making Of'

I wish to elaborate on the words 'context dependent' above as I believe mimicking industry's production of 'Making of' movies, enriches youth media production experiences and enlightens some audience members with deeper intellectual engagement than that offered by the film viewing

---

[8] 'Internalised speech' relates to Vygotskian theories on the role of play in the development of conceptual thought, a discourse which has played an important role in media education theorising since the nineties (Sefton-Green 1998).

alone. Such texts are commonly constructed to provide insight, amusement (the blooper reel) or a tantalising glimpse of film artifice. Setting up a 'Making of' production team has the potential to lay out the tone and constitution of the film's creative processes as well as preserve the golden moments for its participants.

On reflection, I realise that the events pieced together in 'Making of' texts, document the discord, the fun, the challenges, the re-takes, the camaraderie, the finessing in action, in other words, they record a string of selected learning moments. I include links to the 'Making of' movies for Run School Run 1 and 2 in a footnote,[9] as they were a hastily edited afterthought. These particular texts do not constitute research material in and of themselves because they were made by me in teacherly (non-researcherly) cherry-picking mode, but my sense is that it is an area of documentary filmmaking with young people that is under-utilised. My contention is that this potential deficit is down to the default mode of youth film consumption, which is largely one of pure entertainment as opposed to cultural and critical stimulation (not that these categories are mutually exclusive).

On a social level, rendering visible the work that goes on behind the camera and the mess of filming, parallels the disclosure of certain pupils' hitherto undetected ways of being in the school setting, perhaps unsettling adults' and peers' ingrained assumptions about them. For example, in an interview with their class teacher,[10] Clara was described as an occasionally problematic drama queen in the classroom but she transformed into a driven and impassioned actress on screen. Seeing the Clip Club children operating within an entirely different habitus, and in amongst the disarray of backstage film footage, she observed her pupils negotiating altered social relations and self-direction. There are rich pickings to be had in the time and space between filming the shots. In dialogic ways, the 'Making of' gradually unfolds the complicity that film-making fosters and requires, three aspects of which feature in the social interaction

---

[9] Making of Run School Run 1: http://theclipclub.co.uk/2013/07/13/run-school-run-bloopers/-comments [Accessed 21 May 2017].

Making of Run School Run 2: http://theclipclub.co.uk/2014/07/11/run-school-run-1-2-making-of-on-youtube/ [Accessed 21 May 2017].

[10] Year 6 teacher's interview: https://soundcloud.com/shelleuk/clip-club-yr6-teacher/s-89qE0#t=7:30 [Accessed 21 May 2017].

dimension of my interpretive model—(role)play, co-composition and collaborative relations.

Dialogic Co-construction of Knowledge

I conclude this section on reciprocity with thoughts on collaboration as an important social component in an enlarged, participative notion of literacy and to which practices with media composition are seen to contribute. As mentioned in Chap. 4, I refer to the visit to the Clip Club made by professional film-makers and a media education researcher on a scoping exercise. They were researching the possible benefits and shortcomings of using iPads in school film production as opposed to more conventional camera equipment.

Rather than discuss the particulars of the conversation (which is nonetheless fascinating and revelatory[11]), this account looks to the value of its very occurrence. The encounter bears witness to the ways in which reflection on film-making is a valuable and levelling exercise for young people: knowledge was shared and opinions aired on a variety of sophisticated topics from production tactics to programme design. As previously recognised, this experience may have had a beneficial effect on the group's achievements the following week, in that after a fallow filming period, they significantly upped their game. I propose that they had absorbed an unsimulated appeal to their expertise and that this authentic[12] dialogic exchange kindled a mutual trust and respect that in turn boosted their identities as film-makers and participants in a wider social narrative. Processes of media production provide opportunities for pupils' meaningful contact with the outside world, and thus for more porous pedagogies (Haas Dyson 1997; McDougall 2014; McDougall and Potter 2015).

---

[11] Audio available at: https://soundcloud.com/shelleuk/phd-interview-clip-club-john-potter-xube-april-2014/s-pscBO#t=4:10 [Accessed 7 February 2018] and video extract available at: https://vimeo.com/136745476 [Accessed 7 February 2018, password = wizard].

[12] I use the word 'authentic' advisedly. It is questionable the extent to which anything can be described as such. Here it simply means a rare and sincere engagement with the so-called 'real world' outside school—an equally problematic construction that devalues the very 'real world' that school life represents for young people.

Potter has a history of consulting young people in the research context (Selwyn et al. 2010), and I asked him to comment on seeking Year 6 advice for a project in which children could be seen as "ethnographic partners" (McDougall 2016) with "funds of knowledge" (Moll et al. 1992) to share:

> you work with giving and receiving respect for knowledge, however that knowledge is gained… The fact that they were children showing other children was really important because it meant that they felt that they were being treated as, if not experts, at least as advisors, because they've gone out there and made some of the mistakes and done things, or done things well, and would be able to give advice to them, so everybody gains from that situation.
> (Interview with John Potter 2015)
> Available at: https://soundcloud.com/shelleuk/john-potter/s-3P9LY#t= 17:38) [Accessed 7 February 2018]

After confirming his iterative approach to teaching—the explicit to-ing and fro-ing of knowledge building—he went on to lament the uni-directional, common-sense mandating of certain kinds of cultural capital that all pupils should know, and without which many are deemed socially lacking or deficient in some way.

The Clip Club Xube interview was an opportunity for the (adult) researchers to gain access to knowledge that pupils themselves had acquired through their own experience of film-making. Recalling Mr. C.'s observation, they spoke from a position of "knowing rather than having been *told*" because of "the stage of making". There is no doubt that Potter's primary teaching background informs his research practice in rewarding ways, the one role learning from the epistemological and ontological insights of the other. As expounded in Chap. 3, my hybrid teacher/practitioner/researcher status attests to a certain symbiosis between these roles, (albeit in a non-formal capacity) which supports the argument that teachers might be re-cast as critical researcher-practitio-ners (Orr and McDougall 2014) in the development of media education pedagogy.

The less textual and more social connotation of doing film, rather than making it, perhaps captures the broader and inclusive ramifications of pedagogies related to audiovisual production in schools. In terms of strengthening its traction, simply this more prosaic term could seed new spaces in which cultural encounters of dialogic parity might blossom. This is ambitious thinking, which may need some reigning in; indeed, if movie clips can have a punctum, the frame that remains with me from the meeting features G-man and the momentary self-conscious glance he shot at me—and my filming of him—in the final seconds of the clip.[13] He remained silent and guarded throughout the discussion, with slippery eyes and a bearing that was demonstrably ill at ease, recalling Callum at the BFI screening.

If, in film-making programmes, time and space is specifically allocated for reflection and dialogue, there is still some way to go for the likes of G-man and Callum to feel completely included. Fluid and confident behind the camera among their peers, they recoil from the double exposure of my prying lens and an alienating world of adult authority. Although it was very much in evidence in other parts of our circular forum, the pressure of having to speak was disempowering for G-man, and there was little in the way of mutual reciprocity to the right of the room. This conscious opting out complicates simplistic notions of overt social participation and language as the natural order of things, and points to the importance of less threatening non-verbal communication in such circumstances. Indeed, understandings achieved through tacit exchanges was a key finding in terms of the range of learning preferences that film-making supports.

By concentrating on the Clip Club research encounter (and indeed as revealed in my interview with Isaac and Daniel in Film in a Morning), I have shown that collective reflection on media-making, although not without complication, can for some be a valuable exercise in the development of a wider literacy of participation. Fielding warns of the risks of not attending to power relations in the classroom. He identifies a clashing incompatibility between collaborative and performative practices,

---

[13] See 04:43': https://vimeo.com/136745476 [Accessed 7 February 2018, password = wizard].

claiming they can lead to a disruptive 'carping' cross-fire in some formal school spaces:

> The strength of dialogue is in its mutuality. Its transformative potential lies in its reciprocity because it is in these kinds of person-centred ... arrangements that trust and creativity are most likely to grow. If we see and relate to each other within the context of a reciprocal responsibility we will indeed transform what it is to be a teacher, what it is to be a student, and the spectre of schools as nineteenth-century institutions will begin to fade. However, the context of performativity and a narrowly conceived, incessant accountability leads too readily down the path of a carping, antagonistic relationship between students and teachers, one in which students become the new agents of external control ... or regressive pedagogy.
> (Fielding 2004, p. 308, my emphasis)

The reaping of data to demonstrate school effectiveness shows no sign of abating as an ideology, meanwhile the unintended impacts of regressive pedagogy on young people and their relations with teachers, remain relatively unexplored. Issues of educational utilitarianism in formal schooling will be explored in a later section, before this, I consider the ways in which media-making relates to the arts and the difficulties of defining the ineffable in a culture of metrics and expediency.

Rightness of Fit

Aesthetic Experience and the Rightness of Combining

Referring to the affective quality of narrative action research, one of the Finnish principles of validation (Heikkinen et al. 2007) I have been using is translated into English as *evocativeness*. In a move to re-align this principle with media composition, and retain an earthed aesthetic dimension, I adapted it to *everyday artistry* for a more process orientated core concept. *Artistry* captures the abstract and physical processes of aesthetic crafting with analogue and digital tools, as well as the disposition and sensibility of the artist. *Everyday* brings artistry to the level of the quotidian, and the ways in which ordinariness can inspire imaginative leaps. Under this umbrella term, I developed the concept of *rhetorical performance* (A. Reid 2007; Burn 2009a, 2013) to suggest the ways in which we assemble and curate media content, and perform our artistry and our identity, both to ourselves and to a potential public (Burn and Durran 2006, 2007; Potter 2012). This performance (not to be confused with 'performativity' against targets in a political economy), relates to our capacity to combine experience, memories and observations with our imagination, to produce a coherent and affective multi-sensory text. This capacity is described by Lanham as an ability to mobilise "our integrative powers" (1994). The realm of 'combinatory play' (a term attributable to Einstein[14]) is the space that creative media mentors are well placed to occupy, to assist pupils in solving what Clip Club's Leonardo called the "slowly fitting puzzle"[15] of media composition in time and space (Bazalgette 2008).

Goodman's phrase, 'rightness of fit' (1978, p. 132), describes artists' ways of negotiating the relationships between qualities in the act of composition (Eisner 2005/1993, p. 208)—in other words, getting the form or creative act right enough for specific moods, effects and a sense of coherence to emerge. I chose 'rightness of fit' for three reasons that align with the contours of my questions and that go some way to capturing:

- those intricate, contingent and phronetic workings of media composition (such as the choice of camera shot, distance, angle, duration and the infinite nuances of DV editing), that constitute a modern relevant meaning-making practice
- the elusive, 'in solution' nature of an inspiring responsive teaching environment

---

[14] The phrase is quoted in various online texts, as part of a conversation between Einstein and Hadamard, in the context of discussing relationships between the productive thought of mathematicians and mental images. One such instance is available at: http://www.brainpickings. org/2013/08/14/how-einstein-thought-combinatorial-creativity/ [Accessed 21 May 2017].

[15] This is how Leonardo referred to the selection, ordering and pacing of metaphorical images in a beautiful animated montage sequence referred to in this post: http://theclipclub.co.uk/2013/10/16/ the-big-match-analysis/ [Accessed 21 May 2017]. Audio available at: https://soundcloud.com/shelleuk/phd-thesis-interview-2-mrp-leonardo-nimbus-march-2013/s-uhdHC#t=8:00 [Accessed 21 May 2017].

- the awkward complexity of assessing and positioning digital media-making in a data-driven school environment, fragmented by subject

Is media composition, as I have been claiming, an important and pertinent strand of literacy, to be aligned with subject English? or is it a discrete set of technical skills and competences in preparation for the workplace? or further still, does it fit more seamlessly and appropriately into visual and expressive Arts? The next sub-section engages with this latter claim, while issues related to the teaching environment and socio-cultural context will be addressed in the final section of this Chapter.

The 'Work' of Art in the Age of Dynamic and Embodied Literacies[16]

I noted in Chap. 2 Eisner's affiliation of aesthetic experience with the word ineffable. This section grapples with the unutterable and seeks to account for the ways in which aesthetic experience[17] relates to the concrete artistry of multimodal expression. Eisner elucidates thus:

> The phrase "work of art" can have two meanings. It can refer to work of art, or it can refer to the work of art. The former refers to the product created, the latter to the process of creating it. Aesthetic experience can be secured at each location.
> (Eisner 2002, p. 81, original emphasis)

According to Eisner, the word 'artistry' captures the duality of the word work:

---

[16] The title is a play on Benjamin's celebrated essay (1936) in which he critiques the loss of a work of art's 'aura' in the age of 'mechanical reproduction'. I reference it as Benjamin's study on technology's disruption of tradition and its potential impact on the politicisation of artists' work resonates with aspects of this study.

[17] Eisner makes the distinction between aesthetic and anaesthetic experience, the former lays claim to works of art that heighten our senses and the latter to processes that deaden or suppress them (Eisner 2002, p. 81).

Artistry consists in having an idea worth expressing, the imaginative ability needed to conceive of how, the technical skills needed to work effectively with some material, and the sensibilities needed to make the delicate adjustments that will give the forms the moving qualities that the best of them possess.
(Eisner 2002, p. 81)

There are, however, two missing perspectives in Eisner's philosophy that are crucial to modern views of creative, screen-based media artistry—the critical frame and popular cultural understanding.[18] This expanded view of the work of (media) art is supported by Burn's (2013) proposed re-location of school media production into a newly conceived Media Arts discipline, and by his beckoning for the academic development of a Poetics of media education (2009b). In his view, an injection of discursive Media Arts production and performance would feed into and enrich the established critical and cultural frames of Media Studies and Film Studies, respectively.

The study most cognisant of this aesthetic in this text is Le Cinéma: Cent Ans de Jeunesse (CCADJ). As will be recalled, its co-ordinators value the liminal and iterative states of becoming, offered by the programme's va et vient rhythms, shuttling between theory and practice. Teachers, film-makers and pupils engage collaboratively in the joint weaving[19] of theoretically underpinned and affective moving image texts. My study suggests that participants' decisions made in the interstices between conscious and intuitive reckoning correlate with deep learning moments. These moments might for example constitute: re-taking shots, going off script, actors' and directors' improvisations on set, indulging private jokes, anticipating audiences' responses whilst editing, and embracing surprise and serendipity.

Shared social moments that involve imaginative leaps are redolent of Vygotsky's widely acknowledged zone of proximal development (Burn and Durran 2006, 2007; Potter 2012, p. 146; Sefton-Green 1998;

---

[18] Eisner's use of the word 'best' here hints questionably at Arnoldian nineteenth century thinking and elitist views of culture as 'the best that has been thought and said'.

[19] The derivation of the word text is from the Latin texere, to weave, evoking compact strands of intertextual meaning (Burn and Durran 2006, p. 291).

Vygotsky 1978) describing the fertilising effect on learning of social play when combined with teachers' scaffolding: a blend that purports to carry young people beyond current levels of understanding. Indeed, Maria's use of the sound boom as an air guitar updates Vygotsky's analogy of 'the broom that becomes a hobby horse' in children's imaginative play—a motif quoted by Burn (2009a, p. 14) in the context of defining intuitive leaps of the imagination.

Moving beyond Vygotsky, my account puts forward a more granular formulation for understanding the everyday work of digital artistry and editing, drawing on Sennett (2008) and his study on the nature of craftsmanship. I believe that the articulation of literacy as a perceptual craft, involving the adding, re-fashioning and eliminating of sensory material, serves to refresh formal "schooled literacies" (Street 1995), whose emphasis is on accuracy and progress towards predefined goals, following predefined standards, measured with predefined indicators (Thomson et al. 2012, p. 5; Yandell 2014).

My Masters dissertation (Cannon 2011)[20] touched on imaginative patterns of thought in design and craft processes and how, in some respects, they can be seen to parallel meaning-making in DV editing. Like many others (Banaji et al. 2006; Buckingham 2003; Readman 2010), Sennett dispels a tendency towards romantic ideals of creativity and defines the four elements necessary for making intuitive leaps in maker/craft practices:

(a) *reformatting*—an aspect of reality is materially reworked

This calls to mind the aesthetic, phronetic and intertextual re-mixing of image and sound inherent in the re-presenting of assimilated cultural material, as that rehearsed in Film in a Morning. In this project, themes from a novel or poetic verse were unpicked, analysed, and the format of understanding was re-woven and re-imagined as another digital audiovisual entity.

---

[20] Available in blog format at: https://fashioningandflow.wordpress.com/2011/11/10/vygotsky-intuition-flow-theory/ [Accessed 7 February 2018].

(b) adjacency—the juxtaposition of "two unlike domains … the closer they are the more stimulating seems their twined presence" (Sennett 2008, p.210)

My video clips of young people editing, signal the ways in which varied shots, clips and appropriate sounds are provisionally stitched together onto a timeline in processes of multi-layered matching and sequencing. The idea of contrasting or complementary adjacency is fundamental to the creative process. Depending on the audience and the protocols of the medium, the more innovatively or artfully juxtaposed the genres, audio-visual assets, materials and/or ideas, the more compelling the effect (Bordwell and Thompson 2010; Cousins 2012; Monaco 2009; Reisz and Millar 2010).

(c) surprise—"you begin dredging up tacit knowledge into consciousness to do the comparing" and experience wonder. "Surprise is a way of telling yourself that something you know can be other than you assumed" (Sennett 2008, p.211)

Linked with the recognition that original composition can produce arresting work, Sennett introduces a welcome affective dimension that helps us understand the fun element in media production. A frequently observed phenomenon in this research was the element of wonder and surprise that film and moving image manipulation often generates, especially when the work, the people and the productive moment seem to coalesce. There is a sense in which an unconscious process of comparison with one's former experiences meshes with present creative conditions, and precipitates the urge to imitate or re-present—an impulse embodied in Claxton's understanding of acting on one's intuition (1998).[21] From clinching the take, to trusting feelings of 'rightness' in editing, recurrent experiences such as

---

[21] Bruner offered a pleasing definition of intuition that captures the idea of 'temporary rightness' whilst editing: "the intellectual technique of arriving at plausible but tentative formulations without going through the analytical steps by which such formulations would be found to be valid or invalid conclusions" (2009/1960, p. 13).

these beget confidence, pleasure and arguably, a reflexively literate state of being.[22]

(d) gravity—recognition that leaps do not defy gravity and constraints are something of a constant: "The technical import, like any immigrant, will bring with it its own problems" (Sennett 2008, p.212)

So much for the highs; Sennett concedes the inevitable downward arc of the imaginative leap—here articulated as the human or technical hitches and glitches in craft processes. As evinced in the group agency of participants in CCADJ and The Clip Club, their focus and ingenuity defied perceptibly adverse circumstance by working imaginatively with the available resources. This account argues that embracing questioning 'habits of mind' and a disposition for resourcefulness, rehearse the kinds of democratic and responsible decision-making that can unseat the seemingly insurmountable.

Having looked at media composition artistry from aesthetic (Eisner 2005/1985) and craft (Sennett 2008) points of view, there appears to be a lack of emphasis in both cases on the specifics of context from a critical perspective. Media craft work might be rendered a more socially-conscious embodied literacy practice by introducing a fifth element to Sennett's framework, which I have termed rhetorical performance. This integrates the ideas of reaching out in explicit and informed ways to situated audiences, using critical arts practices whose ripples provoke debate as well as aesthetic impact.

Burn goes further to suggest that the popular acronym describing a comprehensive curriculum inclusive of the arts—STEAM (Science, Technology, Engineering, Arts, Maths) as mentioned in Chap. 2—fails to go far enough. He claims that the arts, even in this frame, are still positioned as separate and secondary—"a supplement to the formidable ranks of the 'serious' disciplines" (Burn 2013, p. 60). Instead Burn (2013) introduces the acronym STAMMP (Science, Technology, Arts, Maths, Media and Performance—with Engineering perhaps subsumed in S and

---

[22] Lanham captured the 'surprise' element of literacy work in the phrase "a toggle to boggle the mind" (1994, p. 82) referring to repetitive movements between concrete inscription and abstract conceptualisation that produce anomalies or incongruities.

T), along with a rationale that unites science, computer programming, the analogue and digital arts and humanities, as a more relevant curriculum descriptor.[23] This view is more accommodating of a broad and inclusive interest-base, and checks the advance of instrumentalist STEM lobbies—enthusiastically embraced by some (Gibb 2015a, 2015b) and closely critiqued by others (Crafts Council 2014; Cultural Learning Alliance 2011, 2014)—that fuel the acceleration of computer programming as a stand-alone skill, both in schools and in informal maker-spaces more widely.

My account now moves on to take up Burn's call for unity and continuity between the disciplines and for a more conciliatory view within the media education camp itself. Its trajectories tend to veer in different discursive directions, following cultural, critical and/or creative avenues, or indeed the way of ed-tech evangelism and technological determinism as critiqued by Buckingham (2007) and Watters (2015). Burn and Durran nominate that we "resist and question these rhetorics of rupture" (2006, p. 273) and seek a more even-handed approach, the better to put the arts 'stammp' on cross-disciplinary spaces of learning and their wider contexts.

Spaces of Translation

As will have been apparent over the course of this book, etymology has inspired certain lines of enquiry and this section is no exception. At various points the concept of translation has looped in and out of my prose—translat meaning 'carried across' in Latin. I intend spaces of translation to evoke the social environments in which meanings are carried in one form to another, from one person to another, from one space to another, across certain terrains in iterative movements. I will examine what hinders and what facilitates the fluid translation and unrestricted movement of meanings in and beyond the classroom. In other words, I revisit Quadrant 3 of Fig. 2.3 (the pedagogies that correspond with Composition/Production) to explore hybrid approaches that shape the digital teaching environment

---

[23] See also Potter (2015), for further informed play with acronyms. STEAM(M) works along the same lines, where (M) is the sadly 'ignored' but all-pervading curriculum dimension: Media.

in positive ways, while also engaging with the social conditions of possibility (Scott and Usher 2011). In these ways, I hope to cast light on the discursive factors that delimit media composition practices in schools, and at the same time suggest how teachers might respond to these tensions for new grass root pedagogies to emerge.

As disclosed in Chap. 2 in relation to Crawford's work, attentiveness to interactions between elements and the capacity to make immediate material adjustments on the fly, are key characteristics of craftsmanship, and no less is true of the daily interactions of a teacher. This thesis works on the premise that teaching involves all the nuance and qualitative adjustment required of an artist refining their craft and experimenting with their medium. The medium, rather than any tool or curriculum content, is envisaged as the ether and presence of communicative relations with pupils. One of my questions relates to normative teaching methods and the practices that might be borrowed from creative media environments; it is the constitution of this 'classroom ether' that is put under scrutiny.

Teaching as 'Practical Consciousness of a Present Kind'

The Signature Pedagogies report (Thomson et al. 2012) explains the modus operandi of creative practitioners and the ways in which school environments can be shaped in their hands. The authors extrapolate specific pedagogic platforms, purposes and practices—too large in scope to detail in full here, but some key ideas percolate through to help explore debates in this field. The platforms comprise the foundational approaches common to all the creative pedagogies revealed in their research:

* inclusion
* choice and agency
* scale and ambition
* the carnivalesque (in Bakhtin's playful sense (1981) of norms being overturned)
* the lived experience of the present

All of these components resonate with my research, but the latter promises to illuminate the spaces of translation of interest in this section.

Thomson et al. make use of Williams' structure of feeling (referenced in Chap. 2), to represent the essentially present duality of thought and feeling that creative practitioners are able to conjure in their manipulation of art forms:

> For Williams [the structure of feeling] was a way of describing the moment before meanings and possibilities are closed down. In the present, ideas are being formed, not finished, events are experienced, not remembered... We can find no better term to describe the combination of affect and cognitive attention, the sheer exhilaration, delight and joy that students often displayed during their encounters with creative pedagogies.
> (Thomson et al. 2012, p. 15)

Clearly some teachers, more versed in analogue practice, may already be sensitive to such moments, and might already be actively negotiating a "practical consciousness of a present kind, in a living and interrelating continuity" (Thomson et al. 2012, p. 32; see also Van Manen's (2008) pedagogic 'Knowing-in-Action'). My contention is that filming, editing and working with digital media can help to ground pupils' conceptual, perceptual and representational meaning-making even further, in present and material ways. Interstitial spaces are opened up for constructive dialogue and exchange between actions which, I propose, concretise the conceptual work of literacy. Pursued further, the potential for a world of sophisticated metaphor, nuance and critique is brought to light, thus widening and democratising the palette of expressive representation. These horizons of possibility were revealed to me in my Masters research, and teachers such as Ms. J. and Mr. C. grasp this potential too, working in their own ways to realise it.

At the same time, my research has exposed the erosion of the enabling ether which is rendered anaemic by the deadening imperative to cover compulsory compartmentalised material. For many children, the meaning and value of the present moment is sacrificed on the slab of some other obscure, deferred future moment. Indeed, my data suggests that for some children the future moment that is considered to be of any worth, is one that narrowly relates media-making to the world of work. For some researchers it might be tempting to take the enthusiastic associations young people make between school media production and employment at face value, as an indication of sophisticated forward thinking, whereas what is more likely to be the case is their having imbibed the empty "alienated and alienating blah" (Freire 1993/1970, p. 68, original emphasis) of hegemonic discourse.

There seems to be a conflict here between the enjoyable hands-on experiences that creative media pedagogies fabricate, and the idea that the former have no intrinsic worth except when reified and rationalised with state-endorsed use and value. Even having explained my position as Mr. C.'s friendly impartial researcher, the videoed Riverside Year 7 boys seemed to want to wrap their free reign media-making with adult-work-speak in order to legitimise it. On the other hand, my observations of older students indicated that this constrained outlook did gradually dissipate as they moved through the years, revealing more of an engaged and personal orientation to digital media production. My research suggests that recipients of the one-off media project 'treat', would benefit from a sustained and diversified view of the moving image. Far from an industry-related extracurricular frill, film and media texts are legitimate expressive forms with which to experiment across the curriculum, in the here-and-now.

Schools, Industry and the Participatory Promise

To broker a dialogue that goes beyond audience building or corporate responsibility, it is in the gift of creative media practitioners and professional film educators, to disturb the ready conflation of school film production with vocational work and industry. The stranglehold of instrumental thinking might then be loosened and Media Arts with cross disciplinary frames of reference might be given a chance to establish themselves.

My autoethnographic account in Chap. 4 brings home the extent to which I was enculturating industry practices, occasionally replicating the trappings of "cinematic life" (Furstenau and MacKenzie 2009). For all the benefits of role-taking and the 'Making of', one wonders how else it might be possible for young people to experience informal film production, on their own terms, in ways that are not so in thrall to dominant professional practices, standards and vocabulary. This is a possible area of development for practitioners, educators and young people, who, through the use of mobile and wireless technologies, may come to reinvent and fashion moving image production and consumption norms for their own playful purposes.[24]

Having elaborated in celebratory ways on film-making in schools as a democratic strand of literacy, it must be acknowledged that the process itself is steeped in commercial and cultural constraints. From the designed affordances of the hardware and software, to the very conventions of filming and editing, the empowerment that film-making purports to offer is always-already compromised. Nimbus delights in the choice of sounds available in an iMovie database but my experience suggests that the development of a more critical eye and ear means the novelty of standardised authoring packages wears off as quickly as mobile ring tones. A longer view of learning with digital assets would encourage young people to record, compose and curate their own library of music and Foley sounds from the outset, modelling a more holistic and independent practice.

The Clip Club made good use of the green screen, but this remains the only item in use out of a trunk of low-grade film-making equipment, bought on a whim by a former staff member. This purchase is symptomatic of the ways in which schools are commonly positioned by commercial interests, buoyed by all-in-one, ed-tech solutionism (Buckingham 2007; Selwyn 2012; Watters 2015, Williamson 2017). Writers researching the use of technologies in schools (Selwyn et al. 2010) report the privilege that acquiring tools often occupies over and above the consideration that might be given to their purpose and use in a learning context (Luckin et al. 2012). My concern is that if visual literacy becomes more popular in schools and industry's rhetorical influence goes unexamined,

---

[24] See http://movingcinema.eu/ [Accessed 21 May 2017] for an account of a Spanish-Lithuanian-Portuguese collaboration in which innovative models of film education for young people are being explored and enacted.

commercial interests combined with the magnetising power of the "participatory promise … and access to the movie-dream" (Furstenau and MacKenzie 2009, p. 8) may stultify and delimit agency and variety. Promising spaces of dispersed and diverse translations of meaning could, without informed cultural and critical investment in teacher education, correspond more with the homogenised re-production of familiar texts and genres.

Seeding the Ecotonal Environment

On a more pragmatic note, I now look at the ways in which schools can develop different relationships and more porous borders with cultural organisations. My professional experience with BFI-led film and media projects allowed me to see the advantages of partnerships between schools and external creative, cultural and research agencies. The research interview with Clip Club participants seemed to consolidate the children's hitherto simulated film-making roles. They became the experienced actors, editors, camera operators, directors and producers whose advice was being formally sought, rehearsing the value of interactions which vivify learning and enable more hybrid, permeable pedagogies and practices (Potter 2011).

In the weeks prior to the interview there had been fractious exchanges in the Club, but after adult validation of their identities as film-makers, although cautious of narratives of causation, a more conscious commitment took hold. This switch in dynamic could demonstrate the changeable, undulating terrain that DV work inhabits. With this in mind, I propose that the transactional nature of the Clip Club environment is redolent of the ecotone: a term borrowed from the natural sciences, that describes a space in which juxtaposed biodiverse zones are in constant tension, commingling and effecting a productive and "unstable equilibria"[25] (Barker 2011, p. 68, drawing on Gramsci).

---

[25] 'Unstable equilibria' is Gramsci's way of describing constantly evolving hegemonic practices, bound up with social and consensual power relations that are continually being superceded to maintain the tension.

In the DV production context the ecotonal tension equates to pupils' ongoing diverse talents, dispositions and home-spun interests, operating within non-formal parameters, but also within a formal institutional space. Introducing professional adults and alternative educators into the mix, as indeed was witnessed in Film in a Morning, adds to the complexity in productive ways. Through the skillful management of a sense of social interdependence, the potential for chaos can lead to positive disruptive innovation, making new juxtapositions and alliances. Professor of Architecture, Ann Pendleton-Jullian depicts these transitional learning spaces as permeable corridors between social institutions and innovation hubs, which is redolent of Potter's "semi-permeable membrane" (2011) mentioned in Chap. 2:

> The ecotone's success, both in terms of sustaining itself and evolving, depends upon the ability to self-generate spontaneous events of work, play and communication which can, themselves, evolve improvisationally. And it values the serendipitous connections between events and their content. These events and mechanisms, as the ecotone corridors, seed the ecotone. They bring work from the edges into the system, transfer work into new questions, these questions back into new work, etc., all of which plays back into the system.
>
> Non time and space dependent, the corridors form an ether of connectivity as opposed to point to point conversations or lines of thought. As an indivisible entity, one in which the spontaneous, improvised and serendipitous are valued, the ecotone requires a communication infrastructure that is diverse in its forms, highly responsive in its operations, so easy as to become tacit in nature, and of high capacity. In fact, the ecotone concept can only be realized in our digital age with the new media tools and methods we now have at hand.
>
> (Pendleton-Jullian 2009, p. 52)

With this, and enriched by an incongruous analogy with the natural world, this commentator calls for the structured exploitation of digital tools in learning environments mediated by distinctly human interventions. If the concept of literacy is in need of a digital overhaul, then new moving image production alliances could occupy these corridors[26] carrying innovatory pedagogic practices in from the edges—where inertia and entrenched interests are weaker—across contested state-organised terrain.[27]

Emerging mainly inductively from experience in the field, this Chapter has considered digital moving image literacy from a range of perspectives found to co-exist interdependently. For example, my research supports the re-imagining of schools' engagement with film and the moving image as both a cross-disciplinary critical means of expression and as a Media Arts discipline, a particular dimension of the visual arts. This would require an adjusted view of literacy and pedagogy—as hybrid social practices in a densely networked environment, that mobilise multiple expressive resources, with and on a range of digital tools and platforms. As such, it is worth reflecting further on the contextual challenges with which progressive pedagogies would have to contend if such a vision were to be realised. The final Chapter is devoted to this challenge.

In conclusion, a pre-digital citation from Eisner traces many of the themes and discursive tensions relevant to the introduction of media composition in schools and the complications therein. Originally given in 2002 as the John Dewey Lecture at Stanford University, he entreats:

At the risk of propagating dualisms, but in the service of emphasis, I am talking about a culture of schooling in which more importance is placed on exploration than on discovery, more value is assigned to surprise than to control, more attention is devoted to what is distinctive than to what is standard, more interest is related to what is metaphorical than to what is literal. It is an educational culture that has a greater focus on becoming than on being, places more value on the imaginative than on the factual, assigns greater priority to valuing than to measuring, and regards the qual-

---

[26] In serendipitous ways, the ecotonal corridor metaphor is embodied in microcosm, in the Clip Club's 'corridor shoot' already examined (Clip 2 here: https://vimeo.com/142087018 @ 00:18′ [Accessed 7 February 2018, password = wizard]. We used the Evernote app for wireless shot list management in fluid connected relations with other remote members of the group. In these ways school media production can experience the flow of creative practice in a networked environment, thus disrupting linear, mono-spatial and individually conceived meaning-making practices.

[27] A further analogy inspired by natural forms is made by Sherrington (2013), who compares teachers' working conditions within the current one-size-fits-all 'plantation thinking' frame with those of an imagined lush, complex '(managed) rainforest thinking' model.

ity of the journey as more educationally significant than the speed at which the destination is reached. I am talking about a new vision of what education might become and what schools are for.

(Eisner 2005/1993, p. 213, my emphasis)

Eisner's commitment to the qualitative and the experiential in schooling is clear, what is less clear is how these priorities tally with cultures of performativity and accountability metrics, which are seen as hampering the agency of the teacher and the progress of a critical Media Arts discipline.

What frames the problematic is twofold: the infantilisation of the teaching profession through the enactment of neoliberal discourse, as recognised below:

Teachers are no longer encouraged to have a rationale for practice, account of themselves in terms of a relationship to the meaningfulness of what they do, but are required to produce measurable and 'improving' outputs and performances, what is important is what works.

(Ball and Olmedo 2013, p. 91, my emphases)

and the overweening sheen of 'big data' solutions. Ball and Olmedo's critique sits in contrast with, for example, the popular technologically deterministic (Sivek 2011) speak of Chris Anderson (physicist, former editor of Wired magazine). His promotion of a 'new maker industrial revolution' heralds the inception of an increasingly essentialising grand narrative that celebrates the blind acceptance of progress at the expense of criticality:

This is a world where massive amounts of data and applied mathematics replace every other tool that might be brought to bear. Out with every theory of human behaviour, from linguistics to sociology. Forget taxonomy, ontology, and psychology. *Who knows why people do what they do?* The point is they do it, and we can track and measure it with unprecedented fidelity. With enough data, the numbers speak for themselves.

(Anderson 2008, my emphasis)

Bibliography

Anderson, C. (2008, June 23). The end of theory: The data deluge makes the scientific method obsolete. [online]. *Wired.* Retrieved May 20, 2018, from www.wired.com/2008/06/pb-theory/

Anyon, J. (2009). *Theory and Educational Research: Toward Critical Social Explanation.* New York: Routledge.

Bakhtin, M. (1981). *The Dialogic Imagination: Four Essays.* Austin: University of Texas Press.

Ball, S. J., & Olmedo, A. (2013). Care of the self, resistance and subjectivity under neoliberal governmentalities. *Critical Studies in Education, 54*(1), 85–96.

Banaji, S., Buckingham, D., & Burn, A. (2006). *The Rhetorics of Creativity: A Review of the Literature.* London: Institute of Education, Creative Partnerships, Arts Council England.

Barker, C. (2011). *Cultural Studies: Theory and Practice.* London: Sage Publications.

Barrs, M., & Horrocks, S. (2014). *Educational Blogs and Their Effects on Pupils' Writing.* CFBT (Centre for British Teachers) & LCLC (London Connected Learning Centre).

Bazalgette, C. (2008). Literacy in time and space. *PoV: Journal of the Media Education Association, 1*(1), 12–16. Retrieved February 7, 2018, from http://www.themea.org.uk/wpcontent/uploads/2012/09/Pov_volume1_issue1.pdf.

Benjamin, W. (1936). *The Work of Art in the Age of Mechanical Reproduction* [online]. Retrieved February 7, 2018, from https://www.marxists.org/reference/subject/philosophy/works/ge/benjamin.htm.

BFI Education and Film Education. (2012). *Film: 21st Century Literacy— Integrating Film into Education* [online]. London: British Film Institute, Creative Skillset, Filmclub, Film Education, First Light. Retrieved February 7, 2018, from http://www.independentcinemaoffice.org.uk/media/Misc/film-21st-century-literacy-advocacy-report.pdf.

Bordwell, D., & Thompson, K. (2010). *Film Art: An Introduction* (9th ed.). New York: McGraw-Hill.

Bruner, J. S. (2009/1960). *The Process of Education.* Cambridge, MA: Harvard University Press.

Buckingham, D. (2003). *Media Education: Literacy, Learning and Contemporary Culture.* Cambridge: Polity Press.

Buckingham, D. (2007). *Beyond Technology: Children's Learning in the Age of Digital Culture*. London: Routledge.

Burn, A. (2009a). *Making New Media: Creative Production and Digital Literacies*. New York: Peter Lang.

Burn, A. (2009b, December). Culture, art, technology: Towards a poetics of media education [online]. *Cultuur + Educatie, 26*. Retrieved February 7, 2018, from http://aburn2012.files.wordpress.com/2014/04/burn-towards-a-poetic-of-media-education.pdf.

Burn, A. (2013, June). Six arguments for the media arts: Screen education in the 21st century [online]. *NATE: Teaching English, 2*, 55–60. Retrieved February 7, 2018, from http://www.nate.org.uk/cmsfiles/NATE_TE_Issue2_55-60_Burn.pdf. Also: https://aburn2012.files.wordpress.com/2014/04/six-arguments-for-the-media-arts.pdf

Burn, A., & Durran, J. (2006). Digital anatomies: Analysis as production in media education. In D. Buckingham & R. Willett (Eds.), *Digital Generations: Children, Young People, and the New Media* (pp. 273–293). London: Routledge.

Burn, A., & Durran, J. (2007). *Media Literacy in Schools: Practice, Production and Progression*. London: Paul Chapman.

Cannon, M. (2011). *Fashioning and Flow* [online]. MA Dissertation, Institute of Education, London. Retrieved February 7, 2018, from https://fashioningandflow.wordpress.com/.

Claxton, G. (1998). Investigating human intuition: Knowing without knowing why [online]. *The Psychologist, 11*, 217–220. Retrieved February 7, 2018, from https://thepsychologist.bps.org.uk/volume-11/edition-5/investigating-human-intuition-knowing-without-knowing-why.

Cousins, M. (2012). *The Story of Film*. London: Pavilion Books.

Crafts Council. (2014). *Our Future is in the Making* [online]. London. Retrieved February 7, 2018, from http://www.craftscouncil.org.uk/content/files/7822_Education_manifesto%4014FINAL.PDF.

Csikszentmihalyi, M. (1990). *Flow: The Psychology of Optimal Experience*. New York: Harper & Row.

Cultural Learning Alliance. (2011). *ImagineNation—The Case for Cultural Learning* [online]. London. Retrieved February 7, 2018, from http://www.culturallearningalliance.org.uk/news.aspx?id=125.

Cultural Learning Alliance. (2014). *STEM + ARTS = STEAM* [online]. Retrieved February 7, 2018, from http://www.culturallearningalliance.org.uk/images/uploads/STEAM_report.pdf.

Dezuanni, M. (2014). The building blocks of digital media literacy, socio-material participation and the production of media knowledge. *Journal of Curriculum Studies*, 1–24.

Donaldson, S. (2014). *Maximums and Minimums* [online]. Film Literacy Advisory Group (FLAG) Blog. Retrieved February 7, 2018, from https://filmliteracyadvisorygroup.wordpress.com/2014/11/20/maximums-and-minimums/.

Eisner, E. (2002). *The Arts and the Creation of Mind*. New Haven, CT: Yale University Press.

Eisner, E. (2005/1985). Aesthetic modes of knowing. In E. Eisner (Ed.), *Reimagining Schools* (pp. 95–104). Abingdon: Routledge.

Eisner, E. (2005/1993). Forms of understanding and the future of educational research. In E. Eisner (Ed.), *Reimagining Schools* (pp. 150–162). Abingdon: Routledge.

Fielding, M. (2004). Transformative approaches to student voice: Theoretical underpinnings, recalcitrant realities. *British Educational Research Journal, 30*(2), 295–311.

Freire, P. (1993/1970). *Pedagogy of the Oppressed*. London: Penguin.

Furstenau, M., & Mackenzie, A. (2009). The promise of 'makeability': Digital editing software and the structuring of everyday cinematic life. *Visual Communication, 8*(1), 5–22.

Gibb, N. (2015a). *The Purpose of Education* [online]. Department for Education, London. Retrieved February 7, 2018, from https://www.gov.uk/government/speeches/the-purpose-of-education.

Gibb, N. (2015b). Speech on government's maths reforms [online]. In *London Thames Maths Hub Primary Conference*. London. Retrieved February 7, 2018, from https://www.gov.uk/government/speeches/nick-gibb-speech-on-governments-maths-reforms.

Goodman, N. (1978). *Ways of Worldmaking*. Indianapolis: Hackett Publishing.

Haas Dyson, A. (1997). *Writing Superheroes: Contemporary Childhood, Popular Culture, and Classroom Literacy*. New York: Teachers College Press.

Hearing, T. (2015). *The Documentary Imagination: An Investigation into the Performative Application of Documentary Film in Scholarship*. PhD Thesis, Bournemouth University.

Heikkinen, H. L., Huttunen, R., & Syrjälä, L. (2007). Action research as narrative: Five principles for validation. *Educational Action Research, 15*(1), 5–19.

Joaquin, J. (2010). Digital literacies and hip hop texts. In D. Alvermann (Ed.), *Adolescents' Online Literacies: Connecting Classrooms, Digital Media, and Popular Culture* (pp. 109–124). New York: Peter Lang.

Jones, K., with Hearing, T. (2013). Turning research into film: Trevor hearing in conversation with Kip Jones about the short film, RUFUS STONE. In M. Lichtman (Ed.), *Qualitative Research for the Social Sciences* (pp. 184–188). New York: Sage Publications.

Kendall, A., & McDougall, J. (2013). Telling stories out of school. In G. Merchant, J. Gillen, J. Marsh, & D. Julia (Eds.), *Virtual Literacies: Interactive Spaces for Children and Young People* (pp. 89–100). Abingdon: Routledge.

Lanham, R. A. (1994). *The Electronic Word: Democracy, Technology, and the Arts.* Chicago: University of Chicago Press.

Lardoux, X. (2014). *For a European Film Education Policy* [online]. Paris. Retrieved February 7, 2018, from http://www.europacreativamedia.cat/rcs_media/For_a_European_Film_Education_Policy.pdf.

Lather, P. (1991). Research as Praxis. In *Getting Smart: Feminist Research and Pedagogy With/In the Postmodern* (pp. 50–69). New York: Routledge.

Lord, P., Jones, M., Harland, J., Bazalgette, C., Reid, M., Potter, J., et al. (2007). *Special Effects: The Distinctiveness of Learning Outcomes in Relation to Moving Image Education Projects: Final Report* [online]. London: Creative Partnerships. Retrieved February 7, 2018, from http://www.nfer.ac.uk/publications/SPF01/SPF01.pdf.

Luckin, R., Bligh, B., Manches, A., Ainsworth, S., Crook, C., & Noss, R. (2012). *Decoding Learning: The Proof, Promise and Potential of Digital Education* [online]. London: NESTA. Retrieved February 7, 2018, from http://www.nesta.org.uk/sites/default/files/decoding_learning_report.pdf.

Marsh, J. (2010). *Childhood, Culture and Creativity: A Literature Review* [online]. Newcastle. Retrieved February 7, 2018, from http://www.creativity culture-education.org/wp-content/uploads/CCE-childhood-culture-and-creativity-a-literature-review.pdf.

McDougall, J. (2011). Media education after the media [online]. *Manifesto for Media Education.* Retrieved February 7, 2018, from http://www.manifesto-formediaeducation.co.uk/2011/01/media-education-should-be-4/.

McDougall, J. (2014). Curating media literacy: A porous expertise. *Journal of Media Literacy, 16*(1/2), 6–9.

McDougall, J. (2016). "Mediapting" and curation: Research informed pedagogy for (digital) media education Praxis. In J. Frechette & R. Williams (Eds.), *Media Education for a Digital Generation.* New York: Routledge Section 20.

McDougall, J., & Potter, J. (2015). Curating media learning: Towards a porous expertise. *Journal of E-learning and Digital Media, 12*(2), 199–211.

McKee, H. (2005). Richard Lanham's the electronic word and AT/THROUGH oscillations [online]. *Pedagogy: Critical Approaches to Teaching Literature, Language, Composition, and Culture, 5*(1), 117–129. Retrieved February 7, 2018, from http://www.users.miamioh.edu/mckeeha/lanham_review.pdf.

Merleau-Ponty, M. (1964). The film and the new psychology. In H. L. Dreyfus & P. A. Dreyfus (Eds.), *Sense and Non-sense* (pp. 48–59). Chicago: Northwestern University Press.

Moll, L. C., Amanti, C., Neff, D., & Gonzalez, N. (1992). Funds of knowledge for teaching: Using a qualitative approach to connect homes and classrooms. *Theory Into Practice, 31*(2), 132–141.

Monaco, J. (2009). *How to Read a Film: Movies, Media, and Beyond.* Oxford: Oxford University Press.

New London Group. (1996). A pedagogy of multiliteracies: Designing social futures. *Harvard Educational Review, 66*(1), 60–92.

Orr, S., & McDougall, J. (2014). Enquiry into learning and teaching in arts and creative practice. In E. Cleaver, M. Lintern, & M. McLinden (Eds.), *Teaching and Learning in Higher Education: Disciplinary Approaches to Research* (pp. 162–177). London: Sage.

Pendleton-Jullian, A. (2009). *Design Education and Innovation Ecotones* [online]. Retrieved February 7, 2018, from https://fourplusone.files.wordpress.com/2010/03/apj_paper_14.pdf.

Potter, J. (2011). New literacies, new practices and learner research: Across the semi-permeable membrane between home and school. *Lifelong Learning in Europe, 16*(3), 174–181.

Potter, J. (2012). *Digital Media and Learner Identity: The New Curatorship.* New York: Palgrave Macmillan.

Potter, J. (2015). *Forward to the New Age of STEAM(M)! Digital Media, Education and Computing* [online]. Media Literacy, Learning and Curating. Retrieved February 7, 2018, from http://digitalcurationandlearning.com/2015/02/25/forward-to-the-new-age-of-steamm-digital-media-education-and-computing/.

Readman, M. (2010). *What's in a Word? The Discursive Construction of 'Creativity'.* PhD Thesis, Centre for Excellence in Media Practice (CEMP), University of Bournemouth, Bournemouth.

Reid, A. (2007). *The Two Virtuals: New Media and Composition.* West Lafayette, IN: Parlor Press.

Reisz, K., & Millar, G. (2010). *The Technique of Film Editing.* Burlington, MA: Focal Press.

Rogers, T., & Winters, K.-L. (2010). Textual play, satire, and counter discourses of street youth zining practices. In D. Alvermann (Ed.), *Adolescents' Online Literacies: Connecting Classrooms, Digital Media, and Popular Culture* (pp. 91–108). New York: Peter Lang.

Rorabaugh, P. (2012). Digital Culture and Shifting Epistemology [online]. *Hybrid Pedagogy*. Retrieved February 7, 2018, from http://www.hybridpedagogy.com/journal/digital-culture-and-shifting-epistemology/.

Scott, D., & Usher, R. (2011). *Researching Education: Data, Methods and Theory in Educational Inquiry* (2nd ed.). London: Continuum.

Sefton-Green, J. (1998). *'Writing' Media: An Investigation of Practical Production in Media Education by Secondary School Students*. PhD Thesis, Institute of Education, University of London, London.

Sefton-Green, J. (2000). From creativity to cultural production. In J. Sefton-Green & R. Sinker (Eds.), *Evaluating Creativity: Making and Learning by Young People* (pp. 216–231). London: Routledge.

Selwyn, N. (2012). Making sense of young people, education and digital technology: The role of sociological theory. *Oxford Review of Education, 38*(1), 81–96.

Selwyn, N., Cranmer, S., & Potter, J. (2010). *Primary Schools and ICT. Learning from Pupil Perspectives*. London: Continuum.

Sennett, R. (2008). *The Craftsman*. London: Penguin.

Sherrington, T. (2013). *From Plantation Thinking to Rainforest Thinking* [online]. Retrieved May 20, 2018, from https://teacherhead.com/2013/03/10/from-plantation-thinking-to-rainforest-thinking/.

Sivek, S. C. (2011). 'We need a showing of all hands': Technological Utopianism in MAKE magazine [online]. *Journal of Communication Enquiry, 35*(3), 187–209. Retrieved February 7, 2018, from http://digitalcommons.linfield.edu/mscmfac_pubs/5.

Smith, M. K. (2002/1997). *Paulo Freire: Dialogue, Praxis and Education* [online]. The Encyclopaedia of Informal Education. Retrieved August 17, 2015, from http://infed.org/mobi/paulo-freire-dialogue-praxis-and-education/.

Street, B. (1984). *Literacy in Theory and Practice*. Cambridge: Cambridge University Press.

Street, B. (1995). *Social Literacies: Critical Approaches to Literacy in Development, Ethnography and Education*. London: Longman.

Street, B. (2003). What's 'new' in new literacy studies? Critical approaches to literacy in theory and practice. *Current Issues in Comparative Education, 5*(2), 77–91.

Thomson, P., Hall, C., Jones, K., & Sefton-Green, J. (2012). *The Signature Pedagogies Project: Final Report* [online]. London and Newcastle-upon-Tyne: Creativity, Culture and Education. Retrieved February 7, 2018, from http://www.creativitycultureeducation.org/wp-content/uploads/Signature_Pedagogies_Final_Report_April_2012.pdf.

Van Manen, M. (2008). Pedagogical sensitivity and teachers' practical knowing-in-action. *Peking University Education Review, 1*, 2–20.

Vygotsky, L. (1978). *Mind in Society: The Development of Higher Psychological Processes*. Cambridge, MA: Harvard University Press.

Vygotsky, L. (2002/1933). *Play and its Role in the Mental Development of the Child* [online]. Psychology and Marxism Internet Archive. Retrieved February 7, 2018, from https://www.marxists.org/archive/vygotsky/works/1933/play.htm.

Watters, A. (2015). *Ed-Tech Guide: What Should You Know About Education Technology?* [online]. Retrieved February 7, 2018, from http://guide.hackeducation.com.

Waugh, C. (2016). Connecting text. In J. McDougall & P. Bennett (Eds.), *Doing Text: Teaching Media After the Subject*. Leighton Buzzard: Auteur.

Williamson, B. (2017). *Big Data in Education The Digital Future of Learning, Policy and Practice*. London: Sage Publications.

Yandell, J. (2014). Classrooms as sites of curriculum delivery or meaning-making: Whose knowledge counts? *Forum, 56*(1), 147–155.

7

Wider Literacies with Digital Media

My research draws together five human and social dimensions that when combined, form the who, what, when and where of the study. More importantly, however, as a qualitative investigation it examines the how and the why of creative media practices in schools. It remains to summarise the discussion points in relation to the underpinning research questions and then propose ways forward. The first question forms around creative media work's relation to an inclusive and interactive vision of contemporary literacy—one that encompasses film and the moving image as a core entitlement and relevant meaning-making practice. I suggest that this vision is constituted by:

* iterative social and cognitive engagements with media forms
* concrete inscription and crafting of media assets with digital tools of production
* proactive development of imaginative and conceptual leaps
* sensibility and criticality towards the social and environmental network of relations embedded in everyday living

© The Author(s) 2018
M. Cannon, *Digital Media in Education*,
https://doi.org/10.1007/978-3-319-78304-8_7

Further, this view is imbued with an arts perspective, combining students' interests and popular cultural motifs in collaborative cultural production.

The second question goes on to consider how existing teaching practices might adapt to the proliferation of digital media beyond school, with the kinds of pedagogic repertoires used by creative media practitioners, and their choreography of DV and film production moments and processes. This amounts to creating generative, ecotonal spaces of translation that steward and support social and creative agency with expressive resources. It is argued that hybrid, less hierarchical interactions and a style of teaching that encourages praxis, autonomy, recursive trial and error, and phronetic making opportunities, feed a disposition for present and engaged learning.

Finally, a scan of the socio-cultural landscape accounts for the discursive factors that determine practical media work in schools, on an institutional and practical level. It was found that the external forces that constrain the agency of teachers, in turn constrain the opportunities for young people to engage formally with digital media in many schools, except when it is in some way advantageous to the establishment. The strategy to win a notional 'international STEM education race' starts in the primary years with basic computer programming. Further, the marginalisation of the arts in school curricula (and thereby of creative media practice), is symptomatic of our extrinsically motivated, results-driven era. For many schools in economically challenged areas, this results in the pruning of more ambitious and sustained creative media learning, and the prolonging of pen, paper and Pritt technologies. This is not to dislodge or denigrate established literacy and visual arts practices, but to question the ways in which trends towards STEM could limit many learners' early achievements with digital media and inhibit integrated creative expression.

Previous chapters have explored how the professional development of many teachers is undermined by exigent reform measures, demanding "the enactment of performance data" (Ball et al. 2012) at the expense of self-determined practice. Professional practice of this nature is often the catalyst that drives learners' intrinsic motivation, that human constant once successive technical fads have receded. A critical eye was also cast on the nature of authoring software: in schools that do engage with digital media production, it was found that some commercial packages, even as they stoke the imaginative capacity of learners, can potentially shape and confine creative agency.

In an effort to counter deficit narratives of digital media practices in schools, including those describing the "datafication" of school cultures (Roberts-Holmes 2014; Williamson 2017a, 2017b) recounted at the end of Chap. 6, I advance some pragmatic recommendations by making further use of my interpretive model (Fig. 7.1). The media-related dimensions at its core reflect aspects of the social world that seem to frame:

- what people do, where, how and with what digital tools (workability)
- their critical engagement and 'conviviality' in the process (reflexivity and dialectics)
- what they create and how they are seen to 'perform' in their daily lives (everyday artistry)
- and the nature of the social conditions in which all of this happens (historical continuity)

Figure 7.1 is annotated at the outer edges with five emergent themes and a re-purposed title: Teaching, Learning and Digital Media Composition in a Networked Community of Practice. These extensions are justified as I believe the model could have a broader application as a framework for developing and evaluating programmes of learning and pedagogies that incorporate digital media production. It is hoped that my ethnographic work on the intricacies of media production and pedagogy offers a plausible but tentative starting point for the development of an overarching digital making framework, as Sefton-Green (2013) suggested was necessary.

Signature Pedagogies and Critical Media-Making

Bearing in mind the limitations that regulated educational frameworks place on such endeavours, I itemise hybrid pedagogies that shape the best possible conditions in which collaborative creative media engagements

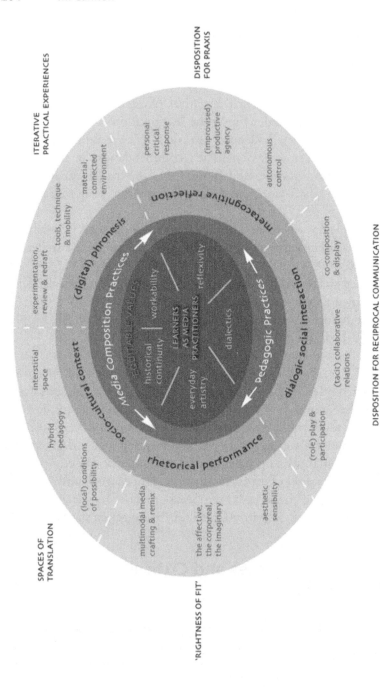

Fig. 7.1 Model for teaching, learning and digital media composition in a networked community of practice

can prosper. In so doing, I nominate the art of critical media-making as a productive practice for raising the consciousness, in the broadest sense, of both maker and audience. In line with a commitment to recognising historical continuity, I then invoke pre-digital literacy ideals that uphold the case for schools' media composition to develop alongside the expressive arts and modern literacy inscription practices.

For many of the following insights I am indebted to the work of Thomson et al. (2012, p. 46) many of whose findings in the Signature Pedagogies report chime with my own. Some of the practices they uncovered in their research with artists and creative practitioners working in schools, will be integrated into five headings which, as stated, relate to the domains of my model. In order then for time-based texts and media production to become established components of literacy teaching and learning—like some arts-based "digital glue" (Brook 2010) that binds subject areas together—I envisage the following.

Managed Time and Space (Workability)

Children and young people are afforded the time and space to develop a phronetic sense; that is, the iterative nature of practical media work is fully realised within the parameters of the possible. Effectively, this amounts to encouraging movements between: watching and making; abstract thought and material representation; the metaphorical and the literal; action and reflection on action; and the repeated drafting and redrafting of outputs. In addition, this means creating the necessary room and mood for learner-practitioners to experience feelings of 'failure' in relatively quick succession ('fast failures' perhaps), as well as technical triumphs and aesthetic successes. Specific attention is paid to the speed and flow of activities underpinned by social connectivity and freedom of movement. The pace is brisk but unhurried: rather than a feeling of time running out towards some remote fixed outcome, the sense is of collective progress towards an ill-defined end.

Film-making in particular is a levelling and trans-disciplinary creative practice that mobilises qualitative tensions. Plans and plot lines change in the midst of production as different ideas are tried, tested and refined. It is this interplay of liquid working relations combined with disciplined, task-oriented roles that appeals to young people, giving them a productive oscillation between structure and agency. In terms of rationale, the infinitely alterable nature of media representations complements cultures of change, possible futures and the practice of Eisnerian judgement in the absence of rule. This opens up the creative process to direction by its participants, and offers an empowered counterpoint to pervasive cultures of external control and performativity.

Recommendation 1: The implications for pedagogy relate to more flexible timetabling and social arrangements. Over a specific period, school leaders would experiment with the structure of the formal day, as well as with more sophisticated after school planning, so that group media projects become a regular embedded social practice both in formal spaces, and in the valuable third space of learning between home and school. Schools would think about their own film and moving image cultures whose forms could more accurately reflect local 'truths', needs and concerns rather than emulating those of industry. Such a strategy would represent a more sincere and therefore more pertinent engagement with the spaces and tools of a wider literacy.

Pedagogic Provocation and Present Sensibility (Reflexivity)

My research indicates that schoolwork that 'matters' is often geared towards national testing, during which process present-ness is often neutralised. To re-balance this deference to an impersonally framed future, creative media production and the development of a film sensibility, proffer a re-engagement with the present, and an alertness to the immediate environment. Creative pedagogic approaches often open with a themed provocation embodied in an artefact or text, coupled with some form of design brief, the dual function of which acts as a stimulus to cognitive and imaginative thought and action. There is an expectation of an autonomous response grounded in the present, with little explicit emphasis on future-oriented learning objectives or success criteria. Success is measured by the group's disposition for praxis that is, the level of theoretical and purposeful engagement with the process. Further, if teachers are to inspire such dispositions for critically informed risk-taking and productive action in their pupils, perhaps the same ought to be encouraged in their practice.

Teaching and learning decisions are in constant negotiation (like Pendleton-Jullian's (2009) kayaker in the rapids). In an earlier section I intimated that pedagogies with media composition processes in particular involve a managed tension between the planned and the improvised, question-posing and problem-solving, autonomous and collaborative learning, and between letting go and adjusting levels of control when necessary. Modelling this kind of agility and versatility, demonstrates to the learner the kind of flexibility and vulnerability they too may have to negotiate as literate practitioners in the digital realm.

Recommendation 2: This study calls for a transformed view of teachers as "public intellectuals" (Giroux 2011, p. 5), rather than as instruments of the state. With less politicised intervention in education design and infrastructure, teachers are empowered to take the long view, and to devise rich curriculum content and relevant assessment routines, in dialogue with the changing needs of young people, and the local and wider community. With fewer utilitarian objectives, time and space for film and moving image production from the early years onwards, become more feasible, and are more likely to gain traction as literacy practices that sharpen critical consciousness and perception.

Make Sociable Meeting Places (Dialectics)

As cited in Chap. 2, one of the framing devices of Signature Pedagogies (Thomson et al. 2012) was taken from the UNESCO commissioned Delors report (1996) relating to the shape of a twenty-first century education. It proposed four foundational pillars of learning—how to know, to do, to live together and to be. Learning to live together is perhaps one of the most overlooked elements of modern schooling, and one which becomes ever more significant in our lived historical moment with respect to mass migration and political intolerance. Without wishing to invest it with all the remedial qualities of a silver bullet, (nor indeed a "silicon bullet"—Lynch 2015, p. 1), the social cohesion that often builds in DV production activity could offer routes to address certain socio-cultural tensions. Creative media practitioners tend towards collaboration as an approach to work, they weave their mediating tools and talents in and out of social interstices and build platforms for debate, dialogue and reciprocal relations.

Group film and media production projects are venues for social gatherings, where, with a specific collective purpose, identities are oxygenated and a particular sense of self is allowed to develop. Strong social bonds are forged within its boundaries, and made all the more complicit with the same tacit understandings and non-verbal cues as those fostered in games and playground interactions. Such practices can encourage playful, dialogic relationships and parity of esteem between its constituents. Mirroring life's vicissitudes, there are peaks and troughs to be negotiated in this burgeoning sense of belonging, and one such peak resides in the moment of display and public address. With appropriate framing and questioning, a media event could function as an interactive, show-tell-and-respond literacy event.

Recommendation 3: In Initial Teacher Training, time should be allocated to the dialogic ways in which film and media projects function and in which unique social spaces for learning and operational excess are generated. With this input, the ground is seeded for genuine cultural partnerships to develop between outside creative agencies and schools, as opposed to the more usual one-off expert-led creative interventions. Teachers should lead the programme with less privilege given to the quality of the textual outcome, and more to pupils' ownership and celebration of the learning process—its intellectual, social and ethereal impact.

Be an Artist! (Everyday Artistry)

Earlier I suggested the ways in which imaginative play is lush terrain for the development of conceptual thought, and how the capacity "to re-imagine the world creates the potential to change it" (Koh 2014). Koh's elaboration of the work of subversive artistry and the disruption of idées reçues, resonates with my research findings. In a comment that recalls the literary stimulus for the Film in a Morning project, she invokes Rushdie's interpretation of the overarching metaphor in the film Brazil (Gilliam 1985). For Rushdie, the film illustrates one of art's great traditions—in which "techniques of comedy, metaphor, heightened imagery, fantasy and so on are used to break down our conventional, habit-dulled certainties about what the world is and has to be" (Rushdie 1991, p. 122). I propose that subversive and imaginative metacognition of this nature is an all-important driver for aesthetic and critical meaning-making with audiovisual media. Instances of wonder and surprise that arise in DV editing and media-crafting make this faculty manifest and can help to nurture a reflexive sense.

Creative pedagogies that combine rich narrative environments with everyday experience and permission to play, render opportunities to rehearse the skill of rhetorical performance. This is a skill which is understood as part of a lifelong process of learning that depends on a strong sense of self, a sensitivity to changing conditions and an awareness of fluctuating audience or peer expectations. The greater the intrinsic desire to refine one's digital creation—to make it better or improve the rightness—the deeper the learning experience. For teachers, this is where acute attention to pupils' aesthetic sensibilities comes to the fore.

Recommendation 4: The development of a critically-inflected Media Arts programme would support moving image and DV editing as a relevant cross-disciplinary expressive practice that amplifies modes of perception. As an extension of this discrete discipline, the professional development of teachers should include support for production skills and for strengthening awareness of young people's dynamic media preferences. Strategies for broadening literacy approaches are thus in a process of continual interest-driven and discursive renewal.

Creating a Distributed Network of Understanding (Historical Continuity)

In Chap. 2, I invoked A. Reid's deliberations on the "material-historical-cultural-space" (2007, p. 25) in which compositional processes are located. I made use of his and others' conceptual armoury to explain the constrained conditions of possibility that surround schools' digital media tools and production. Furthermore, A. Reid loosens cognition from the individual mind, and fashions it materially as a socially distributed network of human and non-human connections. Both these are useful constructs in terms of configuring new spaces in which multiple literacies can thrive and in which translations of meaning can be given a chance to percolate between agents in a community.

This account then, sees schools as porous social hubs with a renewed remit to reach beyond their material confines. Productive roles for pupils are manifold, for example, they could act as junior field agents helping to forge local partnerships and exploring the less familiar realms of their community. Inventive textual capture within the local vicinity creates the potential for intercultural understandings and intergenerational exchanges in a third space of learning (Potter and McDougall 2017). The pedagogies that facilitate this type of engagement are necessarily hybrid, often digitally so, and are backed up with principled and equitable practice. As Stommel states:

> Pedagogy is the place where philosophy and practice meet. It's vibrant and embodied, meditative and productive. Good pedagogy takes both teaching and learning as its subjects.
> (Stommel 2012, original emphasis)

In light of forward-looking pedagogies, one of the areas that will be in need of root and branch reform is that of teaching and learning assessment regimes involving media: digital hybridity aligns maladroitly with linear progress towards sealed numerical standards. It has been suggested in this account that curricula reform increasingly revolves around the needs of its auditors, rather than those of the learning community they purport to serve. I argue that exclusively academic and economically-determined trajectories be short-circuited, and that the needs and interests of pupils and local communities be met as a priority, in dialogue with historical precedent and the wider needs of society.[1]

---

[1] With punitive and performative logic one think-tank proposed that if bureaucratic needs are foiled by exam failure, then a 'resit levy', should be exacted from the offending school and awarded to Further Education institutions dealing with the fall-out. See http://www.policyexchange.org.uk/

Recommendation 5: Inclusivity requires a social and variegated approach to literacy, and permeable borders between classes, year groups, schools, localities, creative agencies and the Inspectorate. School-wide film and interactive media events—some with meaningful local community involvement—would be common practices to be enacted physically and/or shared on open networks. This may be the point at which it is recognised that embedded teacher-practitioners (possibly with pointers on assessment derived from the visual and fine arts), are the ones best placed to assess pupils' group achievements using locally designed criteria.

The above observations on critical media-making practices are entwined in teachers' and pupils' lived experience, and in a sense of freedom of thought, expression and movement. Beyond the fear and control narrative, they support a fundamental trust in young people's integrity as regards their learning, and in their capacity to make more critical choices than might first be assumed—when given the tools, the skills, the time to create, the social space, and the autonomous control.[2] Equally, if teachers were afforded the same 'freedoms' and professional conditions as those just cited for learners, then an environment more auspicious to developing pertinent, interest-driven, media production initiatives may result.

As part of a future-facing, community-oriented approach to education and educational research, this exegesis offers an amalgam of theories that re-frame social practice in three domains: literacy, pedagogy and ethnographic research. My findings suggest that:

* literacy is a disposition towards socio-cultural participation and rhetorical performance reinforced with iterative digital media production, in which young learners are conceived as proto-cultural thinkers and critical producers, within an "(im)material" (Burnett 2011) network of distributed cognition.

---

media-centre/in-the-news/category/item/schools-should-be-fined-for-their-students-gcse-fails-argues-think-tank (Porter 2015) [Accessed 7 February 2018].

[2] Similar sentiments were expressed by Riverside's Mr. C. Available at: https://soundcloud.com/shelleuk/phd-interview-mr-c-riverside-school/s-OSuBH#t=44:49 [Accessed 7 February 2018].

- teachers are professional intellectual media practitioners engaged in developing the knowledge, skills and sensitive pedagogies that facilitate creative engagement and productive learning environments in present and relevant ways.
- ethnographers are "intimate public journalists" (Denzin 2001), equipped with practical media skills and audiovisual sensitivities, whose task is to observe and interpret human, social and material interactions, and produce insightful multi-sensorial narratives.

Literacy: A Disposition Towards Cultural Experience and Production, Made Public

The Cycle of Digital Making in Chap. 2 (Fig. 2.2) offers an interpretation of how cultural products circulate in western societies. Part of that cycle relates to private processes of selection and consumption, and the curation of a personal cultural repertoire, which in large part is made up of media representations. Increasingly the assimilation of digitally mediated 'realities' accounts for a considerable proportion of young people's everyday social encounters—their lived experience. This study proposes that young people's enthusiasm for media production springs from an impulse to "confer a publicly social dimension to cognition" (Eisner 2005/1993, p. 151), and from the desire to "become somebody" (Wexler et al. 1992). My study then, conceives of literacy in the digital age, not simply as a reading and writing threshold, but as the critical capacity and creative sensibility to make and interpret meanings from a range of resources and texts, in/on a range of spaces and platforms. Literacy conceived as multiply sited promises the fullest social and cultural participation.

With thoughts that pre-figure the preoccupations of the digital age, Eisner's understanding of experience and creative action in the public realm throws light on current institutional responsibilities, and young people's disposition to engage with multimodal representation:

> Experience is … private. For experience to become public we must find some means to represent it. Culture makes available to the developing human an array of forms of representation through which the transforma-

tion of consciousness into its public equivalent is created. Schools are culture's agencies for selectively developing competences in the use of these forms. Once public, the content of consciousness is stabilized, and once stabilized it can be edited, revised and shared. But representation is not a one-way street … the act of representation is also an act of invention … it provides its own unpredictable options, options that can only emerge in the course of action.

(Eisner 2005/1993, p. 153, my emphasis)

A more public and socially framed literacy then, is grounded in the freedom to make conceptual leaps with expressive forms, and in the liberty to perform rhetorically as social actors.

Do What You Think!—A Pedagogic Call to Action

Ms. J. persistently urged her Year 6 pupils to act on and trust their own judgement in the unfamiliar world of the editing suite. As an educator, my own guiding impulse is to inspire young people to embrace divergent thinking and take control of their learning through praxis. Recapping Eisner's words above: in order to creatively 'invent' and critically 'represent', with the myriad 'unpredictable options' available to the media author, it is incumbent on schools, as public 'cultural agencies', to widen the 'selection' and opportunities for production of representative forms, in order to make manifest their explanatory power, and their "utility in terms of conceptual understanding and applicability" (Belshaw 2012, p. 160, drawing on Martin 2006). Indeed, as if bolstering such a proposal, film director John Huston made the provocative assertion, that "Film is like thought … it's the closest to thought process of any art" (Huston and Long 2001/1973, p. 44).

The fresh perspective on audiovisual meaning-making offered in this narrative—related to the AT (INTERACT)/THROUGH to-ing and fro-ing between arrangements of digital assets and projected abstractions (Lanham 1994)—offers educators new avenues in the quest to secure pupils' creative, critical and cultural engagement. Furthermore,

Ms. J.'s pedagogic call to action is as much a rallying cry to teachers as it is to students, to resist performing the role of expert, and to consciously embrace the messy imprecision of "in-expertise" (Kendall and McDougall 2012) in matters of media manipulation. In this way, pupil agency and collaborative practices with media surface with more authenticity for the discerning young mind.

Creative Ethnographic Research Practice

For literacy practices to remain relevant and equitable, teaching professionals and the research community would do well to engage critically with the present media interests and representations of children and young people, if only to pull back on imposed 'what works' objectives. In defiance of the teleological, Hall reminds us of the necessarily dialogic and disinterested nature of intellectual work in pursuit of ill-defined gains:

> one moves from one detotalized or deconstructed problematic to the gains of another, recognizing its limitations. That, I think, is the infinite open-endedness of critical work, why critical work is always dialogical. It does have the capacity to establish some important conversations on some ground. That's what I mean by the gain; it gains some ground where thinking can go on around a particular set of problems.
> (Hall 1992, p. 290)

And as technology changes how we access and create knowledge, and communicate understandings to ourselves and to each other, schools' 'particular set of problems' regarding digital media-making is a 'conversation' that becomes increasingly pressing to have and maintain, in a range of contexts, with a range of people, and in/on a range of modes and platforms (Burn et al. 2014, p. 10; Peppler 2013; Sefton-Green 2013).

Doing this study meant negotiating a tension between teacher and researcher roles which often pulled in opposite directions and I felt I never quite managed to do full justice to either. As a researcher, I was processing impressions, and as a teacher I was facilitating the children's meandering paths through different media. Teaching is already a visceral practice[3] and having to toggle between present and future demands on two levels made for a challenging and intense weekly engagement. Teachers and ethnographic researchers share much in common in terms of weighing up conditions and being alert to the moment.

I found that the oscillation in the media production environment between hands-on and hands-off pedagogy is analogous with the practices of the embedded participant-observer. Knowing when and whether to steer events in data reaping mode, or to let go and watch, was a continual struggle. It was towards the end of Clip Club that I felt a release of this tension, which rendered some of the most powerful material. Whilst learners are negotiating cultural material and making and disseminating their own, perhaps successful pupil engagement and profound research insight is down to the improvisations and "skilful neglect" (Loveless 2008, p. 68) of teachers and researchers.

Giving voice to participants has become something of a cliché in qualitative research, but to deny this is to potentially fuel asymmetries in power. Made visible in this account are the observations of a participant-practitioner peering into the often over-looked interstices of creative media practice and pedagogy. What might lend these interpretations theoretical heft is the fact that they are based on rich and textured evidence, mainly generated by the participants themselves—in some instances in impassioned ways—that demand attention and action. Hence the value of this work lies in its capacity to capture excess in unregulated territories and go beyond rigour to the sweet spots of learning at the edges of perceived capability.

Where possible, some of these moments have been presented using the affordances of authoring software for dual representation, such as the inlaid imagery, for a polyvocal perspective. This is surely just the beginning of a technical re-configuration in media education scholarship, in

---

[3] This visceral quality was elaborated on by Mark Reid, former teacher and current Head of Education at the British Film Institute, in a personal interview: "teaching is an experience that engages all of your senses … your heart, your soul and your brain, your gut feeling, your instincts, everything about your being which is lived and in the moment and three dimensional, and physical as well as mental." Available at: https://soundcloud.com/shelleuk/mark-reid/s-wVzWW#t=5:50 [Accessed 7 February 2018].

terms of the potential for creative DV and image data capture, representation and dissemination. Just as teachers and learners are enfranchised by the plural and public embodiment of abstractions that digital media makes possible, so researchers might well feel a similar sense of responsibility to experiment playfully with alternative productive modalities. As Kvale (1996) intimates, as far as research instruments go in the performance of narrative accounts, researchers themselves could be the principals in the orchestra—the ones who experiment with expressive legitimacy. If this study provokes a response from teachers and other researchers, and they are inspired to replicate aspects of it or adapt content or methodology for their own purposes, then I propose this constitutes an extension of Hall's conversation—another stitch in the warp and weft of intellectual work.

Youth Civic Practice

I have already mentioned how school life is often narrowly viewed as preparation for adult working life, but I argue, in a shift to a universalising tone, that school life is a very real existence for all pupils in the here and now, each with largely neglected individual interests and specific circumstances. To counter what seems to be an ever-postponed present, my research supports a future agenda that complements creative fictional outputs with innovative forms of critical documentary. This aligns with McDougall's call for an augmented youth civic praxis to permeate already established literacy networks, and for more dispersed media and social participation pertinent to local youth interests (Goodman 2003; Goodman and Cocca 2014; Mihailidis 2014). Pragmatic partnerships with these and other creative arts agencies will secure:

> a more strategic dialogue between literacy research and media education practice, with a particular emphasis on the aspiration for media educators to foster 'critical' thought and 'civic' action in a new (digital) public sphere … the material (including virtual) conditions for such 'voice' can only be adequately configured with lessons learned from the rich history of 'analogue' literacy enquiry.
> (McDougall 2016)

One of the elegantly argued aims of Alexander's comprehensive Cambridge Primary Review (2010)[4] is indeed the need for citizenship to occupy more space in the scramble for curriculum real estate. In a similar vein, I argued in Chap. 2 that education systems should be devised to maximise the potential for leading a life that can be personally fulfilling, socially rewarding, culturally enriching and economically beneficial, whilst being of benefit to the wider community. In this, my conclusion, I maintain that DV, film and media composition practices and associated pedagogies, have a vital role to play in pursuit of these broad aims and of a transformed school mediascape.

Bibliography

Alexander, R. (Ed.). (2010). *Children, their World, their Education: Final Report and Recommendations of the Cambridge Primary Review*. Abingdon: Routledge.

Ball, S. J., Maguire, M., & Braun, A. (2012). *How Schools Do Policy: Policy Enactments in Secondary Schools*. Abingdon: Routledge.

Belshaw, D. (2012). *What is Digital Literacy? A Pragmatic Investigation* [online]. PhD Thesis, Durham University, Durham. Retrieved February 7, 2018, from http://neverendingthesis.com.

Brazil. (1985). Film, Directed by T. Gilliam. USA: Universal Pictures.

Brook, T. (2010). Digital glue: Creative media in the classroom. In C. Bazalgette (Ed.), *Teaching Media in Primary Schools* (pp. 116–130). London: SAGE Publications.

Burn, A., Potter, J., & Reid, M. (2014). Media arts, digital culture and education—Guest editorial [online]. *Media Education Research Journal, 5*(1), 5–14. Retrieved February 7, 2018, from http://merj.info/wp-content/uploads/2014/11/MERJ_5.1_Introduction.pdf.

Burnett, C. (2011). The (im)materiality of educational space: Interactions between material, connected and textual dimensions of networked technology use in schools. *E-Learning and Digital Media, 8*(3), 214.

Delors, J. (1996). *Learning: The Treasure Within*. The International Commission on Education for the 21st Century. Paris: UNESCO.

---

[4] The twelve aims of the esteemed Cambridge Primary Review (Alexander 2010, pp. 197–199) many of which speckle this account, are succinctly itemised here: http://cprtrust.org.uk/about_cprt/aims/ [Accessed 7 February 2018].

Denzin, N. K. (2001). *Interpretive Interactionism* (2nd ed.). London: Sage.

Eisner, E. (2005/1993). Forms of understanding and the future of educational research. In E. Eisner (Ed.), *Reimagining Schools* (pp. 150–162). Abingdon: Routledge.

Giroux, H. A. (2011). *On Critical Pedagogy*. New York: Continuum.

Goodman, S. (2003). *Teaching Youth Media, A Critical Guide to Literacy, Video Production, and Social Change*. New York: Teachers College Press.

Goodman, S. & Cocca, C. (2014). Spaces of action: Teaching critical literacy for community empowerment in the age of neoliberalism [online]. *English Teaching: Practice and Critique, 13*(3), 210–226. Retrieved May 22, 2018, from http://education.waikato.ac.nz/research/files/etpc/files/2014v13n3dial1.pdf.

Hall, S. (1992). Cultural studies and its theoretical legacies [online]. In L. Grossberg, C. Nelson, & P. Treichler (Eds.), *Cultural Studies* (pp. 277–294). London and New York: Routledge. Retrieved February 7, 2018, from http://msuweb.montclair.edu/~furrg/pursuits/hallcultstuds.html.

Huston, J., & Long, R. E. (2001/1973). *John Huston: Interviews*. Jackson, MS: University Press of Mississippi.

Kendall, A., & McDougall, J. (2012). Critical media literacy after the media [online]. *Revista Comunicar*. Retrieved February 7, 2018, from http://www.revistacomunicar.com/pdf/preprint/38/En-02-PRE-13482.pdf.

Koh, A. (2014). *The Political Power of Play* [online]. Hybrid Pedagogies. Retrieved February 7, 2018, from http://www.hybridpedagogy.com/journal/political-power-of-play/.

Kvale, S. (1996). *Interviews: An Introduction to Qualitative Research Interviewing*. London: Sage Publications.

Lanham, R. A. (1994). *The Electronic Word: Democracy, Technology, and the Arts*. Chicago: University of Chicago Press.

Loveless, A. (2008). Creative learning and new technology? A provocation paper [online]. In J. Sefton-Green (Ed.), *Creative Learning* (pp. 61–71). London: Creative Partnerships, The Arts Council. Retrieved February 7, 2018, from https://www.sussex.ac.uk/webteam/gateway/file.php?name=creative-learning-sept-2008&site=45 .

Lynch, T. L. (2015). *The Hidden Role of Software in Educational Research: Policy to Practice*. New York: Routledge.

Martin, A. (2006). A European framework for digital literacy [online]. *Nordic Journal of Digital Literacy, 1*(2), 151–161. Retrieved February 7, 2018, from http://www.idunn.no/dk/2006/02/a_european_framework_for_digital_literacy.

McDougall, J. (2016). "Mediapting" and curation: Research informed pedagogy for (digital) media education Praxis. In J. Frechette & R. Williams (Eds.), *Media Education for a Digital Generation*. New York: Routledge Section 20.

Mihailidis, P. (2014). *Media Literacy and the Emerging Citizen: Youth, Engagement and Participation in Digital Culture*. New York: Peter Lang.

Pendleton-Jullian, A. (2009). *Design Education and Innovation Ecotones* [online]. Retrieved February 7, 2018, from https://fourplusone.files.wordpress.com/2010/03/apj_paper_14.pdf.

Peppler, K. (2013). *New Opportunities for Interest-Driven Arts Learning in a Digital Age*. New York: The Wallace Foundation.

Porter, N. (2015). *Schools Should be Fined for Their Students' GCSE Fails, Argues Think Tank* [online]. Policy Exchange. Retrieved February 7, 2018, from https://policyexchange.org.uk/schools-should-be-fined-if-pupils-dont-make-the-grade/.

Potter, J., & McDougall, J. (2017). *Digital Media, Culture and Education: Theorising Third Space Literacies*. London: Palgrave Macmillan.

Reid, A. (2007). *The Two Virtuals: New Media and Composition*. West Lafayette, IN: Parlor Press.

Roberts-Holmes, G. (2014). The 'datafication' of early years pedagogy 'if the teaching is good, the data should be good and if there's bad teaching, there is bad data'. *Journal of Education Policy, 30*(3), 302–315.

Rushdie, S. (1991). *Imaginary Homelands*. London: Granta.

Sefton-Green, J. (2013). *Mapping Digital Makers: A Review Exploring Everyday Creativity, Learning Lives and the Digital*. State of the Art Reviews. London: Nominet Trust.

Stommel, J. (2012). Hybridity, pt. 2: What is Hybrid Pedagogy? [online]. *Hybrid Pedagogy* [online]. Retrieved February 7, 2018, from http://www.hybridpedagogy.com/journal/hybridity-pt-2-what-is-hybrid-pedagogy/.

Thomson, P., Hall, C., Jones, K., & Sefton-Green, J. (2012). *The Signature Pedagogies Project: Final Report* [online]. London and Newcastle-upon-Tyne: Creativity, Culture and Education. Retrieved February 7, 2018, from https://www.creativitycultureeducation.org/publication/the-signature-pedagogies-project/ .

Wexler, P., Crichlow, W., Kern, J., & Matusewicz, R. (1992). *Becoming Somebody: Toward a Social Psychology of School*. Abingdon: Routledge.

Williamson, B. (2017a). *Big Data in Education The Digital Future of Learning, Policy and Practice*. London: Sage Publications.

Williamson, B. (2017b). Learning in the "platform society": Disassembling an educational data assemblage. *Research in Education, 98*(1), 59–82.

Bibliography

Aberdare, Lord A. L., (2015). *Parliamentlive.tv* [online]. *House of Lords debate* [online]. Retrieved February 7, 2018, from http://www.parliamentlive.tv/Event/Index/8ae0f3a3-e276-48e1-b921-b6b6e7a148d8 (Time code: 11:14:22–11:23:00).

Abrams, F. (2012). Cultural literacy Michael Gove's school of hard facts. *BBC Radio 4's Analysis* [online]. Retrieved February 7, 2018, from http://www.bbc.co.uk/news/education-20041597.

Adams, J. (2013). The English baccalaureate: A new Philistinism? *International Journal of Art & Design Education, 32*(1), 2–5.

Alasuutari, P. (1995). *Researching Culture: Qualitative Method and Cultural Studies.* California: Sage Publications.

Alexander, R. (Ed.). (2010). *Children, their World, their Education: Final Report and Recommendations of the Cambridge Primary Review.* Abingdon: Routledge.

Alexander, R. (2014). The best that has been thought and said. *Forum, 56*(1) [online]. Retrieved February 7, 2018, from http://www.robinalexander.org.uk/wp-content/uploads/2014/02/19_Alexander_FORUM_56_1_web.pdf.

Alma. (2009) [online]. Short Film, Directed by R. Blaas. Spain. Retrieved February 7, 2018, from https://vimeo.com/4749536.

Anderson, C. (2008, June 23). The end of theory: The data deluge makes the scientific method obsolete. [online]. *Wired.* Retrieved May 20, 2018, from www.wired.com/2008/06/pb-theory/

© The Author(s) 2018
M. Cannon, *Digital Media in Education,*
https://doi.org/10.1007/978-3-319-78304-8

Anderson, C. (2012). *Makers: The New Industrial Revolution*. London: Random House Business Books.

Animatou. (2007). Short Film. Directed by C. Luyet. Switzerland.

Anyon, J. (2009). *Theory and Educational Research: Toward Critical Social Explanation*. New York: Routledge.

Appadurai, A. (1986). *The Social Life of Things: Commodities in Cultural Perspective*. Cambridge: Cambridge University Press.

Arendt, H. (1981/1971). *The Life of the Mind*. San Diego: Houghton Mifflin Harcourt.

Atkinson, P., & Hammersley, M. (2007). *Ethnography Principles in Practice* (3rd ed.). London: Routledge.

Back, L. (2013). *The Art of Listening*. London: Bloomsbury Academic.

Bakhtin, M. (1981). *The Dialogic Imagination: Four Essays*. Austin: University of Texas Press.

Ball, S. J. (1995). Intellectuals or technicians? The urgent role of theory in educational studies. *British Journal of Educational Studies, 43*(3), 255–271.

Ball, S. J. (2013). *The Education Debate* (2nd ed.). Bristol: Policy Press.

Ball, S. J., Maguire, M., & Braun, A. (2012). *How Schools Do Policy: Policy Enactments in Secondary Schools*. Abingdon: Routledge.

Ball, S. J., & Olmedo, A. (2013). Care of the self, resistance and subjectivity under neoliberal governmentalities [online]. *Critical Studies in Education, 54*(1), 85–96. Retrieved February 7, 2018, from https://www.fe.unicamp.br/TEMPORARIOS/cse-resistance.pdf.

Banaji, S., Buckingham, D., & Burn, A. (2006). *The Rhetorics of Creativity: A Review of the Literature*. London: Institute of Education, Creative Partnerships, Arts Council England.

Barker, C. (2011). *Cultural Studies: Theory and Practice*. London: Sage Publications.

Barker, M. (2001). On the problems of being a 'trendy travesty'. In M. Barker & J. Petley (Eds.), *Ill Effects: The Media/Violence Debate* (pp. 202–224). London: Routledge.

Barone, T. (2001). Pragmatizing the imaginary: A response to a fictionalized case study of teaching [online]. *Harvard Educational Review, 71*(4), 734–741. Retrieved February 7, 2018, from http://hepg.org/her-home/issues/harvard-educational-review-volume-71-issue-4/herarticle/a-response-to-a-fictionalized-case-study-of-teachi.

Barone, T. (2007). A return to the gold standard? Questioning the future of narrative construction as educational research. *Qualitative Inquiry, 13*(4), 454–470.

Barrs, M., & Horrocks, S. (2014). *Educational Blogs and Their Effects on Pupils' Writing.* CFBT (Centre for British Teachers) & LCLC (London Connected Learning Centre).

Barthes, R. (1977). *Image—Music—Text* (Stephen Heath trans.). London: Fontana Press.

Barthes, R. (1979). *Camera Lucida: Reflections on Photography.* London: Vintage.

Bassey, M. (1998). Fuzzy generalisation: An approach to building educational theory [online]. In *BERA: British Educational Research Association Annual Conference.* The Queen's University of Belfast, Northern Ireland. Retrieved February 7, 2018, from http://www.leeds.ac.uk/educol/documents/000000801.htm.

Bassey, M., Wrigley, T., Maguire, M., & Pring, R. (2013, March 19). Gove will bury pupils in facts and rules. *The Independent* [online]. Retrieved February 7, 2018, from http://www.independent.co.uk/voices/letters/letters-gove-will-bury-pupils-in-facts-and-rules-8540741.html.

Bazalgette, C. (1989). *Primary Media Education: A Curriculum Statement.* London: British Film Institute.

Bazalgette, C. (2000). A stitch in time: Skills for the new literacy. *English in Education, 34*(1), 42–49.

Bazalgette, C. (2008). Literacy in time and space. *PoV: Journal of the Media Education Association, 1*(1), 12–16. Retrieved May 24, 2018, from http://english.hias.hants.gov.uk/pluginfile.php/1718/mod_resource/content/0/LitTimeSpace_1_.pdf.

Bazalgette, C. (2010). *Teaching Media in Primary Schools.* London: Sage.

Bazalgette, C. (2011). Rethinking text [online]. In *Empowerment Through Literacy: Literacy Shaping Futures—UKLA 47th International Conference.* Chester: UKLA, 20–31. Retrieved February 7, 2018, from http://www.ukla.org/downloads/UKLA_Chester_International_Conference_Papers_2011.pdf.

Bazalgette, C. (2012). *Key Findings of the Persistence of Vision: Animation and Poetry Project* [online]. Retrieved February 7, 2018, from http://www.themea.org.uk/archive/persistence-of-visionanimation-and-poetry-in-primary-schools/.

Bazalgette, C. (2018). *Some Secret Language: How Toddlers Learn to Understand Movies.* PhD Thesis, UCL, Institute of Education, University of London, London.

Bazalgette, C., & Bearne, E. (2010). *Beyond Words: Developing Children's Understanding of Multimodal Texts.* Leicester: UKLA.

Bazalgette, C., & Buckingham, D. (2013). Literacy, media and multimodality: A critical response. *Literacy, 47*(2), 95–102.

Bazalgette, C., Parry, B., & Potter, J. (2011). Creative, cultural and critical: Media literacy theory in the primary classroom [online]. In *Creative Engagements: Thinking with Children*. Oxford: Inter-Disciplinary.net. Retrieved February 7, 2018, from http://www.inter-disciplinary.net/wp-content/uploads/2011/06/bazalgettecpaper.pdf.

Bazalgette, C., & Staples, T. (1995). Unshrinking the kids: Children's cinema and the family film. In C. Bazalgette & D. Buckingham (Eds.), *In Front of the Children: Screen Entertainment and Young Audiences* (pp. 92–108). London: British Film Institute.

BECTA. (2003). *What the Research Says About Digital Video in Teaching and Learning* [online]. Coventry: BECTA ICT Research. Retrieved February 7, 2018, from http://www.nsead.org/ict/resources/downloads/Research15_DigitalVideo.pdf.

Belshaw, D. (2011). *The Essential Elements of Digital Literacies* [online]. Presentation to the Association of Independent Schools of New South Wales (Australia) ICT Managers Conference. Retrieved February 7, 2018, from http://www.slideshare.net/dajbelshaw/the-essential-elements-of-digital-literacies.

Belshaw, D. (2012). *What is Digital Literacy? A Pragmatic Investigation* [online]. PhD Thesis, Durham University, Durham. Retrieved February 7, 2018, from http://neverendingthesis.com.

Benedict, R. (1934). *Patterns of Culture*. New York: Houghton Mifflin Harcourt.

Benjamin, W. (1936). *The Work of Art in the Age of Mechanical Reproduction* [online]. Retrieved February 7, 2018, from https://www.marxists.org/reference/subject/philosophy/works/ge/benjamin.htm.

Bennett, D., & Doherty, D. (2010). Innovation, education, and the maker movement [online]. In *Innovation, Education, and the Maker Movement*. New York: New York Hall of Science. Retrieved February 7, 2018, from http://nysci.org/wp-content/uploads/Maker-Faire-Report-Final.pdf.

Bennett, S., Maton, K., & Kervin, L. (2008). The 'digital natives' debate: A critical review of the evidence. *British Journal of Educational Technology, 39*(5), 775–786.

Bennett, T. (2013). *Teacher Proof: Why Research in Education Doesn't Always Mean What It Claims, and What You Can Do About It*. London: Routledge.

BERA. (2011). *Ethical Guidelines for Educational Research* [online]. London. Retrieved February 7, 2018, from https://www.bera.ac.uk/wp-content/uploads/2014/02/BERA-Ethical-Guidelines-2011.pdf.

Bergala, A. (2002). *L'hypothèse cinéma. Petit traité de transmission du cinéma à l'école et ailleurs*. Paris: Cahiers du cinéma.

Bergala, A., Whittle, M., & Bachmann, A. (2016). *The Cinema Hypothesis— Teaching Cinema in the Classroom and Beyond*. Vienna: Austrian Film Institute.

Berger, R., & Zezulkova, M. (2018). A remaking pedagogy: Adaptation and archetypes in the child's multimodal reading and writing. *Education 3–13, 46*(1), 64–75.

Bergeron, P. J. (2017). *How to Engage in Pseudoscience with Real Data: A Criticism of John Hattie's Arguments in Visible Learning from the Perspective of a Statistician* [online]. Retrieved February 7, 2018, from http://mje.mcgill.ca/article/view/9475/7229.

BFI Education. (2008). *Reframing Literacy* [online]. London: British Film Institute. Retrieved February 7, 2018, from http://www.bfi.org.uk/sites/bfi.org.uk/files/downloads/bfi-education-reframing-literacy-2013-04.pdf.

BFI Education and Film Education. (2012). *Film: 21st Century Literacy— Integrating Film into Education* [online]. London: British Film Institute, Creative Skillset, Filmclub, Film Education, First Light. Retrieved February 7, 2018, from http://www.independentcinemaoffice.org.uk/media/Misc/film-21st-century-literacy-advocacy-report.pdf.

Bhabha, H. K. (1994). *The Location of Culture*. London: Routledge.

Black, P., & Wiliam, D. (1998). Inside the black box: Raising standards through classroom assessment [online]. *Phi Delta Kappan, 80*, 139–148. Retrieved February 7, 2018, from http://weaeducation.typepad.co.uk/files/blackbox-1.pdf.

Blum-Ross, A. (2013). 'It made our eyes get bigger': Youth film-making and place-making in East London. *Visual Anthropology Review, 29*(2), 89–106.

Bold, C. (2012). *Using Narrative in Research*. London: Sage.

Bordwell, D., & Thompson, K. (2010). *Film Art: An Introduction* (9th ed.). New York: McGraw-Hill.

Bourdieu, P. (1984). *Distinction: A Social Critique of the Judgement of Taste*. London: Routledge.

boyd, d. (2008). Why youth (♥) youth social network sites: The role of networked publics in teenage social life. In D. Buckingham (Ed.), *Youth, Identity, and Digital Media*. The John D. and Catherine T. MacArthur Foundation Series on Digital Media and Learning (pp. 119–142). Cambridge, MA: MIT Press.

boyd, d. (2014). *It's Complicated—The Social Lives of Networked Teens* [online]. New Haven, CT: Yale University Press. Retrieved February 7, 2018, from http://www.danah.org/books/ItsComplicated.pdf.

Bradford City of Film (2010–2015). *Bradford Film Literacy Programme* [online]. Retrieved February 7, 2018, from http://bradfordfilmliteracy.com/about/.

Bragg, S., & Manchester, H. (2011). *Creativity, School Ethos and the Creative Partnerships Programme* [online]. Newcastle upon Tyne. Retrieved February 7, 2018, from http://www.creativitycultureeducation.org/wp-content/uploads/may-2011-final-report-ou-creativity-school-ethos-and-creative-partnerships-282.pdf.

Brazil. (1985). Film, Directed by T. Gilliam. USA: Universal Pictures.

Brook, T. (2010). Digital glue: Creative media in the classroom. In C. Bazalgette (Ed.), *Teaching Media in Primary Schools* (pp. 116–130). London: SAGE Publications.

Bruner, J. S. (1990). *Acts of Meaning.* Cambridge, MA: Harvard University Press.

Bruner, J. S. (1996). *The Culture of Education.* Cambridge, MA: Harvard University Press.

Bruner, J. S. (2009/1960). *The Process of Education.* Cambridge, MA: Harvard University Press.

Bryer, T., Lindsay, M., & Wilson, R. (2014). A take on a Gothic poem: Tablet film-making and literary texts. *Changing English: Studies in Culture and Education, 21*(3), 235–251.

Bryman, A. (2008). *Social Research Methods* (3rd ed.). Oxford: Oxford University Press.

Buckingham, D. (1986). Against demystification: A response to teaching the media. *Screen, 27*, 80–85.

Buckingham, D. (1990). *Watching Media Learning: Making Sense of Media Education.* London: The Falmer Press.

Buckingham, D. (2003). *Media Education: Literacy, Learning and Contemporary Culture.* Cambridge: Polity Press.

Buckingham, D. (2007). *Beyond Technology: Children's Learning in the Age of Digital Culture.* London: Routledge.

Buckingham, D. (2009). 'Creative' visual methods in media research: Possibilities, problems and proposals. *Media Culture and Society, 31*(4), 633–652.

Buckingham, D. (2010). Do we really need media education 2.0? Teaching in the age of participatory media. In K. Drotner & K. Schroder (Eds.), *Digital Content Creation: Perceptions, Practices and Perspectives* (pp. 287–304). New York: Peter Lang.

Buckingham, D., 2014a. The Success and failure of media education [online]. *Media Education Research Journal, 4*(2), 5–17. Retrieved February 7, 2018, from http://merj.info/wp-content/uploads/2014/01/MERJ_4-2-Editorial.pdf.

Buckingham, D. (2014b). The (re-)making of media educators: Teacher identities in changing times. In P. Benson & A. Chik (Eds.), *Popular Culture, Pedagogy and Teacher Education: International Perspectives* (pp. 125–137). London: Routledge.

Buckingham, D. (2017). *The Strangulation of Media Studies* [online]. Retrieved January 1, 2018, from https://ddbuckingham.files.wordpress.com/2017/08/strangulation-final-2.pdf.

Buckingham, D., & Sefton-Green, J. (1994). *Cultural Studies Goes to School*. London: Taylor & Francis.

Buckingham, D., & Sefton-Green, J. (2003). Gotta catch 'em all: Structure, agency and pedagogy in children's media culture. *Media, Culture & Society, 25*(3), 379–399.

Bulfin, S., & Koutsogiannis, D. (2012). New literacies as multiply placed practices: Expanding perspectives on young people's literacies across home and school. *Language and Education, 26*(4), 331–346.

Bull, E. (2012). *Rationales for Film in Secondary English: Subject Identity, Situated Practice and Professional Histories*. Masters Dissertation, UCL, Institute of Education, University of London, London.

Burke, C. (2008). 'Play in focus': Children's visual voice in participative research. In P. Thomson (Ed.), *Doing Visual Research with Children and Young People* (pp. 23–36). Abingdon: Routledge.

Burn, A. (2009a). *Making New Media: Creative Production and Digital Literacies*. New York: Peter Lang.

Burn, A. (2009b, December). Culture, art, technology: Towards a poetics of media education [online]. *Cultuur + Educatie, 26*. Retrieved February 7, 2018, from http://aburn2012.files.wordpress.com/2014/04/burn-towards-a-poetic-of-media-education.pdf.

Burn, A. (2011). Beyond the heuristic of suspicion: The value of media literacy [online]. In A. Goodwyn & C. Fuller (Eds.), *The Great Literacy Debate: A Critical Response to the Literacy Strategy and the Framework for English* (pp. 8–27). London: Routledge. Retrieved February 7, 2018, from http://aburn2012.files.wordpress.com/2014/04/beyond-the-heuristic-of-suspicion.pdf.

Burn, A. (2013, June). Six arguments for the media arts: Screen education in the 21st century [online]. *NATE: Teaching English, 2*, 55–60. Retrieved February 7, 2018, from http://www.nate.org.uk/cmsfiles/NATE_TE_Issue 2_55-60_Burn.pdf.

Burn, A., Brindley, S., Durran, J., Kelsall, C., Sweetlove, J., & Tuohey, C. (2001). The rush of images: A research report into digital editing and the moving image. *English in Education, 35*(2), 34–47.

Burn, A., & Durran, J. (2006). Digital anatomies: Analysis as production in media education. In D. Buckingham & R. Willett (Eds.), *Digital Generations: Children, Young People, and the New Media* (pp. 273–293). London: Routledge.

Burn, A., & Durran, J. (2007). *Media Literacy in Schools: Practice, Production and Progression.* London: Paul Chapman.

Burn, A., & Parker, D. (2001). Making your mark: Digital inscription, animation and a new visual semiotic. *Education, Communication and Information, 1*(2), 155–179.

Burn, A., & Parker, D. (2003). *Analysing Media Texts.* Continuum Research Methods. London: Continuum.

Burn, A., Potter, J., & Parry, B. (2012). *Montage, Mash-up, Machinima* [online]. DARE: Digital, Arts, Research, Education. Institute of Education, University College London. Retrieved February 7, 2018, from http://darecollaborative. net/2012/06/20/montage-mash-up-and-machinima/.

Burn, A., Potter, J., & Reid, M. (2014). Media arts, digital culture and education—Guest editorial [online]. *Media Education Research Journal, 5*(1), 5–14. Retrieved February 7, 2018, from http://merj.info/wp-content/ uploads/2014/11/MERJ_5.1_Introduction.pdf.

Burnett, C. (2009). Research into literacy and technology in primary classrooms: An exploration of understandings generated by recent studies [online]. *Journal of Research in Reading (Special Issue: New Developments in Literacy and Technology), 31*(1), 22–37. Retrieved March 6, 2018, from http://shura.shu. ac.uk/1307/1/Research_into_literacy.pdf.

Burnett, C. (2011a). The (im)materiality of educational space: Interactions between material, connected and textual dimensions of networked technology use in schools. *E-Learning and Digital Media, 8*(3), 214.

Burnett, C. (2011b). Shifting multiple spaces in classrooms: An argument for investigating learners' boundary-making around digital networked texts [online]. *Journal of Literacy and Technology, 12*(3). Retrieved February 7, 2018, from http://www.literacyandtechnology.org/uploads/1/3/6/8/136889/ jlt_v12_3_burnett.pdf.

Burnett, C. (2016). *The Digital Age and its Implications for Learning and Teaching in the Primary School.* York. Retrieved February 7, 2018, from http://cprtrust. org.uk/wp-content/uploads/2016/07/Burnett-report-20160720.pdf.

Burnett, C., & Bailey, C. (2014). Conceptualising collaboration hybrid sites: Playing *Minecraft* together and apart in a primary classroom. In J. Davies, G. Merchant, & J. Rowsell (Eds.), *New Literacies around the Globe: Policy and Pedagogy (Routledge Research in Literacy)* (pp. 50–71). Abingdon: Routledge.

Burnett, C., & Merchant, G. (2015). The challenge of 21st-century literacies. *Journal of Adolescent & Adult Literacy, 59*(3), 271–274.

Burnett, C., Merchant, G., Pahl, K., & Rowsell, J. (2012). The (im)materiality of literacy: The significance of subjectivity to new literacies research. *Discourse: Studies in the Cultural Politics of Education, 35*(1), 90–103.

Cannon, M. (2011). *Fashioning and Flow* [online]. MA Dissertation, Institute of Education, London. Retrieved February 7, 2018, from https://fashioningandflow.wordpress.com/.

Cannon, M. (2013). *Ann Pendleton-Jullian & Design Education* [online]. Retrieved February 7, 2018, from http://makingislearning.com/2013/04/13/ann-pendleton-jullian-design-education/.

Cannon, M., Bryer, T., & Lindsey, M. (2014). Media production and disruptive innovation: Exploring the interrelations between children, tablets, teachers and texts in subject English settings. *Media Education Research Journal, 5*(1), 16–31.

Cannon, M., Potter, J., & Burn, A. (2018). Dynamic, playful and productive literacies. *Changing English, 25*(2).

Cantrill, C., Filipiak, D., Antero, G., Bud, H., Lee, C., Mirra, N., et al. (2014). Teaching in the connected learning classroom [online]. In A. Garcia (Ed.), *Report Series on Connected Learning*. Irvine, CA: The Digital Media and Learning Research Hub. Retrieved February 7, 2018, from http://dmlhub.net/wp-content/uploads/files/teaching-in-the-CL-classroom.pdf.

Charmas, K. (2014). *Constructing Grounded Theory* (2nd ed.). London: Sage Publications.

Clandinin, D. J., & Murphy, S. (2009). Relational ontological commitments in narrative research. *Educational Researcher, 38*(8), 598–602.

Clandinin, D. J., & Rosiek, J. (2007). Mapping a landscape of narrative inquiry: Borderland spaces and tensions. In D. J. Clandinin (Ed.), *Handbook of Narrative Inquiry: Mapping a Methodology* (pp. 35–75). Thousand Oaks, CA: Sage Publications Inc.

Claxton, G. (1998). Investigating human intuition: Knowing without knowing why [online]. *The Psychologist, 11*, 217–220. Retrieved February 7, 2018, from https://thepsychologist.bps.org.uk/volume-11/edition-5/investigating-human-intuition-knowing-without-knowing-why.

Claxton, G. (2003). *Creativity: A Guide for the Advanced Learner (and Teacher)* [online]. Adapted from an article in the National Association of Head Teachers' Leadership Papers. Retrieved February 7, 2018, from http://www.s7colleges.com/learning-innovation/_pdf/A%20Guide%20for%20the%20Advanced%20Learner.pdf.

Clough, P. (2002). *Narratives and Fictions in Educational Research*. Maidenhead: Open University Press.

Cohen, L., Manion, L., & Morrison, K. (2007). *Research Methods in Education* (6th ed.). London: Routledge.

Commons Select Committee. (2013, September 26). *Culture, Media and Sport Committee.* Third Report [online]. Paragraph 117. Retrieved February 7, 2018, from http://www.publications.parliament.uk/pa/cm201314/cmselect/cmcumeds/674/67409.htm.

Connected Learning Alliance. (2015). *Why Connected Learning?* [online]. Retrieved February 7, 2018, from http://clalliance.org/why-connected-learning/.

Conteh, J., Gregory, E., Kearney, C., & Mor-Sommerfeld, A. (2005). *On Writing Educational Ethnographies: The Art of Collusion*. Stoke on Trent: Trentham Books.

Cope, B., & Kalantzis, M. (2000). *Multiliteracies: Literacy Learning and the Design of Social Futures*. New York: Routledge.

Cousins, M. (2012). *The Story of Film*. London: Pavilion Books.

Craft, A. (2013). Childhood, possibility thinking and wise, humanising educational futures. *International Journal of Educational Research, 61*, 126–134.

Crafts Council. (2014). *Our Future is in the Making* [online]. London. Retrieved February 7, 2018, from http://www.craftscouncil.org.uk/content/files/7822_Education_manifesto%4014FINAL.PDF.

Crawford, M. (2009). *The Case for Working with your Hands: Or Why Office Work is Bad for Us and Fixing Things Feels Good*. London: Penguin.

Csikszentmihalyi, M. (1990). *Flow: The Psychology of Optimal Experience*. New York: Harper & Row.

Cultural Learning Alliance. (2011). *ImagineNation—The Case for Cultural Learning* [online]. London. Retrieved February 7, 2018, from http://www.culturallearningalliance.org.uk/news.aspx?id=125.

Cultural Learning Alliance. (2014). *STEM + ARTS = STEAM* [online]. Retrieved February 7, 2018, from http://www.culturallearningalliance.org.uk/images/uploads/STEAM_report.pdf.

Curriculum Review Group. (2004). *A Curriculum for Excellence* [online]. Education Scotland. Retrieved February 7, 2018, from https://education. gov.scot/scottish-education-system/policy-for-scottish-education/policy-drivers/cfe-(building-from-the-statement-appendix-incl-btc1-5)/ Experiences%20and%20outcomes#arts.

Dall'Alba, G., & Barnacle, R. (2007). An ontological turn for higher education. *Studies in Higher Education, 32*(6), 679–691.

Delors, J. (1996). *Learning: The Treasure Within.* The International Commission on Education for the 21st Century. Paris: UNESCO.

Denzin, N. K. (2001). *Interpretive Interactionism* (2nd ed.). London: Sage.

Dewey, J. (1997/1938). *Experience and Education.* New York: Touchstone.

Dewey, J. (2008/1916). *The Middle Works of John Dewey, 1899–1924, Volume 9: 1916, Democracy and Education* (Vol. 9). Southern Illinois: SIU Press.

Dezuanni, M. (2011). *Media Education as a Basic Entitlement for all Children and Young People* [online]. Manifesto for Media Education. Retrieved February 7, 2018, from http://www.manifestoformediaeducation.co.uk/2011/06/michael-dezuanni/.

Dezuanni, M. (2014). The building blocks of digital media literacy, socio-material participation and the production of media knowledge. *Journal of Curriculum Studies*, 1–24.

Dezuanni, M., & Woods, A. (2014). Developing media production skills for literacy in a primary school classroom: Digital materials, embodied knowledge and material contexts. In G. Barton (Ed.), *Literacy in the Arts: Retheorising Learning and Teaching* (pp. 143–160). Heidelberg: Springer.

DfCMS, Department for Culture, Media and Sport. (2013). *Culture, Media and Sport: Commons Select Committee—Third Report* [online]. Paragraphs 117 and 118. Retrieved February 7, 2018, from http://www.publications. parliament.uk/pa/cm201314/cmselect/cmcumeds/674/67409.htm.

DfE, Department for Education. (2010). *Foreword to The Importance of Teaching* [online]. London. Retrieved February 7, 2018, from https://www.gov.uk/government/uploads/system/uploads/attachment_data/file/175429/CM-7980.pdf.

DfE, Department for Education. (2013). *National Curriculum in England: Computing Programmes of Study* [online]. London. Retrieved February 7, 2018, from https://www.gov.uk/government/publications/national-curriculum-in-england-computing-programmes-of-study.

DfE, Department for Education. (2015). *Reading: The Next Steps* [online]. London. Retrieved February 7, 2018, from https://www.gov.uk/government/uploads/system/uploads/attachment_data/file/409409/Reading_the_next_steps.pdf.

DfES, Department for Education and Skills. (2005). *Primary National Strategy: Excellence and Enjoyment—Social and Emotional Aspects of Learning* [online]. Retrieved February 7, 2018, from http://webarchive.nationalarchives.gov.uk/20130401151715/http://www.education.gov.uk/publications/eOrderingDownload/DFES0110200MIG2122.pdf.

Donaldson, G. (2015). *Successful Futures: Independent Review of Curriculum and Assessment Arrangements in Wales* [online]. Retrieved February 7, 2018, from http://gov.wales/docs/dcells/publications/150225-successful-futures-en.pdf.

Donaldson, S. (2014). *Maximums and Minimums* [online]. Film Literacy Advisory Group (FLAG) Blog. Retrieved February 7, 2018, from https://filmliteracyadvisorygroup.wordpress.com/2014/11/20/maximums-and-minimums/.

EEF. (2015a). *About the Education Endowment Foundation* [online]. Retrieved February 7, 2018, from https://educationendowmentfoundation.org.uk/about/.

EEF. (2015b). *Phonics | Teaching and Learning Toolkit* [online]. Phonics Teaching and Learning Toolkit. Retrieved February 7, 2018, from https://educationendowmentfoundation.org.uk/resources/teaching-learning-toolkit/phonics/.

Eisner, E. (1986). The role of the arts in cognition and curriculum. *Journal of Art & Design Education, 5*(1–2), 57–67.

Eisner, E. (1997). The promise and perils of alternative forms of data representation. *Educational Researcher, 26*(6), 4–10.

Eisner, E. (2002). *The Arts and the Creation of Mind*. New Haven, CT: Yale University Press.

Eisner, E. (2005/1985). Aesthetic modes of knowing. In E. Eisner (Ed.), *Reimagining Schools* (pp. 95–104). Abingdon: Routledge.

Eisner, E. (2005/1993). Forms of understanding and the future of educational research. In E. Eisner (Ed.), *Reimagining Schools* (pp. 150–162). Abingdon: Routledge.

Eisner, E. (2005/2002a). What can education learn from the arts about the practice of education? [online]. In E. Eisner (Ed.), *Reimagining Schools* (pp. 205–214). Abingdon: Routledge. Retrieved February 7, 2018, from http://www.infed.org/biblio/eisner_arts_and_the_practice_of_education.htm.

Eisner, E. (2005/2002b). From episteme to phronesis to artistry in the study and improvement of teaching. In E. Eisner (Ed.), *Reimagining Schools* (pp. 193–204). Abingdon: Routledge.

Eisner, E. (2006). *What Do the Arts Teach?* [online]. Chancellors Lecture Series, Vanderbilt University, Nashville, TN. Retrieved February 7, 2018, from http://www.youtube.com/watch?v=h12MGuhQH9E.

Eisner, E. (2008). Art and knowledge. In J. G. Knowles & A. L. Cole (Eds.), *Handbook of the Arts in Qualitative Research: Perspectives, Methodologies, Examples, Issues* (pp. 3–12). Thousand Oaks, CA: Sage Publications, Inc.

ESRO. (2015). *Children's Media Lives* [online]. London. Retrieved February 7, 2018, from http://stakeholders.ofcom.org.uk/binaries/research/media-literacy/childrens-media-lives-year-1/childrens_media_lives_report_FINAL1.pdf.

Fielding, M. (2004). Transformative approaches to student voice: Theoretical underpinnings, recalcitrant realities. *British Educational Research Journal, 30*(2), 295–311.

Fisher, T., Higgins, C., & Loveless, A. (2006). *Teachers Learning with Digital Technologies: A Review of Research and Projects.* Bristol: Futurelab at NFER. Retrieved February 7, 2018, from https://www.nfer.ac.uk/publications/FUTL67.

FLAG (Film Literacy Advisory Group). (2013). *Screening Literacy* [online]. London: British Film Institute, Institute of Education, Film Education. Retrieved February 7, 2018, from http://www.bfi.org.uk/screening-literacy-film-education-europe.

FLAG (Film Literacy Advisory Group). (2015). *A Framework for Film Education* [online]. London: British Film Institute. Retrieved February 7, 2018, from http://www.bfi.org.uk/sites/bfi.org.uk/files/downloads/ bfi-a-framework-for-film-education-brochure-2015-06-12.pdf.

Frayling, C. (1993). Research in art and design [online]. *Royal College of Art Research Papers, 1*(1), 1–5. Retrieved February 7, 2018, from http://www.transart.org/wp-content/uploads/group-documents/79/1372332724-Frayling_Research-in-Art-and-Design.pdf.

Frayling, C. (2011). *On Craftsmanship Towards a New Bauhaus.* London: Oberon Books.

Freedman, A. (1990). Teaching the text: English and media studies. In *Watching Media Learning: Making Sense of Media Education* (pp. 194–211). London: The Falmer Press.

Freire, P. (1993/1970). *Pedagogy of the Oppressed.* London: Penguin.

Furedi, F. (2013). Keep the scourge of scientism out of schools. Retrieved February 7, 2018, from http://www.frankfuredi.com/site/article/keep_the_scourge_of_scientism_out_of_schools.

Furstenau, M., & Mackenzie, A. (2009). The promise of 'makeability': Digital editing software and the structuring of everyday cinematic life. *Visual Communication, 8*(1), 5–22.

Le Gallais, T. (2008). Wherever I go there I am: Reflections on reflexivity and the research stance. *Reflective Practice: International and Multidisciplinary Perspectives, 9*(2), 145–155.

Gardner, H. (2009). *Five Minds for the Future.* Boston, MA: Harvard Business School Press.

Gauntlett, D. (2007). Wide angle: Is it time for Media Studies 2.0? *Media Education Association Newsletter, 5*, 3–5.

Gauntlett, D. (2011a). *Making is Connecting.* Cambridge: Polity Press.

Gauntlett, D. (2011b). Extended book review: Making is connecting: The social meaning of creativity, from DIY and knitting to You Tube and Web 2.0 (A Conversation with McDougall, J., Readman, M., Trotman, D.) [online]. *Media Education Research Journal, 2*(1). Retrieved February 7, 2018, from http://merj.info/wp-content/uploads/2011/08/Gauntlett-review.pdf.

Gee, J. P. (2004). *Situated Language and Learning: A Critique of Traditional Schooling.* New York: Routledge.

Gee, J. P. (2011/1990). *Social Linguistics and Literacies: Ideology in Discourses.* Abingdon: Routledge.

Gee, J. P. (2015a). The new literacy studies. In J. Rowsell & K. Pahl (Eds.), *The Routledge Handbook of Literacy Studies* (pp. 35–48). Abingdon: Routledge.

Gee, J. P. (2015b). *Literacy and Education.* New York: Routledge.

Geertz, C. (1973). *The Interpretation of Cultures* [online]. London: Hutchinson. Retrieved February 7, 2018, from http://www.csub.edu/~mault/pdffiles/ch1.pdf.

Gell, A. (1998). *Art and Agency: An Anthropological Theory.* Oxford: Oxford University Press.

Gergen, K. J. (1995). Social construction and the educational process. In L. P. Steff & J. Gale (Eds.), *Constructivism in Education* (pp. 17–39). Hillsdale, NJ: Lawrence Erlbaum Associates.

Gibb, N. (2015a, January 7). Schools minister Nick Gibb sets out his timetable for educational reform in Britain 2015 [online]. *The Independent.* Retrieved February 7, 2018, from http://www.independent.co.uk/news/education/schools/schools-minister-nick-gibb-sets-out-his-timetable-for-educational-reform-in-2015-9963751.html.

Gibb, N. (2015b). *The Purpose of Education* [online]. Department for Education, London. Retrieved February 7, 2018, from https://www.gov.uk/government/speeches/the-purpose-of-education.

Gibb, N. (2015c). Speech on government's maths reforms [online]. In *London Thames Maths Hub Primary Conference.* London. Retrieved February 7, 2018, from https://www.gov.uk/government/speeches/nick-gibb-speech-on-governments-maths-reforms.

Giddens, A. (1991). *Modernity and Self-identity: Self and Society in the Late Modern Age*. Cambridge: Polity Press.

Giroux, H. A. (2011). *On Critical Pedagogy*. New York: Continuum.

Goffman, E. (1990). *The Presentation of Self in Everyday Life*. London: Penguin.

Gold, R. L. (1958). Roles in sociological fieldwork. *Social Forces, 36*, 217–223.

Goodman, N. (1978). *Ways of Worldmaking*. Indianapolis: Hackett Publishing.

Goodman, S. (2003). *Teaching Youth Media, A Critical Guide to Literacy, Video Production, and Social Change*. New York: Teachers College Press.

Goodman, S. (2014). Spaces of action: Teaching critical literacy for community empowerment in the age of neoliberalism. *English Teaching: Practice and Critique, 13*(3), 210–226. Retrieved November 23, 2017, from http://education.waikato.ac.nz/research/files/etpc/files/2014v13n3dial1.pdf.

Gove, M. (2013). *Michael Gove Speaks at the SMF* [online]. Social Market Foundation. Retrieved February 7, 2018, from http://www.smf.co.uk/michael-gove-speaks-at-the-smf/.

Grady, J. (2004). Working with visible evidence: An invitation and some practical advice. In C. Knowles & P. Sweetman (Eds.), *Picturing the Social Landscape: Visual Methods and the Sociological Imagination* (pp. 18–31). Abingdon: Routledge.

Green, B. (1995). Post-curriculum possibilities: English teaching, cultural politics, and the postmodern turn. *Journal of Curriculum Studies, 27*(4), 391–409.

Greig, A. D., MacKay, T., & Taylor, J. (2013). *Doing Research with Children: A Practical Guide* (3rd ed.). London: Sage.

Grossberg, L. (2013). *Cultural Studies in the Future Tense*. Durham, NC: Duke University Press.

Grundin, H. (2018). Policy and evidence: A critical analysis of the year 1 phonics screening check in England. *Literacy, 52*(1), 39–46.

Gutiérrez, K. D. (2008). Developing a sociocritical literacy in the third space. *Reading Research Quarterly, 43*(2), 148–164.

Haas Dyson, A. (1997). *Writing Superheroes: Contemporary Childhood, Popular Culture, and Classroom Literacy*. New York: Teachers College Press.

Hagel, J., & Seely Brown, J. (2005). *From Push to Pull—Emerging Models for Mobilizing Resources* [online]. Retrieved February 7, 2018, from http://www.johnhagel.com/paper_pushpull.pdf.

Hall, S. (1991). Ethnicity: Identity and difference. *Radical America, 23*(4), 9–20.

Hall, S. (1992). Cultural studies and its theoretical legacies [online]. In L. Grossberg, C. Nelson, & P. Treichler (Eds.), *Cultural Studies* (pp. 277–294). London and New York: Routledge. Retrieved February 7, 2018, from http:// msuweb.montclair.edu/~furrg/pursuits/hallcultstuds.html.

Harré, R. (1983). *Personal Being—A Theory for Individual Psychology.* Oxford: Basil Blackwell.

Hattie, J. (2012). *Visible Learning for Teachers: Maximizing Impact on Learning.* Abingdon: Routledge.

Hattie, J., & Yates, G. (2014). *Visible Learning and the Science of How We Learn.* Abingdon: Routledge.

Hawkins, J., & Blakeslee, S. (2005). *On Intelligence.* New York, NY: Henry Holt.

He Dies At The End. (2010) [online]. Short Film. Directed by D. McCarthy. Ireland. Retrieved February 7, 2018, from https://www.youtube.com/ watch?v=YRlvnDUtBbI.

Hearing, T. (2015). *The Documentary Imagination: An Investigation into the Performative Application of Documentary Film in Scholarship.* PhD Thesis, Bournemouth University.

Heath, S. B. (1983). *Ways with Words: Language, Life and Work in Communities and Classrooms.* Cambridge: Cambridge University Press.

Heikkinen, H. L., Huttunen, R., & Syrjälä, L. (2007). Action research as narrative: Five principles for validation. *Educational Action Research, 15*(1), 5–19.

Heikkinen, H. L., Jong, F. P. C. M. d., & Vanderlinde, R. (2016). What is (good) practitioner research? *Vocations and Learning, 9*(1), 1–19.

Heron, J., & Reason, P. (1997). A participatory inquiry paradigm [online]. *Qualitative Inquiry, 3*(3), 274–294. Retrieved February 7, 2018, from http:// www.peterreason.eu/Papers/Participatoryinquiryparadigm.pdf.

Hill Bulman, J. (2014). *Developing a Progression Framework for Children's Reading of Film.* PhD Thesis, School of Education, University of Sheffield, Sheffield.

Hirsch, E. D. (2006). *The Knowledge Deficit: Closing the Shocking Education Gap for American Children.* Boston, MA: Houghton Mifflin Company.

Hollway, W., & Jefferson, T. (2000). *Doing Qualitative Research Differently: Free Association, Narrative and the Interview Method.* London: Sage Publications.

Hughes, E. C. (1971). *The Sociological Eye: Selected Papers.* Chicago: Aldine-Atherton.

Husbands, C. (2015). *Twenty-seven Years on From the National Curriculum* [online]. UCL, Institute of Education blog. Retrieved February 7, 2018, from https://ioelondonblog.wordpress.com/2015/06/22/twenty-seven-years-on-from-the-national-curriculum/.

Huston, J., & Long, R. E. (2001/1973). *John Huston: Interviews*. Jackson, MS: University Press of Mississippi.

Hymes, D. H. (1981). Ethnographic monitoring. In H. T. Trueba, G. P. Guthrie, & K. H. Au (Eds.), *Culture and the Bilingual Classroom: Studies in Classroom Ethnography* (pp. 56–68). Newbury House: Rowley, MA.

Illich, I. (1973). *Tools for Conviviality* [online]. New York: Marion Boyars. Retrieved February 7, 2018, from http://eekim.com/ba/bookclub/illich/tools.pdf.

Instrell, M. (2011). Breaking barriers: Multimodal and media literacy in the curriculum for excellence. *Media Education Journal, 49*, 4–11.

Ito, M. (2009). *Hanging Out, Messing Around, and Geeking Out: Kids Living and Learning with New Media*. The John D. and Catherine T. MacArthur Foundation Series on Digital Media and Learning. Cambridge, MA: MIT Press.

Ito, M., Livingstone, S., Penuel, B., Rhodes, J., Salen, K., Schor, J., et al. (2013). *Connected Learning: An Agenda for Research and Design* [online]. Digital Media and Learning Research Hub. Retrieved February 7, 2018, from http://dmlhub.net/wp-content/uploads/files/Connected_Learning_report.pdf.

Jenkins, H. (1992). *Textual Poachers: Television Fans and Participatory Culture*. New York: Routledge.

Jenkins, H. (2011). *From New Media Literacies to New Media Expertise: 'Confronting the Challenges of a Participatory Culture' Revisited* [online]. Manifesto for Media Education. Retrieved February 7, 2018, from http://www.manifestoformediaeducation.co.uk/2011/01/henryjenkins/.

Jenkins, H., Ito, M., & boyd, d. (2016). *Participatory Culture in a Networked Era: A Conversation on Youth, Learning, Commerce, and Politics*. Cambridge: Polity Press.

Jenkins, H., Purushota, R., Clinton, K., & Robinson, A. J. (2006). *Confronting the Challenges of Participatory Culture: Media Education for the 21st Century* [online]. Chicago: The John D. & Catherine T. MacArthur Foundation. Retrieved February 7, 2018, from https://www.macfound.org/media/article_pdfs/JENKINS_WHITE_PAPER.PDF.

Jewitt, C. (2008). *The Visual in Learning and Creativity: A Review of the Literature* [online]. Creative Partnership Series, Institute of Education, University of London. Retrieved February 7, 2018, from http://www.creativitycultureeducation.org/wp-content/uploads/the-visual-in-learning-and-creativity-92.pdf.

Joaquin, J. (2010). Digital literacies and hip hop texts. In D. Alvermann (Ed.), *Adolescents' Online Literacies: Connecting Classrooms, Digital Media, and Popular Culture* (pp. 109–124). New York: Peter Lang.

Jones, K. (2004). The turn to a narrative knowing of persons: Minimalist passive interviewing technique and team analysis of narrative qualitative data. In F. Rapport (Ed.), *New Qualitative Methodologies in Health and Social Care Research* (pp. 35–54). New York: Routledge.

Jones, K. (2006). A Biographic researcher in pursuit of an aesthetic: The use of arts-based (re)presentations in 'performative' dissemination of life stories [online]. *Qualitative Sociology Review, 2*(1), 66–85. Retrieved February 7, 2018, from http://www.qualitativesociologyreview.org/ENG/Volume3/QSR_ 2_1_Jones.pdf.

Jones, K. (2012). Short film as performative social science: The story behind 'princess margaret'. In P. Vannini (Ed.), *Popularizing Research* (pp. 13–18). New York: Peter Lang.

Jones, K. (2013). Infusing biography with the personal: Writing Rufus Stone. *Creative Approaches to Research, 6*(2), 4.

Jones, K., & Fenge, L.-A. (2017). Gifted stories: How well do we retell the stories that research participants give us? *Creative Approaches to Research, 10*(1), 35–35. Retrieved February 7, 2018, from http://creativeapproachestoresearch.net/wp-content/uploads/CAR10_1_Jones_Fenge.pdf.

Jones, K., with Hearing, T. (2013). Turning research into film: Trevor hearing in conversation with Kip Jones about the short film, RUFUS STONE. In M. Lichtman (Ed.), *Qualitative Research for the Social Sciences* (pp. 184–188). New York: Sage Publications.

Kafai, Y. B., & Peppler, K. A. (2011). Youth, technology, and DIY: Developing participatory competencies in creative media production. *Review of Research in Education, 35*(1), 89–119.

Kaplan, I. (2008). Being 'seen', being 'heard': Engaging with students on the margins of education through participatory photography. In P. Thomson (Ed.), *Doing Visual Research with Children and Young People* (pp. 175–191). Abingdon: Routledge.

KAVI, Finnish Media Education Authority. (2013). Finnish Media Education [online]. Helsinki: National Audiovisual Institute. Retrieved from https://kavi.fi/sites/default/files/documents/mil_in_finland.pdf

Kendall, A., & McDougall, J. (2012). Critical media literacy after the media [online]. *Revista Comunicar.* Retrieved February 7, 2018, from http://www.revistacomunicar.com/pdf/preprint/38/En-02-PRE-13482.pdf.

Kendall, A., & McDougall, J. (2013). Telling stories out of school. In G. Merchant, J. Gillen, J. Marsh, & D. Julia (Eds.), *Virtual Literacies: Interactive Spaces for Children and Young People* (pp. 89–100). Abingdon: Routledge.

Knobel, M., & Lankshear, C. (2008). Remix: The art and craft of endless hybridization. *Journal of Adolescent & Adult Literacy, 52*(1), 22–33.

Knobel, M., & Lankshear, C. (2010). *DIY Media: Creating, Sharing and Learning with New Technologies.* New York: Peter Lang.

Koh, A. (2014). *The Political Power of Play* [online]. Hybrid Pedagogies. Retrieved February 7, 2018, from http://www.hybridpedagogy.com/journal/political-power-of-play/.

Kress, G., & Van Leeuwen, T. (2001). *Multimodal Discourse: The Modes and Media of Contemporary Communication.* London: Hodder Arnold.

Kvale, S. (1996). *Interviews: An Introduction to Qualitative Research Interviewing.* London: Sage Publications.

Lanham, R. A. (1994). *The Electronic Word: Democracy, Technology, and the Arts.* Chicago: University of Chicago Press.

Lankshear, C., & Knobel, M. (2003). *New Literacies: Changing Knowledge and Classroom Learning.* Buckingham: Open University Press.

Lankshear, C., & Knobel, M. (2011). *New Literacies: Everyday Practices and Social Learning.* Maidenhead: Open University Press.

Lardoux, X. (2014). *For a European Film Education Policy* [online]. Paris. Retrieved February 7, 2018, from http://www.europacreativamedia.cat/rcs_media/For_a_European_Film_Education_Policy.pdf.

Lather, P. (1991). Research as Praxis. In *Getting Smart: Feminist Research and Pedagogy With/In the Postmodern* (pp. 50–69). New York: Routledge.

Lather, P. (2006). Paradigm proliferation as a good thing to think with: Teaching research in education as a wild profusion. *International Journal of Qualitative Studies in Education, 19*(1), 35–57.

Laughey, D. (2012). Media Studies 1.0: Back to basics. *Media Education Research Journal, 2*(2), 57–64.

Lave, J., & Wenger, E. (1991). *Situated Learning: Legitimate Peripheral Participation.* Cambridge, UK: Cambridge University Press.

Law, J. (2004). *After Method: Mess in Social Science Research (International Library of Sociology).* Abingdon: Routledge.

Law, J., & Urry, J. (2003). *Enacting the Social* [online]. Department of Sociology and the Centre for Science Studies, Lancaster University. Retrieved February 7, 2018, from http://www.lancaster.ac.uk/fass/resources/sociology-online-papers/papers/law-urry-enacting-the-social.pdf.

Leander, K., & Frank, A. (2006). The aesthetic production and distribution of image/subjects among online youth. *E-Learning, 3*(2), 185–206.

Lévi-Strauss, C. (1966). *The Savage Mind.* Chicago: University of Chicago Press.

Lincoln, Y. S., & Guba, E. G. (1985). *Naturalistic Inquiry*. Beverley Hills, CA: Sage Publications, Inc.

Lincoln, Y. S., & Guba, E. G. (2000). Paradigmatic controversies, contradictions, and emerging confluences. In Y. S. Lincoln & E. G. Guba (Eds.), *Handbook of Qualitative Research* (pp. 163–188). Thousand Oaks, CA: Sage Publications, Inc.

Liu, E., & Noppe-Brandon, S. (2009). *Imagination First: Unlocking the Power of Possibility*. San Francisco, CA: John Wiley & Sons.

Livingstone, I., & Hope, A. (2011). *Next Gen Report*. London: NESTA.

Livingstone, S. (2009). *Children and the Internet*. Cambridge: Polity Press.

Livingstone, S., & Bulger, M. (2014). A global research agenda for children's rights in the digital age [online]. *Journal of Children and Media*, 8(4) 317–335.

Livingstone, S., & Sefton-Green, J. (2016). *The Class: Living and Learning in the Digital Age*. New York: NYU Press. Retrieved February 7, 2018, from http://connectedyouth.nyupress.org/book/9781479824243/.

Lord, P., Jones, M., Harland, J., Bazalgette, C., Reid, M., Potter, J., et al. (2007). *Special Effects: The Distinctiveness of Learning Outcomes in Relation to Moving Image Education Projects: Final Report* [online]. London: Creative Partnerships. Retrieved February 7, 2018, from http://www.nfer.ac.uk/publications/SPF01/SPF01.pdf.

Loveless, A. (2008a). Creative learning and new technology? A provocation paper [online]. In J. Sefton-Green (Ed.), *Creative Learning* (pp. 61–71). London: Creative Partnerships, The Arts Council. Retrieved February 7, 2018, from http://www.creativitycultureeducation.org/wp-content/uploads/creative-learning-booklet-26-233.pdf.

Loveless, A. (2008b). Moving from the margins creating space with digital technology: Wonder, theory and action [online]. In C. Palmer & D. Torevell (Eds.), *The Turn to Aesthetics: An Interdisciplinary Exchange of Ideas in Applied and Philosophical Aesthetics* (pp. 189–198). Liverpool: Liverpool Hope University Press. Retrieved February 7, 2018, from http://works.bepress.com/cgi/viewcontent.cgi?article=1001&context=clive_palmer.

Loveless, A. (2012). Body and soul: A study of narratives of learning lives of creative people who teach. In I. Goodson, A. Loveless, & D. Stephens (Eds.), *Explorations in Narrative Research: Studies in Professional Life and Work* (pp. 107–122). Rotterdam: Sense Publishers.

Luckin, R., Bligh, B., Manches, A., Ainsworth, S., Crook, C., & Noss, R. (2012). *Decoding Learning: The Proof, Promise and Potential of Digital Education* [online]. London: NESTA. Retrieved February 7, 2018, from http://www.nesta.org.uk/sites/default/files/decoding_learning_report.pdf.

Lundvall, A. (2010). *Finnish Media Education Policies: Approaches in Culture and Education* [online]. Helsinki. Retrieved February 7, 2018, from http://www.mediakasvatus.fi/publications/mediaeducationpolicies.pdf.

Lynch, T. L. (2015). *The Hidden Role of Software in Educational Research: Policy to Practice*. New York: Routledge.

Lyotard, J. F. (1984). *The Postmodern Condition: A Report on Knowledge*. Minneapolis: University of Minneapolis Press.

Maeda, J. (2013). Foreword to. In R. Somerson & M. L. Hermano (Eds.), *The Art of Critical Making: Rhode Island School of Design on Creative Practice* (pp. 5–9). Hoboken, NJ: Wiley.

Mäkelä, M. (2007). Knowing through making: The role of the artefact in practice-led research. *Knowledge, Technology & Policy, 20*(3), 157–163.

Maker Faire. (2017). *World Maker Faire | New York 2017* [online]. Retrieved February 7, 2018, from http://makerfaire.com/.

Maker Faire UK. (2015). *Brighton Mini Maker Faire* [online]. Retrieved February 7, 2018, from http://makerfairebrighton.com/.

Maker Media Inc. (2014). *Maker Faire: A Bit of History* [online]. Retrieved February 7, 2018, from http://makerfaire.com/makerfairehistory/.

Manovich, L. (2001). *The Language of New Media*. Cambridge, MA: MIT Press.

Marsh, J. (2009). Play, creativity and digital cultures. In R. Willett, M. Robinson, & J. Marsh (Eds.), *Play, Creativity and Digital Cultures* (pp. 216–218). Abingdon: Routledge.

Marsh, J. (2010). *Childhood, Culture and Creativity: A Literature Review* [online]. Newcastle. Retrieved February 7, 2018, from http://www.creativitycultureeducation.org/wp-content/uploads/CCE-childhood-culture-and-creativity-a-literature-review.pdf.

Marsh, J., & Bearne, E. (2008). *Moving Literacy On: Evaluation of the BFI Lead Practitioner Scheme for Moving Image Media Literacy*. UKLA, University of Sheffield.

Martin, A. (2006). A European framework for digital literacy [online]. *Nordic Journal of Digital Literacy, 1*(2), 151–161. Retrieved February 7, 2018, from http://www.idunn.no/dk/2006/02/a_european_framework_for_digital_literacy.

Massumi, B. (2002). *Parables for the Virtual: Movement, Affect, Sensation*. Durham, NC: Duke University Press.

Masterman, L. (1985). *Teaching the Media*. London: Comedia.

McDougall, J. (2011). Media education after the media [online]. *Manifesto for Media Education*. Retrieved February 7, 2018, from http://www.manifestoformediaeducation.co.uk/2011/01/media-education-should-be-4/.

McDougall, J. (2014). Curating media literacy: A porous expertise. *Journal of Media Literacy, 16*(1/2), 6–9.

McDougall, J. (2016). "Mediapting" and curation: Research informed pedagogy for (digital) media education Praxis. In J. Frechette & R. Williams (Eds.), *Media Education for a Digital Generation*. New York: Routledge Section 20.

McDougall, J., & Berger, R. (2012). What is media education for? *Media Education Research Journal, 3*(1), 5–20.

McDougall, J., & Potter, J. (2015). Curating media learning: Towards a porous expertise. *Journal of E-learning and Digital Media, 12*(2), 199–211.

McIntyre, J., & Jones, S. (2014). Possibility in impossibility? Working with beginning teachers of english in times of change. *English in Education, 48*(1), 26–40.

McKee, H. (2005). Richard Lanham's the electronic word and AT/THROUGH oscillations [online]. *Pedagogy: Critical Approaches to Teaching Literature, Language, Composition, and Culture, 5*(1), 117–129. Retrieved February 7, 2018, from http://www.users.miamioh.edu/mckeeha/lanham_review.pdf.

MEA, Media Education Association. (2015). *MEA Response to the Consultations* [online]. Retrieved February 7, 2018, from http://www.themea.org.uk/2015/09/mea-response-to-the-consultations/.

Mee, J., & Gittings, R. (2002). *John Keats: Selected Letters (Oxford World's Classics)*. Oxford: Oxford University Press.

Merchant, G. (2006). Identity, social networks and online communication. *E-Learning and Digital Media, 3*(2), 235–244.

Merchant, G. (2009). Web 2.0, new literacies, and the idea of learning through participation [online]. *English Teaching: Practice and Critique, 8*(3), 8–20. Retrieved February 7, 2018, from http://shura.shu.ac.uk/1102/1/Merchant_draft2.pdf.

Merchant, G. (2010). 3D virtual worlds as environments for literacy learning [online]. *Educational Research, 52*(2), 135–150. Retrieved February 7, 2018, from http://shura.shu.ac.uk/1206/1/Final_GM_Ed_Res.pdf.

Merleau-Ponty, M. (1964a). *The Primacy of Perception*. Evanston, IL: Northwestern University Press.

Merleau-Ponty, M. (1964b). The film and the new psychology. In H. L. Dreyfus & P. A. Dreyfus (Eds.), *Sense and Non-sense* (pp. 48–59). Chicago: Northwestern University Press.

Merrin, W. (2009). Media studies 2.0: Upgrading and open-sourcing the discipline [online]. *Interactions: Studies in Communication and Culture, 1*(1). Retrieved February 7, 2018, from http://mediastudies2point0.blogspot.co.uk/2010/03/studying-me-dia-problem-of-method-in.html.

Merrin, W. (2014). *Media Studies 2.0*. Abingdon: Routledge.

Mihailidis, P. (2014). *Media Literacy and the Emerging Citizen: Youth, Engagement and Participation in Digital Culture*. New York: Peter Lang.

Miller, D. (2008). *The Comfort of Things*. Cambridge, UK: Polity.

Moll, L. C., Amanti, C., Neff, D., & Gonzalez, N. (1992). Funds of knowledge for teaching: Using a qualitative approach to connect homes and classrooms. *Theory Into Practice, 31*(2), 132–141.

Monaco, J. (2009). *How to Read a Film: Movies, Media, and Beyond*. Oxford: Oxford University Press.

Monbiot, G. (2016). *Neoliberalism—The Ideology at the Root of All Our Problems* [online]. Retrieved February 7, 2018, from http://www.theguardian.com/books/2016/apr/15/neoliberalism-ideology-problem-george-monbiot.

Morgan, N. (2014, November 10). *Nicky Morgan Speaks at Launch of Your Life Campaign* [online]. Retrieved February 7, 2018, from https://www.gov.uk/government/speeches/nicky-morgan-speaks-at-launch-of-your-life-campaign.

Morgan, N. (2015). Education secretary Nicky Morgan: 'Arts subjects limit career choices' [online]. *The Stage News*. Retrieved February 7, 2018, from http://www.thestage.co.uk/news/2014/11/education-secretary-nicky-morgan-arts-subjects-limit-career-choices/.

Morozov, E. (2013). *To Save Everything, Click Here: Technology, Solutionism, and the Urge to Fix Problems That Don't Exist*. London: Allen Lane.

Mumford, S., Parry, B., & Walker, G. (2013). *Pockets of Excellence: Film Education in Yorkshire and the Humber* [online]. Leeds: IVE Creative (formerly CAPEUK). Retrieved February 7, 2018, from https://weareive.org/impact/pockets-excellence-film-education-yorkshire-humber/.

Murch, W. (2001). *In the Blink of an Eye: A Perspective on Film Editing*. Los Angeles: Silman-James Press.

NACCE, National Advisory Committee on Creative and Cultural Education. (1999). *All Our Futures: Creativity, Culture and Education* [online]. London: DCMS. Retrieved February 7, 2018, from http://sirkenrobinson.com/pdf/allourfutures.pdf.

New London Group. (1996). A pedagogy of multiliteracies: Designing social futures. *Harvard Educational Review, 66*(1), 60–92.

NI DOE, Northern Ireland Department of Education. (2010). *The Big Picture at Key Stages 1 and 2* [online]. Belfast: Northern Ireland. Retrieved February 7, 2018, from http://www.nicurriculum.org.uk/docs/key_stages_1_and_2/Big-PicturePrimary-KS12.pdf.

NIFTC, Northern Ireland Film & Television Council, and BFI Education. (2004). *A Wider Literacy: The Case for Moving Image Media Education in Northern Ireland* [online]. Belfast: Northern Ireland Film & Television Council, BFI Education Policy Working Group. Retrieved February 7, 2018, fromhttp://www.bfi.org.uk/sites/bfi.org.uk/files/downloads/bfi-case-for-moving-image-media-education-in-northern-ireland.pdf.

NUT, National Union of Teachers. (2014). *Reclaiming Schools—The Evidence and the Arguments* [online]. National Union of Teachers. Retrieved February 7, 2018, from https://radicaled.files.wordpress.com/2015/03/reclaiming-schools.pdf.

NYHS, New York Hall of Science, Maker Faire. (2012). Design-make-play conference: Growing the next generation of science innovators [online]. In *Design-Make-Play Conference: Growing the Next Generation of Science Innovators*. New York: New York Hall of Science. Retrieved February 7, 2018, from http://www.yingtrsef.org/wp-content/uploads/DesignMakePlay_Report-2012.pdf.

OFSTED, Office for Standards in Education. (2012). *Changes to Education Inspections Announced* [online]. Retrieved February 7, 2018, from https://www.gov.uk/government/news/changes-to-education-inspections-announced.

Ong, W. (2002/1982). *Orality and Literacy: The Technologizing of the Word* [online]. London: Routledge. Retrieved February 7, 2018, from http://dss-edit.com/prof-anon/sound/library/Ong_orality_and_literacy.pdf.

O'Reilly, T. (2017). *WTF?: What's the Future and Why It's Up to Us*. Louth: R H Business Books.

Orr, S. (2013). *Making Teaching Work in Media* [online]. Media Education Summit, Sheffield Hallam University. Retrieved February 7, 2018, from https://www.youtube.com/watch?v=SI0jep9bNBs.

Orr, S., & Blythman, M. (2002). The process of design is almost like writing an essay [online]. *The Writing Center Journal*, 22 (2), 39–54. Retrieved February 7, 2018, from http://casebuilder.rhet.ualr.edu/wcrp/publications/wcj/wcj22.2/WCJ22.2_Orr_Blythman.pdf.

Orr, S., & McDougall, J. (2014). Enquiry into learning and teaching in arts and creative practice. In E. Cleaver, M. Lintern, & M. McLinden (Eds.), *Teaching and Learning in Higher Education: Disciplinary Approaches to Research* (pp. 162–177). London: Sage.

Parry, B. (2013). *Children, Film and Literacy*. Basingstoke: Palgrave Macmillan.

Parry, B. (2014). Popular culture, participation and progression in the literacy classroom. *Literacy*, 48(1), 14–22.

Parry, B., & Hill Bulman, J. (2017). *Film Education, Literacy and Learning*. Leicester: UKLA.

Pendleton-Jullian, A. (2009). *Design Education and Innovation Ecotones* [online]. Retrieved February 7, 2018, from https://fourplusone.files.wordpress.com/2010/03/apj_paper_14.pdf.

Peppler, K. (2013). *New Opportunities for Interest-Driven Arts Learning in a Digital Age*. New York: The Wallace Foundation.

Peppler, K., & Kafai, Y. (2007). From Supergoo to Scratch: Exploring creative digital media production in informal learning. *Learning, Media and Technology, 32*(2), 149–166.

Petersen, S. M. (2008). Loser generated content: From participation to exploitation [online]. *First Monday*. Retrieved February 7, 2018, from http://journals.uic.edu/ojs/index.php/fm/article/view/2141/1948.

Pink, D. (2009). *Drive: The Surprising Truth About What Motivates Us*. London: Penguin.

Pink, S. (2013). *Doing Visual Ethnography* (3rd ed.). London: Sage.

Polanyi, M. (2009/1967). *The Tacit Dimension*. Chicago: University of Chicago Press.

Polkinghorne, D. (1988). *Narrative Knowing and the Human Sciences*. Albany: State University of New York Press.

Ponyo. (2008). Film, Directed by H. Miyazaki. Japan: Toho Company.

Porter, N. (2015). *Schools Should be Fined for Their Students' GCSE Fails, Argues Think Tank* [online]. Policy Exchange. Retrieved February 7, 2018, from https://policyexchange.org.uk/schools-should-be-fined-if-pupils-dont-make-the-grade/.

Potter, J. (2009). *Curating the Self: Media Literacy and Identity in Digital Video Production by Young Learners*. PhD Thesis, Institute of Education, University of London, London.

Potter, J. (2011). New literacies, new practices and learner research: Across the semi-permeable membrane between home and school. *Lifelong Learning in Europe, 16*(3), 174–181.

Potter, J. (2012). *Digital Media and Learner Identity: The New Curatorship*. New York: Palgrave Macmillan.

Potter, J. (2015). *Forward to the New Age of STEAM(M)! Digital Media, Education and Computing* [online]. Media Literacy, Learning and Curating. Retrieved February 7, 2018, from http://digitalcurationandlearning.com/2015/02/25/forward-to-the-new-age-of-steamm-digital-media-education-and-computing/.

Potter, J., & Bryer, T. (2014). *Out of the Box: A Project Evaluation Report for Shoot Smart*. London: DARE, Digital, Arts, Research, Education.

Potter, J., & Bryer, T. (2016). 'Finger flowment' and moving image language: Learning filmmaking with tablet devices. In B. Parry, C. Burnett, & G. Merchant (Eds.), *Literacy, Media, Technology: Past, Present and Future* (pp. 111–128). London: Bloomsbury.

Potter, J., & Gilje, Ø. (2015). Curation as a new literacy practice. *E-Learning and Digital Media, 12*(2), 123–127.

Potter, J., & McDougall, J. (2017). *Digital Media, Culture and Education: Theorising Third Space Literacies*. London: Palgrave Macmillan.

Prensky, M. (2001). Digital natives, digital immigrants part 1. *On the Horizon, 9*(5), 1–6.

Prensky, M. (2012). *From Digital Natives to Digital Wisdom: Hopeful Essays for 21st Century Learning*. Thousand Oaks, CA: Sage Publications.

Pring, R. (2004). *Philosophy of Educational Research* (2nd ed.). London: Continuum.

Prosser, J., & Loxley, A. (2008). *Introducing Visual Methods* [online]. ESRC National Centre for Research Methods, NCRM Review Papers 010. Retrieved February 7, 2018, from http://eprints.ncrm.ac.uk/420/1/MethodsReview PaperNCRM-010.pdf.

Qian, Y. (2009). New media literacy in 3-D virtual learning environments. In L. Hin & R. Subramaniam (Eds.), *Handbook of Research on New Media Literacy at the K-12 Level: Issues and Challenges* (pp. 257–270). New York: IGI Global.

Quinlan, O. (2015). *Young Digital Makers: Surveying Attitudes and Opportunities for Digital Creativity Across the UK* [online]. London. Retrieved February 7, 2018, from http://www.nesta.org.uk/sites/default/files/youngdigmakers.pdf.

Readman, M. (2010). *What's in a Word? The Discursive Construction of 'Creativity'*. PhD Thesis, Centre for Excellence in Media Practice (CEMP), University of Bournemouth, Bournemouth.

Reid, A. (2007). *The Two Virtuals: New Media and Composition*. West Lafayette, IN: Parlor Press.

Reid, M. (2003). Writing film: Making inferences when viewing and reading. *Literacy (formerly Reading), 37*(3), 111–115.

Reid, M. (2009). Reframing literacy: A film pitch for the 21st century. *English Drama Media: The Professional Journal of the National Association for the Teaching of English, 14*, 19–23.

Reid, M. (2013). Film 21st century literacy: Re/defining film education—Notes towards a definition of film education. In *Film: 21st Century Literacy Strategy Seminar*. London. Retrieved February 7, 2018, from http://www.bfi.org.uk/sites/bfi.org.uk/files/downloads/film-21st-century-literacy-redefining-film-education.pdf.

Reid, M. (2014). Film, literacy and cultural participation. In S. Brindley & B. Marshall (Eds.), *Master Class in English Education: Transforming Teaching and Learning* (pp. 84–98). London: Bloomsbury.

Reid, M. (2017). Little Film about Cinema Cent Ans de Jeunesse (CCAJ). Retrieved February 7, 2018, from https://markreid1895.wordpress.com/2017/01/27/little-film-about-ccaj/.

Reid, M., Burn, A., & Parker, D. (2002). *Evaluation Report of the BECTA Digital Video Pilot* [online]. BECTA/BFI. Retrieved February 7, 2018, from http://archive.teachfind.com/becta/research.becta.org.uk/index9a09.html.

Reisz, K., & Millar, G. (2010). *The Technique of Film Editing*. Burlington, MA: Focal Press.

ResearchEd. (2015). *ResearchEd Conference 2015* [online]. Retrieved February 7, 2018, from http://www.workingoutwhatworks.com/en-GB/About.

Roberts, B. (2008). Performative social science: A consideration of skills, purpose and context [online]. *Forum: Qualitative Social Research, 9*(2), Art.58 [99]. Retrieved February 7, 2018, from http://www.qualitative-research.net/index.php/fqs/article/view/377/822.

Roberts-Holmes, G. (2014). The 'datafication' of early years pedagogy 'if the teaching is good, the data should be good and if there's bad teaching, there is bad data'. *Journal of Education Policy, 30*(3), 302–315.

Robinson, K. (2006). How schools kill creativity [online]. *TED.com*. Retrieved February 7, 2018, from http://www.ted.com/talks/ken_robinson_says_schools_kill_creativity.html.

Robinson, K. (2011). *Out of our Minds: Learning to be Creative* (2nd ed.). Chichester: Capstone.

Robinson, K. (2013). *Finding Your Element: How to Discover Your Talents and Passions and Transform Your Life*. London: Allen Lane.

Rogers, T., & Winters, K.-L. (2010). Textual play, satire, and counter discourses of street youth zining practices. In D. Alvermann (Ed.), *Adolescents' Online Literacies: Connecting Classrooms, Digital Media, and Popular Culture* (pp. 91–108). New York: Peter Lang.

Rorabaugh, P. (2012). Digital Culture and Shifting Epistemology [online]. *Hybrid Pedagogy*. Retrieved February 7, 2018, from http://www.hybridpedagogy.com/journal/digital-culture-and-shifting-epistemology/.

Rose, G. (2006). *Visual Methodologies. An Introduction to the Interpretation of Visual Materials*. London: Sage.

Rosen, M. (2012). *Who Owns Literacy?* [online]. Michael Rosen's blog. Retrieved February 7, 2018, from http://michaelrosenblog.blogspot.co.uk/2012/02/who-owns-literacy.html.

Rosen, M. (2013). Michael Rosen: Phonics: A summary of my views. Retrieved February 7, 2018, from http://michaelrosenblog.blogspot.co.uk/2013/01/phonics-summary-of-my-views.html.

Ross, M., Mitchell, S., Bierton, C., & Radnor, H. (1993). *Assessing Achievement in the Arts*. Buckingham; Philadelphia: Open University Press.

Rushdie, S. (1990). *Haroun and the Sea of Stories*. London: Puffin/Penguin.

Rushdie, S. (1991). *Imaginary Homelands*. London: Granta.

Schmidt, E. (2011). *MacTaggart Lecture, Edinburgh TV Festival* [online]. Edinburgh TV Festival. Retrieved February 7, 2018, from http://www.theguardian.com/media/interactive/2011/aug/26/eric-schmidt-mactaggart-lecture-full-text.

Scollon, R., & Scollon, S. B. K. (1981). *Narrative, Literacy, and Face in Interethnic Communication*. Norwood, NJ: Ablex.

Scott, D., & Usher, R. (2010). *Researching Education: Data, Methods and Theory in Educational Inquiry* (2nd ed.). London: Continuum.

Scottish Screen. (2006). *Moving Image Education & a Curriculum for Excellence* [online]. Glasgow. Retrieved February 7, 2018, from http://www.movingimageeducation.org/files/pdfs/mie-and-a-curriculum-for-excellence-2006-booklet.pdf.

Sefton-Green, J. (1990). Teaching and learning about representation: Culture and The Cosby Show in a North London comprehensive. In D. Buckingham (Ed.), *Watching Media Learning: Making Sense of Media Education* (pp. 127–150). London: The Falmer Press.

Sefton-Green, J. (1998). *'Writing' Media: An Investigation of Practical Production in Media Education by Secondary School Students*. PhD Thesis, Institute of Education, University of London, London.

Sefton-Green, J. (2000). From creativity to cultural production. In J. Sefton-Green & R. Sinker (Eds.), *Evaluating Creativity: Making and Learning by Young People* (pp. 216–231). London: Routledge.

Sefton-Green, J. (2005). Timelines, timeframes and special effects: Software and creative media production. *Education, Communication & Information, 5*(1), 99–103.

Sefton-Green, J. (2008). *Creative Learning* [online]. London: Creative Partnerships, Arts Council England. Retrieved February 7, 2018, from http://www.creativitycultureeducation.org/wp-content/uploads/creative-learning-booklet-26-233.pdf.

Sefton-Green, J. (2013a). *Mapping Digital Makers: A Review Exploring Everyday Creativity, Learning Lives and the Digital.* State of the Art Reviews. London: Nominet Trust.

Sefton-Green, J. (2013b). *Learning at Not-School: A Review of Study, Theory, and Advocacy for Education in Non-formal Settings.* The John D. and Catherine T. MacArthur Foundation Reports on Digital Media and Learning. Cambridge, MA: MIT & MITE.

Sefton-Green, J., & Sinker, R. (2000). *Evaluating Creativity: Making and Learning by Young People.* London: Routledge.

Sellar, S., Rutkowski, D., & Thompson, G. (2017). *The Global Education Race: Taking the Measure of PISA and International Testing.* Edmonton, Canada: Brush Education Inc.

Selwyn, N. (2006). Dealing with digital inequality: Rethinking young people, technology and social Inclusion. Conference paper: *Cyberworld Unlimited? Digital Inequality and New Spaces of Informal Education for Young People,* Bielefeld, Germany, 9 February 2006.

Selwyn, N. (2009). The digital native—Myth and reality. *Aslib Proceedings, 61*(4), 364–379.

Selwyn, N. (2012a). Ten suggestions for improving academic research in education and technology. *Learning, Media and Technology, 37*(3), 213–219.

Selwyn, N. (2012b). Making sense of young people, education and digital technology: The role of sociological theory. *Oxford Review of Education, 38*(1), 81–96.

Selwyn, N. (2016). *Is Technology Good for Education?* Cambridge: Polity Press.

Selwyn, N., Bulfin, S., & Johnson, N. (2016). Toward a digital sociology of school. In J. Daniels, K. Gregory, & T. McMillan Cottom (Eds.), *Digital Sociologies.* Bristol: Policy Press.

Selwyn, N., Cranmer, S., & Potter, J. (2010). *Primary Schools and ICT. Learning from Pupil Perspectives.* London: Continuum.

Sennett, R. (2008). *The Craftsman.* London: Penguin.

Sherrington, T. (2013). *From Plantation Thinking to Rainforest Thinking* [online]. Retrieved February 7, 2018, from http://headguruteacher.com/2013/03/10/from-plantation-thinking-to-rainforest-thinking/.

Shirky, C. (2009). *Here Comes Everybody: How Change Happens When People Come Together.* London: Penguin.

Shirky, C. (2011). *Cognitive Surplus: Creativity and Generosity in a Connected Age*. London: Penguin.

Sinker, R. (2000). Making multimedia—Evaluating young people's creative multimedia production. In *Evaluating Creativity* (pp. 187–215). London: Routledge.

Sivek, S. C. (2011). 'We need a showing of all hands': Technological Utopianism in MAKE magazine [online]. *Journal of Communication Enquiry, 35*(3), 187–209. Retrieved February 7, 2018, from http://digitalcommons.linfield.edu/mscmfac_pubs/5.

Smith, M. K. (2002/1997). *Paulo Freire: Dialogue, Praxis and Education* [online]. The Encyclopaedia of Informal Education. Retrieved August 17, 2015, from http://infed.org/mobi/paulo-freire-dialogue-praxis-and-education/.

Snow, C. P. (1961). *The Two Cultures and the Scientific Revolution* [online]. New York: Cambridge University Press. Retrieved February 7, 2018, from http://sciencepolicy.colorado.edu/students/envs_5110/snow_1959.pdf.

Soja, E. (1999). Third space: Expanding the scope of the geographical imagination. In D. Massey, J. Allen, & P. Sarre (Eds.), *Human Geography Today* (pp. 260–278). Cambridge: Polity Press.

Somerson, R., & Hermano, M. L. (2013). *The Art of Critical Making: Rhode Island School of Design on Creative Practice*. Hoboken, NJ: Wiley.

Stommel, J. (2012). Hybridity, pt. 2: What is Hybrid Pedagogy? [online]. *Hybrid Pedagogy* [online]. Retrieved February 7, 2018, from http://www.hybridpedagogy.com/journal/hybridity-pt-2-what-is-hybrid-pedagogy/.

Street, B. (1984). *Literacy in Theory and Practice*. Cambridge: Cambridge University Press.

Street, B. (1995). *Social Literacies: Critical Approaches to Literacy in Development, Ethnography and Education*. London: Longman.

Street, B. (2003). What's 'new' in new literacy studies? Critical approaches to literacy in theory and practice. *Current Issues in Comparative Education, 5*(2), 77–91.

Teachmeet Wiki. (2015). *TeachMeet/FrontPage* [online]. Retrieved February 7, 2018, from http://teachmeet.pbworks.com/w/page/19975349/FrontPage.

Teachmeet Wiki. (2018). TeachMeet/FrontPage [online]. Retrieved May 20, 2018, from http://teachmeet.pbworks.com/w/page/19975349/FrontPage

Thomas, M. (Ed.). (2011). *Deconstructing Digital Natives: Young People, Technology, and the New Literacies*. New York: Routledge.

Thomson, P. (2008). Children and young people: Voices in visual research. In P. Thomson (Ed.), *Doing Visual Research with Children and Young People* (pp. 1–19). Abingdon: Routledge.

Thomson, P., Coles, R., Hallewell, M., & Keane, J. (n.d.). *A Critical Review of the Creative Partnerships Archive: How was Cultural Value Understood, Researched and Evidenced?* [online]. Nottingham. Retrieved February 7, 2018, from http://www.creativitycultureeducation.org/a-critical-review-of-the-creative-partnerships-archive.

Thomson, P., & Gunter, H. (2007). The methodology of students-as-researchers: Valuing and using experience and expertise to develop methods. *Discourse: Studies in the Cultural Politics of Education, 28*(3), 327–342.

Thomson, P., & Gunter, H. (2011). Inside, outside, upside down: The fluidity of academic researcher 'identity' in working with/in school [online]. *International Journal of Research & Method in Education, 34*(1), 17–30. Retrieved February 7, 2018, from http://www.researchgate.net/publication/233282142_Inside_outside_upside_down_the_fluidity_of_academic_researcher_identity_in_working_within_school.

Thomson, P., Hall, C., Jones, K., & Sefton-Green, J. (2012). *The Signature Pedagogies Project: Final Report* [online]. London and Newcastle-upon-Tyne: Creativity, Culture and Education. Retrieved February 7, 2018, from http://www.creativitycultureeducation.org/wp-content/uploads/Signature_Pedagogies_Final_Report_April_2012.pdf.

Truss, E. (2013). *Elizabeth Truss Speaks about Curriculum Reform* [online]. Retrieved February 7, 2018, from https://www.gov.uk/government/speeches/elizabeth-truss-speaks-about-curriculum-reform.

Turkle, S., & Papert, S. (1992). Epistemological pluralism and the revaluation of the concrete [online]. *Journal of Mathematical Behavior, 11*(1), 3–33. Retrieved February 7, 2018, from http://www.papert.org/articles/EpistemologicalPluralism.html.

Two Cars, One Night. (2004) [online]. Short film. Directed by T. Waititi. New Zealand: Defender Films Ltd. Retrieved February 7, 2018, from https://www.youtube.com/watch?v=R6Pc6cBP-8U.

Van Manen, M. (1977). Linking ways of knowing with ways of being practical. *Curriculum Inquiry, 6*(3), 205–228.

Van Manen, M. (2008). Pedagogical sensitivity and teachers' practical knowing-in-action. *Peking University Education Review, 1*, 2–20.

Vygotsky, L. (1978). *Mind in Society: The Development of Higher Psychological Processes.* Cambridge, MA: Harvard University Press.

Vygotsky, L. (2002/1933). *Play and its Role in the Mental Development of the Child* [online]. Psychology and Marxism Internet Archive. Retrieved February 7, 2018, from https://www.marxists.org/archive/vygotsky/works/1933/play.htm.

Vygotsky, L. (2012/1934). *Thought and Language*. Cambridge, MA: MIT Press.

Wall-E. (2008). Film. Directed by A. Stanton. USA: Disney-Pixar.

Watters, A. (2015). *Ed-Tech Guide: What Should You Know About Education Technology?* [online]. Retrieved February 7, 2018, from http://guide.hackeducation.com.

Waugh, C. (2015). *The Edutronic* [online]. Retrieved February 7, 2018, from http://www.edutronic.net/.

Waugh, C. (2016). Connecting text. In J. McDougall & P. Bennett (Eds.), *Doing Text: Teaching Media After the Subject*. Leighton Buzzard: Auteur.

Waugh, C. (2017). *Rebel Education: Pick Your Teacher—Democratic Schooling in the UK*. Aljazeera website. Retrieved March 12, 2017, from http://www.aljazeera.com/programmes/rebel-education/2016/12/pick-teacher-democratic-schooling-uk-161220141451434.html.

Wenger, E. (1998). *Communities of Practice: Learning, Meaning, and Identity. Systems Thinker*. Cambridge: Cambridge University Press.

Wenger-Trayner, E. (2015). *Introduction to Communities of Practice* [online]. Retrieved February 7, 2018, from http://wenger-trayner.com/introduction-to-communities-of-practice/.

Wexler, P., Crichlow, W., Kern, J., & Matusewicz, R. (1992). *Becoming Somebody: Toward a Social Psychology of School*. Abingdon: Routledge.

What Works Network. (2015). Guidance from the Cabinet Office on Public Services. Retrieved February 7, 2018, from https://www.gov.uk/guidance/what-works-network.

Williams, F. (2004). What matters is who works: Why every child matters to new labour. Commentary on the DfES Green Paper *Every Child Matters*. *Critical Social Policy, 24*(3), 406–427.

Williams, R. (1961). *The Long Revolution*. London: Chatto and Windus.

Williams, R. (1977). *Marxism and Literature*. Oxford: Oxford University Press.

Williamson, B. (2014). Political computational thinking: Cross-sector policy networks in the construction of learning to code in the new computing curriculum. In *British Educational Research Association Annual Conference*, Institute of Education, University of London, 23–25 September 2014.

Williamson, B. (2017a). *Big Data in Education The Digital Future of Learning, Policy and Practice*. London: Sage Publications.

Williamson, B. (2017b). Learning in the "platform society": Disassembling an educational data assemblage. *Research in Education, 98*(1), 59–82.

Willingham, D. T. (2012). *When Can You Trust the Experts? How to Tell Good Science from Bad in Education*. San Francisco, CA: Jossey Bass.

Wohlwend, K., & Peppler K. (2015). All rigor and no play is no way to improve learning [online]. *Phi Delta Kappan, 96*(8), 22–26. Retrieved February 7, 2018, from http://kpeppler.com/Docs/2015_Peppler_All-Rigor-No-Play. pdf.

Wolf, A. (2011). *Review of Vocational Education: The Wolf Report* [online]. London. Retrieved February 7, 2018, from https://www.gov.uk/government/ publications/review-of-vocational-education-the-wolf-report.

Wright Mills, C. (1959). *The Sociological Imagination.* New York: Oxford University Press.

Yandell, J. (2014). Classrooms as sites of curriculum delivery or meaning-making: Whose knowledge counts? *Forum, 56*(1), 147–155.

Index[1]

---

[1] Note: Page numbers followed by 'n' refer to notes.

© The Author(s) 2018
M. Cannon, *Digital Media in Education*,
https://doi.org/10.1007/978-3-319-78304-8

Printed by Printforce, the Netherlands